Exploring Translation T

Exploring Translation Theories presents a comprehensive analysis of the core and contemporary paradigms of Western translation theory.

The book starts with a survey of the classic twentieth-century linguistic approaches before moving on to more recent models such as cultural translation. Each central paradigm and its associated theories is addressed in turn, including equivalence, purpose, description, uncertainty, localization, and cultural translation. Readers are encouraged to explore the various theories and consider their strengths and implications for translation today and in the future. The book concludes with a survey of the way translation is used as a model in postmodern cultural studies and sociologies, extending the scope beyond traditional Western notions.

Each chapter includes a wealth of features, such as an introduction outlining the main points, key concepts, illustrative examples with translations, a chapter summary and discussion points and exercises. Examples are drawn from a range of languages, although knowledge of no language other than English is assumed.

This comprehensive and highly engaging book is ideal both for self-study and as the main textbook on Translation Theory courses within Translation Studies and Applied Linguistics programs.

Anthony Pym is Director of postgraduate programs in Translation and Intercultural Studies at Rovira i Virgili University in Tarragona, Spain. He is also a member of the International Advisory Board for the journal *Translation Studies*.

Exploring Translation Theories

ANTHONY PYM

Routledge
Taylor & Francis Group

LONDON AND NEW YORK

First published 2010
by Routledge
2 Park Square, Milton Park, Abingdon, Oxon OX14 4RN

Simultaneously published in the USA and Canada
by Routledge
270 Madison Ave, New York, NY 10016

Routledge is an imprint of the Taylor & Francis Group, an informa business

© 2010 Anthony Pym

Typeset in Akzidenz Grotesque by
Keystroke, Tettenhall, Wolverhampton
Printed and bound in Great Britain by
MPG Books Group, UK

British Library Cataloguing in Publication Data
A catalogue record for this book is available from the British Library

Library of Congress Cataloging-in-Publication Data
Pym, Anthony, 1956–
Exploring translation theories / Anthony Pym.
p. cm.
1. Translating and interpreting. I. Title.
P306.P95 2010
418′.0201–dc22
2009013647

ISBN 10: 0-415-55362-8 (hbk)
ISBN 10: 0-415-55363-6 (pbk)
ISBN 10: 0-203-86929-X (ebk)

ISBN 13: 978-0-415-55362-9 (hbk)
ISBN 13: 978-0-415-55363-6 (pbk)
ISBN 13: 978-0-203-86929-1 (ebk)

Contents

List of figures and tables

FIGURES

TABLES

Preface

This is a course on the main paradigms of Western translation theories since the 1960s. It adopts a view of translation that includes interpreting (spoken translation) but does not give any special attention to the problems of interpreting. The course is not primarily designed to make anyone a better translator; it is mainly for academic work at advanced levels, although it should be accessible to anyone interested in how the theories invite debate. The basic idea is that all the theories respond to the one central problem: translation can be defined by equivalence, but there are many reasons why equivalence is not a stable concept. So how can we think about translation beyond equivalence? The answers to that question have been more numerous than many suspect, and are often creative and surprising.

The general view taken here is that what we say about translation has a *performative* value; this course is not just a matter of knowing who said what. In seeking to develop greater awareness about what translation can be, we enact confrontations between the paradigms. Our mission will have been accomplished whenever anyone finds pleasure in the contest of ideas, or better, whenever the issues of translation are debated, ideally as part of a pluralist learning project.

This book accompanies some of the best introductory works in the field. Jeremy Munday's *Introducing Translation Studies* (2001/2008) and Franz Pöchhacker's *Introducing Interpreting Studies* (2004) are indispensable guides to "who has done what" in the field of research. Our aim here is to focus more squarely on the main *theories*, not the research or applications, and to make those theories actively engage with each other. This means presenting rather more criticisms than the overviews do. It also means that many fields of research, particularly those that have not made strong original contributions to translation theory, have been sidelined here. Some readers will be surprised to find no real treatment of empirical research on interpreting, adaptation studies of film or theater, or the ways translation has been dealt with from the perspective of gender studies, for example. Those areas are very much part of Translation Studies; they have adopted many of the concepts and methods of neighboring disciplines; but they have not played key roles in the development of translation theory as such. We thus leave them to the companion volumes.

This book also accompanies *The Translation Studies Reader* (2000/2004) edited by Lawrence Venuti, along with *The Interpreting Studies Reader* (2001) edited by Franz Pöchhacker and Miriam Shlesinger. Both those volumes are superb collections of key texts. Our aim has not been to replace those texts: anyone who wants to know about translation theory must read the theorists, in context and in all their complexity. Only with first-hand knowledge of the fundamental texts can one really follow the adventures of critical thought.

Preface

Acknowledgements

I am grateful to the following publishers and authors for permission to adapt material of various kinds: John Benjamins Publishing Company (Amsterdam/Philadelphia. www.benjamins.com) for passages from my article "Natural and Directional Equivalence in Theories of Translation," published in *Target* 19(2) (2007), 271–294, which forms the basis for Chapters 2 and 3; Ricardo Muñoz Martín for Table 2.2; Christiane Nord for Table 4.1 and Figure 4.1; Daniel Gouadec for Table 4.2.

My sincere thanks to those who have helped revise parts of the text: Gideon Toury, Itamar Even-Zohar, Christiane Nord, Tal Goldfajn, José Ramón Biau Gil, Christina Schäffner, John Milton, Serafima Khalzanova, Ester Torres Simón, Humberto Burcet Rojas, Kayoko Takeda, Yukiko Muranaga, and Chie Okada.

Special thanks go to the many students and colleagues who have participated in the seminars that have comprised this course since it was first offered in 2003: at Monash University in Melbourne, Australia; in the PhD program in Translation and Intercultural Studies at the Rovira i Virgili University in Tarragona, Spain; and at the Monterey Institute of International Studies in the United States.

I am also extremely grateful for the editorial guidance provided by Louisa Semlyen and Eloise Cook, who are responsible for the book's title.

CHAPTER 1

What is a translation theory?

This short chapter explains what we mean by the terms "theory" and "paradigm," and how theorization can be related to translation practice. We also detail the overall chapter plan of this course, some reasons for studying translation theory, and the ways this book may be used as part of a learning process based on debate.

1.1 FROM THEORIZING TO THEORIES

Translators are theorizing all the time. Once they have identified a translation problem, they usually have to decide between several possible solutions. Let us say you have to translate the English term "Tory," employed to designate the Conservative Party in Britain. According to the situation, you might consider things like using the English term and inserting information to explain it, or adding a footnote, or just giving a word-for-word equivalent of "Conservative Party," or naming the corresponding part of the political spectrum in the target culture, or just leaving out the problematic name altogether. All those options could be legitimate, given the appropriate text, purpose, and client. Formulating them (*generating* possible translations) and then choosing between them (*selecting* a definitive translation) can be a difficult and complex operation, yet translators are doing precisely that all the time, in split seconds. Whenever they do it, whenever they decide to opt for one rendition and not others, they bring into play a series of ideas about what translation is and how it should be carried out. They are theorizing.

The word "theory" probably comes from the Greek *theā*, view + *-horan*, to see – to theorize is to look at a view (the word *theater* has the same origins). A theory sets the scene where the generation and selection process takes place. Translators are thus constantly theorizing as part of the regular practice of translating.

This private, internal theorizing becomes public when translators discuss what they do. They occasionally theorize out loud when talking with other translators or with clients, sometimes with fellow students or instructors. Sometimes this out-loud theorizing involves no more than a few shared terms for the things we are dealing with. For example, here we will refer to the "**source text**" as the one we translate from, and to the "**target text**" as the translation we produce. By extension, we can talk about the "source language" and the "target language," or the "source culture" and the "target culture." "**Translating**" would then be a set of processes leading from one side to the other.

Do these terms mean that we are already using a theory? Probably not, at least not in the sense of having an explicit theory and defending it. Then again, these interrelated names-for-things do tend to form **models of translation**, and those models conceal some very powerful guiding ideas. Why, for example, should our terms reduce translation to an affair of just two sides ("source" and "target")? Surely each source can be traced back to a number of previous sources? And each target is only a link towards further actions and aims. For that matter, each text may contain elements of more than one language and culture. In all these aspects there are usually more than just two sides involved. Further, when we put the "source" and "target" concepts next to the "trans-" part of "translation," we see that the terms build a very *spatial* image in which our actions just go from one side to the other. The words suggest that translators affect the target culture but not the source, thanks to a transitivity that happens in space. Now, is this always true?

Compare that model with "**anuvad**," a Sanskrit and Hindi term for written translation that basically means, we are told, "repeating" or "saying later" (cf. Chesterman 2006; Spivak 2007: 274). According to this alternative term, the main difference between one text and the other could be not in space, but in time. Translation might then be seen as a constant process of updating and elaborating, rather than as some kind of physical movement across cultures.

Our interrelated names-for-things form models, and those models become theories, scenes set by ideas about what could or should be in a translation. In other words, our basic terms encapsulate theories, even though we are mostly not aware of those theories.

This does not mean that all our inner theorizing is constantly turned into public theories. When translators talk with each other, they mostly accept the common terms without too much argument. Straight mistakes are usually fixed quickly, through reference to usage, to linguistic knowledge, or to common sense. For instance, we might correct a translator who identifies the term "Tory" with extreme right-wing politics. Any ensuing discussion could be interesting but it will have no great need of translation theory (political theory, perhaps, but not ideas about translation). Only when there are **disagreements over different ways of translating** does private theorization tend to become public theory. If different translators have come up with alternative renditions of the term "Tory," one of them might argue that "translation should explain the source culture" (so they will use the English term and add a long footnote). Another might say that "translation should make things understandable to the target culture" (so they will just put "the main right-wing party"). A third might consider that "the translation should re-situate everything in the target culture" (so they would give the name of a conservative target-culture party). And a fourth will perhaps insist that since the source text was not primarily about politics, there is no need to waste time on an ornamental detail (so they might calmly eliminate all reference to the term).

When those kinds of arguments are happening, practical theorizing is turning into explicit theories. The arguments turn out to be between different theoretical positions. Sometimes the exchanges turn one way rather than the other, and two initially opposed positions will find they are compatible within a larger theory. Often, though, people remain with their fixed positions; they keep arguing.

1.2 FROM THEORIES TO PARADIGMS

As theorizing turns into theory, some theories develop names and explanations for multiple aspects of translation (including names for the presumed blindness of other theories). When that stage is reached, we can legitimately talk about different "**paradigms**," here understood as sets of principles that underlie different groups of theories (in the general sense outlined by Kuhn 1962). This particularly occurs when we find general ideas, relations, and principles for which there is internal coherence and a shared point of departure. For example, one set of theories uses the common terms "source," "target," and "equivalence." They agree that the term "equivalence" names a substantial relation between the "source" and the "target"; their shared point of departure is the comparison of source texts with target texts. People using those theories of equivalence can discuss translation with each other fairly well. They share the same vague terms and general ideas about the aims of a translation. They can even reach some kind of consensus about various modes of equivalence. They are theorizing within the one paradigm.

On the other hand, we sometimes find people arguing about translation problems and reaching nothing but constant disagreement. In such cases, the ideas are probably working within quite different paradigms, with different points of departure. For example, one kind of description works from comparisons between translations and non-translations (both in the same language). People engaged in that activity come up with results that could be of interest to psycholinguistics (the language used in translations is different from the language found in non-translations). But that finding will appear almost totally irrelevant to anyone working within the equivalence paradigm. If the language in translations is different, the theorist of equivalence can still serenely argue that it *should* not be different. Each side thus continues the discussion without appreciating the other side's perspective. The paradigms enter into conflict. The outcome may be continued tension (debate without resolution), revolution (one paradigm wins out over the other), or more commonly silence (people choose to travel along separate paths).

1.3 HOW THIS BOOK IS ORGANIZED

This book is structured in terms of paradigms rather than individual theories, theorists, or schools. We will be talking about paradigms based on equivalence, purposes, descriptions, uncertainty, localization, and, for want of a better term, cultural translation. Equivalence is broken down into two sub-paradigms, corresponding to "natural" and "directional" equivalence. We do this in order to underscore the complexity of equivalence, since some current theorists tend to dismiss it as a naïve non-theory. The **website associated with this course** presents supplementary materials, particularly on the intellectual background of the descriptive paradigm, which is sometimes unfairly dismissed as nothing more than empiricism.

The **order of the paradigms** is very roughly chronological, starting around the 1960s and reaching the present day, except for the "uncertainty" paradigm, which was present in one form or another at the beginning. In fact, the fundamental conflict between uncertainty and equivalence would be the basic problem to which all the paradigms respond.

This order does not mean that the newer theories have automatically replaced the older ones. If that were true, you would only have to read the last chapter of this book. On the contrary, we spend a lot of time on equivalence precisely to indicate its complexity and longevity – a lot of equivalence theory lives on within the localization paradigm. Theories can, of course, become ever better, more refined, or more exact in their descriptions and predictions, in accordance with an accumulation of knowledge. This sometimes happens in the field of translation, since the newer theories occasionally do try to accommodate the perspectives of the older ones. For example, German-language *Skopos* theory can accept the equivalence paradigm as being appropriate to a "special case" scenario. That kind of accumulation is not, however, to be found in any move to the uncertainty paradigm (here including deconstruction), which would regard both equivalence and purpose as indefensible essentialisms. In such cases, we can indeed talk about quite different paradigms without trying to fit one inside the other. Those paradigms differ right from the very basic questions of what translation is, what it can be, and how a translator should act in the world. When the paradigms clash, people are often using the one word "translation" to refer to quite different phenomena. Debate might then become pointless, at least until someone attempts to rise above their initial paradigm. Only then, when an attempt is made to understand a new view of translation, can there be productive theorizing in the public domain.

You may have to read all the chapters after all.

1.4 WHY STUDY TRANSLATION THEORIES?

Why study these theories? Instructors and trainers sometimes assume that a translator who knows about different theories will work better than one who knows nothing about them. As far as we know, there is no empirical evidence for that claim, and there are good reasons to doubt its validity. All translators theorize, not just the ones who can express their theories in technical terms. Untrained translators may work faster and more efficiently because they know *less* about complex theories. They have fewer doubts and do not waste time reflecting on the obvious. On the other hand, some awareness of different theories might be of practical benefit when confronting problems for which there are no established solutions, where significant creativity is required. The theories can pose productive questions, and sometimes suggest successful answers. Theories can also be significant agents of change, especially when moved from one professional culture to another, or when they are made to challenge endemic thought (think about the Sanskrit idea of translation as "saying later"). And public theories can help foster awareness of the complexities of translation, thus enhancing the public image of translators and interpreters.

The practical advantage we want to defend here is that of a **plurality of paradigms**. Rather than set out to defend one paradigm against all others, we are interested in promoting awareness that there are many valuable ways of approaching translation, any of which may prove useful or stimulating in a given situation.

Awareness of a range of theories can help the translation profession in several ways. When arguments occur, theories provide translators with valuable tools not just to defend their positions but also to find out about other positions. The theories might simply name things that people had not previously thought about. If a client complains that the term "Tory" has disappeared from the translation, you could say you have achieved "compensatory correspondence" by comparing the British party with a target-culture party two pages later in your target text. The client may not be entirely convinced, but the terms could help explain some of the possibilities of translation. In fact, that piece of theory might be of as much practical use to the client as to the translator. The more terms and ideas you have, the more you and your client can explore the possibilities of translation.

Some knowledge of different theories can also be of direct assistance in the translation process itself. At the beginning of this chapter we have presented a simple theory of translation: a problem is identified, possible solutions are generated, and one solution is selected. That is our own model (a set of related names-for-things), not a transcendent truth. In terms of our model, a plurality of theories can widen the range of potential solutions that translators think of. On the selective side, theories can also provide a range of reasons for choosing one solution and discarding the rest, as well as defending that solution when necessary. Some theories are very good for the *generative* side, since they criticize the more obvious options and make one think about a wider range of factors. Descriptive, deconstructionist, and cultural-translation approaches might all fit the bill there. Other kinds of theory are needed for the *selective* moment of translating, when decisions have to be made between the available alternatives. That is where reflections on ethics, on the basic purposes of translation, could provide guidelines. Unfortunately that second kind of theory, which should give reasons for selective decisions, has become unfashionable in some circles. That is why we indulge in plurality, to try to redress the balance.

1.5 HOW SHOULD TRANSLATION THEORIES BE STUDIED?

Since all translators are always theorizing, it would be quite wrong to separate the theory from the practice of which it is already a part. The best uses of theory are actually in active discussions about different ways of solving translation problems. You can promote that kind of discussion on the basis of translations that students have already done. You will find that, at some points, one group of students will disagree with another group. Get those groups to debate the point, then suggest the appropriate terms and concepts once the students have demonstrated their need for those things. In this way, students come to theories only when they find they need them. Classes on individual theories or paradigms can then build on that practical basis.

Unfortunately our educational institutions tend to separate theory from practice, often demanding a separate course in "translation theory." If necessary, that can be done. However, the theories and their implications should still be drawn out from a series of practical tasks, structured as discovery processes. This book has been designed to allow such use. Towards the end of each chapter we list some "**frequently had arguments**," most of which do not have any clear resolution, and many of which are not really as frequent as we would like them to be. Then, at the end of each chapter we suggest some "**projects and activities**" that can be carried out in class or given as assignments. No solutions are given to the problems, and in many cases there *are* no correct solutions. Discussions and further suggested activities are available on the course website. Of course, the examples should always be adapted for use in a particular class. More important, the activities should be integrated into the learning process; they should probably come at the beginning of a class, rather than be used as an appendage at the end.

In a sense, the challenge of this book is to work against its fixed written form. The real learning of theory, even for the self-learner, should be in dialogue and debate.

CHAPTER 2

Natural equivalence

This chapter starts from the idea that what we say in one language *can* have the same value (the same worth or function) when it is translated into another language. The relation between the source text and the translation is then one of equivalence ("equal value"), no matter whether the relation is at the level of form, function, or anything in between. Equivalence does not say that languages are the same; it just says that values can be the same. The many theories that share this assumption can be fitted into a broad "equivalence paradigm," which can be broken down into two sub-paradigms. Here we focus on the sub-paradigm where the things of equal value are presumed to exist *prior* to the act of translation. This means that it makes no difference whether you translate from language A into language B or vice versa. This kind of equivalence is considered "natural," and it will be opposed to what we call "directional" equivalence in Chapter 3. Natural equivalence stands at the base of a strong and robust sub-paradigm closely allied with Applied Linguistics. It is also close to what many translators, clients, and translation users believe about translation. It should thus be appreciated in all its complexity. On the one hand, theories of natural equivalence were an intellectual response to the structuralist vision of languages as world-views. On the other, they have produced lists of equivalence-maintaining procedures that try to describe what translators do. In this chapter we cover in some detail the list of translation procedures proposed by Vinay and Darbelnet (1958/1972). One should not forget, however, that the sub-paradigm has produced several such categorizations, and that all the lists were, in their day, a response to an important problem within structuralist linguistics.

The term "equivalence," in various European languages, became a feature of Western translation theories in the second half of the twentieth century. Its heyday was in the 1960s and 1970s, particularly within the frame of structuralist linguistics. The term roughly assumes that, on some level, a source text and a translation can share the same value ("equi-valence" means "equal value"), and that this assumed sameness is what distinguishes translations from all other kinds of texts. Within the paradigm, to talk about translations is to talk about different kinds of equivalence. In the course of the 1980s, however, the equivalence paradigm came to be regarded as naïve or limited in scope. **Mary Snell-Hornby**, for example, jettisoned equivalence as presenting "an illusion of symmetry between languages which hardly exists beyond the level of vague approximations and which distorts the basic problems of translation" (1988: 22).

Here we take the unpopular view that the equivalence paradigm was and remains far richer than such quick dismissals would suggest. It merits a serious place alongside and within the more recent paradigms. This is because, if you look closely, the theorizing of

The main points covered in this chapter are:

- Equivalence is a relation of "equal value" between a source-text segment and a target-text segment.
- Equivalence can be established on any linguistic level, from form to function.
- Natural equivalence is presumed to exist between languages or cultures prior to the act of translating.
- Natural equivalence should not be affected by directionality: it should be the same whether translated from language A into language B or the other way around.
- Structuralist linguistics, especially of the kind that sees languages as world-views, would consider natural equivalence to be theoretically impossible.
- The equivalence paradigm solves this problem by working at levels lower than language systems. This can be done by focusing on contextual signification rather than systemic meaning, by undertaking componential analysis, by assuming reference to a *tertium comparationis*, by assuming that deverbalization is possible, or by rendering features that are marked.
- Following Vinay and Darbelnet, there are several categorizations of the procedures by which equivalence can be maintained.
- The sub-paradigm of natural equivalence is historical, since it assumes the production of stable texts in languages with equal expressive capacity.

equivalence has in fact involved two competing conceptualizations, which here we call "natural" as opposed to "directional" equivalence. The intertwining duality of those notions allows for considerable subtlety in some past and present theories. It also creates confusion, not only in some of the theories of equivalence themselves but also in the many current arguments *against* equivalence.

First we should understand what "natural" equivalence entails.

2.1 NATURAL EQUIVALENCE AS A CONCEPT

Most discussions of equivalence concern typical misunderstandings. For instance, Friday the thirteenth is an unlucky day in English-language cultures but not in most other cultures. In Spanish, the unlucky day is *Tuesday* the thirteenth. So when we translate the name of that day, we have to know exactly what kind of information is required. If we are just referring to the calendar, then Friday will do; if we are talking about bad luck, then a better translation would probably be "Tuesday the thirteenth" (actually "martes 13," or "martes y 13" in some varieties). The world is full of such examples. The color of death is mostly black in the West, mostly white in the East. A nodding head means agreement in Western Europe, disagreement in Turkey. That is all boring textbook stuff.

The concept of equivalence underlies all these cases. Equivalence, we have posited, says that **a translation will have the same value** as (some aspect of) its corresponding source text. Sometimes the value is on the level of form (two words translated by two words); sometimes it is reference (Friday is always the day before Saturday); sometimes it is function (the function "bad luck on 13" corresponds to Friday in English, to Tuesday in Spanish). Equivalence need not say exactly which kind of value is supposed to be the same in each case; it just says that equal value can be achieved on one level or another.

Equivalence is a very simple idea. Unfortunately it becomes quite complex, both as a term and as a theory.

As for the term, it seems that the first uses of "equivalence" in a technical sense described the kind of relation that allows us to equate, more or less, the English "Friday the 13th" with the Spanish "martes 13." When Friday becomes Tuesday, the two terms are equivalent because they are considered to activate approximately the same cultural function. This is the sense in which **Vinay and Darbelnet** used the term *équivalence* in 1958, and **Vázquez-Ayora** used *equivalencia* in 1977. That is, for the initial period of contemporary equivalence theories, the term referred to only one kind of translation option among many (we shall soon look at the various alternative procedures described by Vinay and Darbelnet). Equivalence was determined by function (the value "bad-luck day" in our example), which is the opposite sense to what Snell-Hornby supposes when she talks about a "symmetry between languages." In this initial period, equivalence referred to what could be done at points where there was precisely no symmetry between linguistic forms. Hence much confusion.

It was not long before other theorists, particularly the American linguist and Bible scholar **Eugene Nida**, would be talking about different kinds of equivalence. Nida, for example, might look at the Spanish "martes 13" and see that there are two ways of rendering it: either as "Tuesday the thirteenth" or as "Friday the thirteenth." The first option would be "**formal equivalence**" (since it mimics the form of what is said in Spanish); the second would be what Nida calls "**dynamic equivalence**" (since it activates the same or similar cultural function). As soon as theorists started talking about different kinds of equivalence, the meaning of the term "equivalence" obviously became much broader, referring to a relation of value on any level. It is in this wider sense that we are using it here.

On the level of practice, things are scarcely simpler. Consider for a moment the television game shows that are popular all over the world. English audiences usually know a show called *The Price is Right*. In French this becomes *Le juste prix*, and in Spanish, *El precio justo*. Equivalence here is not on the level of form (four words become three, and the rhyme has been lost), but it might be operative on the level of reference or function. In German this show became *Der Preis ist heiss*, which changes the semantics (it back-translates as "The price is hot," as when children play the game of rising temperatures when one comes closer to an object). The German name cleverly retains the rhyme, which might be what counts. It could be getting very warm in its approach to equivalence.

If you start picking up examples like this and try to say what stays the same and what has changed, you soon find that a translation can be equivalent to many different things. For example, in the game show *Who Wants to be a Millionaire?* (which retains the structure of that name in many languages), the contestants have a series of "lifelines" in English, "jokers" in French and German, and a "comodín" (wild-card) in Spanish. Although those are all very different images or metaphors, they do have something in common. Describing that commonness can be a difficult operation. More intriguing is the fact that the reference to "millionaire" is retained even though different local currencies make the amount quite different. Given that the show format came from the United Kingdom, we should perhaps translate the pounds into euros or dollars. This might give *Who Wants to Win $1,867,500?*. The title has more money but is decidedly less catchy. One suspects that equivalence was never really a question of exact values.

This is the point at which it makes some sense to talk about what is "natural" in equivalence. Why does no one calculate the exact sum of money to be won? Because, it appears, what counts is what is *usually* said in the target culture. If there is common agreement that the term "millionaire" functions only to say "more money than most of us can imagine possessing," then all you need in any target language is the common term corresponding to that very vague notion. The common expression on one side should correspond to the common expression on the other. This is the sense in which we find the word "natural" in definitions like the following:

> Translating consists in *reproducing* in the receptor language the *closest natural equivalent* of the source-language message.
>
> (Nida and Taber 1969: 12; italics added)

Of course, the theory becomes a little more sophisticated when we realize that not everything we find in source texts is always "natural" or "common." If it were, the texts would be so boring that there would be little reason to translate them. We might then suppose that whatever is uncommon (or better, "marked") on one side be rendered as something similarly uncommon ("marked") on the other. For example, "The Price is Light" would theoretically give rise to a more varied set of equivalents than does the more normal "The Price is Right," since you might try to render the **markedness** of "light." The notion of markedness, however, simply says that some things are natural and others are less natural. It thus remains a theory of natural equivalence, since if there were no such thing as naturalness ("unmarkedness"), the theory would make no sense.

2.2 EQUIVALENCE VS. STRUCTURALISM

In the second half of the twentieth century, translation theorists mostly dealt with this kind of problem against the background of structuralist linguistics. A strong line of thought leading from Wilhelm von Humboldt to Edward Sapir and Benjamin Whorf argued that **different languages express different views of the world**. This connected with the views of the Swiss linguist **Ferdinand de Saussure**, who in the early years of the twentieth century explained how languages form systems that are meaningful only in terms of the differences between the items. The word *sheep*, for example, has a value in English because it does not designate a cow (or any other animal for which there are names in English) and it does not refer to *mutton*, which is the meat, not the animal (the difference between names for animals and names for their meat is fairly systemic in English) (Saussure 1916/1974: 115). In French, on the other hand, the word *mouton* designates both the animal and the meat, both *sheep* and *mutton*.

Such relations between terms were seen as different "structures." Languages were considered to be sets of such structures (and hence different "systems"). **Structuralism** said we should study those relations rather than try to analyze the things themselves. Do not look at actual sheep; do not ask what we want to do with those sheep; do not ask about the universal ethics of eating sheep meat. Just look at the relations, the structures, which are what make language meaningful. One should therefore conclude, according to structuralist linguistics, that the words *sheep* and *mouton* have very different values. They thus cannot translate each other with any degree of certainty. In fact, since different languages cut the world up in very different ways, no words should be completely translatable out of their language system. Translation should simply not be possible.

That kind of linguistics is of little help to anyone trying to translate television game shows. It is not of any greater help to anyone trying to understand how translations are actually carried out, so something must be wrong in the linguistics. As the French theorist **Georges Mounin** argued in the early 1960s, "if the current theses on lexical, morphological, and syntactic structures are accepted, one must conclude that translation is impossible. And yet translators exist, they produce, and their products are found to be useful" (1963: 5; our translation). Either translation did not really exist, or the dominant linguistic theories were inadequate. That is the point at which the main theories of equivalence developed. They tried to explain something that the linguistics of the day could not explain or somehow did not want to explain.

Think for a moment about the kinds of arguments that could be used here. What should we say, for example, to someone who claims that the whole system of Spanish culture (not just its language) gives meaning to "martes 13" (Tuesday the thirteenth) in a way that no English system could ever reproduce? *Martes y 13* is the stage name, for example, of a popular pair of television comedians. Or what do we say to Poles who once argued that, since the milk they bought had to be boiled before it could be drunk, their name for milk could never be translated by the normal English term *milk* (cf. Hoffman 1989)? In fact, if the structuralist approach is pushed, we can never be sure of understanding anything beyond our own linguistic and cultural systems, let alone translating the little that we do understand.

Theories of equivalence then got to work. Here are some of the arguments that were used to address this cluster of problems.

- **Signification**: Within linguistic approaches, close attention was paid to what is meant by "meaning." **Saussure** had actually distinguished between a word's "value" (which it has in relation to the language system) and its "signification" (which it has in actual use). To cite a famous example from chess, the *value* of the knight is the sum of all the moves it is allowed to make, whereas the *signification* of an actual knight depends on the position it occupies at any stage of a particular game. "Value" would thus depend on the language system (which Saussure called *langue*), while "signification" depends on the actual use of language (which Saussure termed *parole*). For theorists like **Coseriu**, those terms could be mapped on to the German distinction between *Sinn* (stable meaning) and **Bedeutung** (momentary signification). If translation could not reproduce the former, it might still convey the latter. French, for example, has no word for *shallow* (as in "shallow water"), but the signification can be conveyed by the two words *peu profond* ("not very deep") (cf. Coseriu 1978). The language structures could be different, but equivalence was still possible.

- **Language use**: Some theorists then took a closer look at the level of language use (*parole*) rather than at the language system (*langue*). Saussure had actually claimed that there could be no systematic scientific study of *parole*, but theorists like the Swiss-German **Werner Koller** (1979/1992) were quite prepared to disregard the warning. If something like equivalence could be demonstrated and analyzed, then there were systems beyond that of *langue*.

■ **Text levels**: Others stressed that translation operates not on isolated words but on whole texts, and texts have many linguistic layers. The linguist **John Catford** (1965) pointed out that equivalence need not be on all these layers at once, but could be "rank-bound." We might thus strive for equivalence to the phonetics of a text, to the lexis, to the phrase, to the sentence, to the semantic function, and so on. Catford saw that most translating operates on one or several of these levels, so that "in the course of a text, equivalence may shift up and down the rank scale" (1965: 76). This was a comprehensive and dynamic theory of equivalence.

■ **Componential analysis**: A related approach, more within lexical semantics, was to list all the functions and values associated with a source-text item, and then see how many of them are found in the target-side equivalent. This kind of componential analysis might analyze *mouton* as "+ animal + meat − young meat (*agneau*)," *mutton* as "+ meat − young meat (lamb)," and *sheep* as "+ animal." Then we would make our translation selections in accordance with the components active in the particular source text. We could go further: *lifeline* could be turned into something like "amusing metaphor + way of solving a problem with luck rather than intelligence + no guarantee of success + need for human external support + nautical." We would then find that the translations *joker* and *wild-card* reproduce at least three of the five components, and would thus be equivalent to no more than that level. There could be no guarantee, however, that different people would recognize exactly the same components.

All of those ideas were problematic to some degree. All of them named or implied a relation of equivalence, and they did so in a way that defended the existence of translation in the face of structuralist linguistics. Their confrontational virtue is not to be belittled.

An example of comparative componential analysis

Comparative linguistics can provide ways of isolating semantic components. Bascom (2007) gives the following analysis of the potential equivalents *key* and the Spanish *llave*:

Wrench	Llave (inglesa)
Faucet	Llave (grifo)
Key	Llave (de casa)
Piano key	Tecla de piano
Computer key	Tecla de ordenador
Key of a code	Clave de un código
Key of music	Clave de música

According to this analysis, the Spanish *llave* would only correspond to the component "instrument for turning;" *tecla* corresponds to the component "thing to press down," and *clave* is only an equivalent of *key* when an abstract or metaphorical sense is involved. This distinction between these components seems not to be made in English.

2.3 PROCEDURES FOR MAINTAINING NATURAL EQUIVALENCE

Another way to defend translation was to record and analyze the equivalents that can actually be found in the world. One of the most entertaining texts in translation theory is the introduction to **Vinay and Darbelnet's** *Stylistique comparée du français et de l'anglais*, first published in 1958. The two French linguists are driving from New York to Montreal, noting down the street signs along the way:

> We soon reach the Canadian border, where the language of our forefathers is music to our ears. The Canadian highway is built on the same principles as the American one, except that its signs are bilingual. After SLOW, written on the road-surface in enormous letters, comes LENTEMENT, which takes up the entire width of the highway. What an unwieldy adverb! A pity French never made an adverb just using the adjective LENT. . . . But come to think of it, is LENTEMENT really the equivalent of SLOW? We begin to have doubts, as one always does when shifting from one language to another, when our SLIPPERY WHEN WET reappears around a bend, followed by the French GLISSANT SI HUMIDE. Whoa!, as the Lone Ranger would say, let's pause a while on this SOFT SHOULDER, thankfully caressed by no translation, and meditate on this SI, this "if," more slippery itself than an acre of ice. No monolingual speaker of French would ever have come straight out with the phrase, nor would they have sprayed paint all over the road for the sake of a long adverb ending in – MENT. Here we reach a key point, a sort of turning lock between two languages. But of course – *parbleu!* – instead of LENTEMENT [adverb, as in English] it should have been RALENTIR [verb in the infinitive, as in France]!
>
> (Vinay and Darbelnet 1958/1972: 19; our translation)

What kind of equivalence is being sought here? The kind the linguists actually find is exemplified by the long French adverb "lentement," which says virtually the same thing as the English adverb "slow." It changes the length, but apparently there is room on the road. What worries the linguists is that the sign "Lentement" is not what one would find on roads in France. For them, the equivalent should be the verb "ralentir," since that is what would have been used if no one had been translating from English (and as if Canada were itself within France). This second kind of equivalence is thus deemed "natural." It is what different languages and cultures seem to produce from within their own systems. This natural equivalence is also reciprocal: "slow" should give "ralentir," which should give "slow," and so on.

Natural equivalents do exist, but rarely in a state of untouched nature. As the East German theorist **Otto Kade** (1968) argued, they are most frequently the stuff of terminology, of artificially standardized words that are *made* to correspond to each other. All specialized fields of knowledge have their terminologies; they are unnaturally creating "natural" equivalents all the time. In Vinay and Darbelnet, however, the artificially imposed glossaries are to be avoided where possible. The linguists are seeking equivalents characterized as "natural" precisely because those equivalents are supposed to have developed without interference from meddling linguists, translators, or other languages. In terms of this naturalism, the best translations are found when you are not translating. We use this mode of thought whenever we look for solutions in "**parallel texts**" (non-translational target-language texts on the same topic as the source text).

In the late 1950s and 1960s, equivalence was often thought about in this way. The problem was not primarily to show what the "thing" was or what one wanted to do with it (Vinay and Darbelnet might have asked what words were best at actually making Canadian drivers slow down). The problem was to describe ways in which equivalence could be attained in all the situations where there were no obvious natural equivalents.

Vinay and Darbelnet worked from examples to define seven general procedures ("procédés," although others sometimes call them "strategies") that could be used in this kind of translation. Table 2.1 is a version of how they summarize their findings.

The seven procedures each come with examples on three levels of discourse. They go from the most literal (at the top) to the most re-creative (at the bottom). Vinay and Darbelnet actually describe this progression as being from the easiest to the most difficult, and this makes some sense if we consider that the bottom situations are the ones where the translator probably has the most options to choose from.

Note, though, that what the linguists are comparing are really the results of what translators are *presumed* to do; the categories are based on no evidence of how a translator might *actually* get from the source to the target. A simple model is nevertheless possible: the translator might first try the "literal" procedure to see what that gives; if that does not work, the translator can either go up the table (closer to the source) or down the table (closer to the target culture). This means that not all the procedures necessarily count as good

Table 2.1 Vinay and Darbelnet's General Table of Translation Procedures (our translation from Vinay and Darbelnet 1958/1972: 55)

	Lexis	Collocation	Message
1. Loan	Fr. Bulldozer Eng. Fuselage	Fr. Science fiction Eng. À la mode	Fr. Five o'clock tea Eng. Bon voyage
2. Calque	Fr. Économiquement faible Eng. Normal School	Fr. Lutétia Palace Eng. Governor General	Fr. Compliments de la saison Eng. Take it or leave it
3. Literal translation	Fr. Encre Eng. Ink	Fr. L'encre est sur la table Eng. The ink is on the table	Fr. Quelle heure est-il? Eng. What time is it?
4. Transposition	Fr. Expéditeur: Eng. From:	Fr. Depuis la revalorisation du bois Eng. As timber becomes more valuable	Fr. Défense de fumer Eng. No smoking
5. Modulation	Fr. Peu profond Eng. Shallow	Fr. Donnez un peu de votre sang Eng. Give a pint of your blood	Fr. Complet Eng. No vacancies
6. Correspondence (*équivalence*)	Fr. (milit.) La soupe Eng. (milit.) Tea	Fr. Comme un chien dans un jeu de quilles Eng. Like a bull in a china shop	Fr. Château de cartes Eng. Hollow triumph
7. Adaptation	Fr. Cyclisme Br. Eng. Cricket Am. Eng. Baseball	Fr. En un clin d'œil Eng. Before you could say Jack Robinson	Fr. Bon appetit! Am. Eng. Hi!

ways to produce natural equivalence – in each case, translators are only required to do the best they can. For example, the use of **loans and calques** is only legitimate when there is no more natural equivalent available (the examples in Table 2.1 are not meant to translate each other). "**Literal translation**," which here means fairly straightforward word-for-word, is quite possible between cognate languages but can also frequently be deceptive, since languages abound with "**false friends**" (lexical, phraseological and syntactic forms that look similar but have different functions in different languages). Literalism is what gives the French *Lentement* as the equivalent of *Slow*, and this is not what Vinay and Darbelnet consider natural. The procedures of real interest to the linguists are **transposition** (where there is a switching of grammatical categories) and **modulation** (where adjustments are made for different discursive conventions). The remaining two procedures concern cultural adjustments: **correspondence** (actually called *équivalence* in the French version) would use all the corresponding proverbs and referents (like "Friday the thirteenth), and **adaptation** would then refer to different things with loosely equivalent cultural functions: cycling is to the French what cricket is to the British, or baseball to the Americans, we are told. At this end of the table there are many very vague equivalents available, and translators can spend hours exploring the possibilities (gardening is to the English what having lovers is to the Italians, perhaps). In all, Vinay and Darbelnet's procedures range from artificial or marked at one end to the vague but naturalistic at the other. The French linguists were thus able to recognize not only the desirability of natural equivalence, but also the practical need for translators to produce other kinds of renditions as well.

In addition to the list of general procedures, Vinay and Darbelnet outline a series of "**prosodic effects**" resulting from the above procedures. This gives a further list of "stylistic procedures" operating closer to the sentence level. In most cases, the translator may be seen as following the constraints imposed by the target language, without many alternatives to choose between.

■ *Amplification*: The translation uses more words than the source text to express the same idea. Example: "the charge against him" (four words) becomes "l'accusation portée contre lui" (back-translation: "the charge brought against him" (five words)). When the amplification is obligatory, the effect is called *dilution*. Example: "le bilan" ("the balance") becomes "the balance sheet" (1958/1972: 183). This category also covers what Vinay and Darbelnet call *étoffement* (perhaps "completion" or "lengthening") (1958/1972: 109ff.), where a target-text word grammatically needs the support of another word. Example: "To the trains" becomes "Accès aux quais," where the preposition for "to" (*à*) grammatically needs the support of the noun meaning "access."

■ *Reduction* (*économie*): The opposite of amplification (just take the above examples in the opposite direction, since that is what natural equivalence invites us to do).

■ *Explicitation*: Procedure whereby the translation gives specifications that are only implicit in the source text (1958/1972: 9). Example: "students of St. Mary's" becomes "étudiantes de l'école St. Mary," where the French specifies that the students are women and St. Mary's is a school (1958/1972: 117).

■ *Implicitation*: The opposite of explicitation (again, the directionality of the above example can be reversed, if and when it is common knowledge in the target culture that St. Mary's is a school for girls).

■ *Generalization*: When a specific (or concrete) term is translated as a more general (or abstract) term. Example: "mutton" (the meat) becomes "mouton" (both the animal and the meat; Vinay and Darbelnet refer to Saussure's example), or the American "alien" becomes "étranger" (which includes the concepts of both "foreigner" and "alien").

■ *Particularization*: The opposite of *generalization* (reverse the above examples).

There are actually more terms than these in Vinay and Darbelnet. The above should suffice, however, to illustrate several points. First, these categories seem to be saying much the same thing; the translation can give more (amplification, explicitation, generalization) or less (reduction, implicitation, particularization). Second point: these terms have been used throughout the equivalence paradigm, but in many different ways. **Kinga Klaudy** (2001), for example, uses "**explicitation**" to cover everything that is "more," and "**implicitation**" to cover everything that is "less" (we will see other uses of the term "explicitation" in Chapter 6). Third, the dominant factor in all these cases is the nature of the target language, or better, the **systemic differences** between the source and the target languages. The individual translator does not really have much choice. This is why the examples can all be read in both directions. Even when Vinay and Darbelnet claim that French is more "abstract" than English, so that there will be more generalization when moving in that direction, the difference is in order to preserve the balance between the languages; it is not something affecting the cognitive processes of the translator. To that extent, Vinay and Darbelnet consistently defend the virtues of natural equivalence.

Not all procedures are consistently of this kind, however. Consider the example of **explicitation** where "students at St. Mary's" become explicitly female students in the French translation (where the language obliges the noun to be male or female). Compare this with a much-discussed example from **Hönig and Kussmaul** (1982/1996), where the term "Eton" is rendered into German as "eine der englischen Eliteschulen" (one of the elite English schools — we analyze the example in 5.6.2 below). This could be considered amplification and explication, since it uses more words to convey the idea, and it makes explicit the information that English readers would attach to the term "Eton." The added information, however, is not natural equivalence, and it is not really considered "explicitation" in the sense in which Vinay and Darbelnet use the term. This is because the **directionality** does not work in both senses. One can get from the English to the German with some surety, but will the phrase "one of the elite English schools" necessarily bring us back to "Eton"? Probably not, given that there are quite a few schools to choose from. Directionality is playing a far more important role here, since we have started to think about what the *users* of the translation might actually need to know. That is not something that Vinay and Darbelnet took into account.

Vinay and Darbelnet actually mention one further procedure, a very important one, which we present separately because it can be used in a particularly directional way:

■ *Compensation*: "Procedure whereby the tenor of the whole piece is maintained by playing, in a stylistic detour, the note that could not be played in the same way and in the same place as in the source" (1958/1972: 189). Our translation of Vinay and Darbelnet here maintains the analogy with music. The examples are nevertheless clear enough. French must choose between the intimate and formal second-person pronouns (*tu* or *vous*); contemporary English cannot. To render the distinction, where pertinent, the translator might opt for a switch from the family name to the given name, or to a nickname, as in "My friends call me Bill," to render "On se tutoie . . ." (meaning, "We can use the intimate second-person pronoun . . ."). Compensation may also be used to indicate various points of emphasis (for example, italics being used in English to render a syntactic emphasis in French), or to render a switch from one linguistic variety to another (examples may be found in Fawcett 1997).

There are quite a few theories that list procedures like this. Vinay and Darbelnet's work was inspired by **Malblanc** (1944/1963), who compared French and German. They in turn became one of the points of reference for **Vázquez-Ayora** (1977), who worked on Spanish and English. Different kinds of equivalence-maintaining procedures have been described in a Russian tradition including **Fedorov** (1953), **Shveitser** (1973/1987) and **Retsker** (1974), and by the American **Malone** (1988), all usefully summarized in Fawcett (1997). When Muñoz Martín presents a comparison of several categorizations of what he calls "translation strategies" (Table 2.2), the most striking aspect is perhaps that there could be so many ways to cut up the same conceptual space. The terms for the procedures (or strategies) have clearly not been standardized even within the sub-paradigm of natural equivalence. Then again, perhaps the best evidence for the existence of the sub-paradigm is the fact that these and many other linguists have agreed that this is the space where the terms and concepts are needed.

The lists of procedures tend to make perfect sense when they are presented alongside carefully selected examples. On the other hand, when you analyze a translation and you try to say exactly which procedures have been used where, you often find that several categories explain the same equivalence relation, and some relations do not fit comfortably into any category. Vinay and Darbelnet recognize this problem:

> The translation (on a door) of PRIVATE as DÉFENSE D'ENTRER [Prohibition to Enter] is at once a transposition, a modulation, and a correspondence. It is a transposition because the adjective *private* is rendered by a noun phrase; it is a modulation because the statement becomes a warning . . ., and it is a correspondence because the translation has been produced by going back to the situation without bothering about the structure of the English-language phrase.
>
> (Vinay and Darbelnet 1958/1972: 54; our translation)

If three categories explain the one phenomenon, do we really need all the categories? Or are there potentially as many categories as there are equivalents? This is a theoretical problem to which we will return in Chapter 3.

Even more serious questions are raised when we try to apply these categories to translation between **European and Asian languages**. Let us go back to Table 2.1 and consider the classical list of procedures. Since they were working between French and English, Vinay and Darbelnet could more or less assume that the general default procedure is "literal translation," and only when that procedure does not work would the translator look for alternative solutions higher on the list ("loan" or "calque"), or harder solutions a little further down ("transposition," "modulation," etc.). Chinese, Japanese, and Korean, however, do not have the explicit syntactic relations of Germanic or Romance languages, so the default procedure is more usually at the level of "transposition" rather than "literal translation," and it is very difficult to make any consistent distinction between "transposition" and "modulation." At the same time, Japanese and Chinese (and perhaps to a lesser extent Korean) are very open to borrowing when dealing with new "international" subject matter, so that loans and

Table 2.2 Comparison of proposed "translation strategies," adapted from Muñoz Martín (1998)

Vinay and Darbelnet (1958)		*Vázquez Ayora (1977)*			*Malone (1988)*	
More difficulty less	Loan	more ← translation proper → less		Literal translation	Matching	Equation $A \rightarrow E$
	Calque					Substitution $A \rightarrow S$
	Literal translation					
	Transposition		Oblique	Transposition	Reordering $AB \rightarrow BA$	
	Modulation			Modulation		
	Correspondance (équivalence)			Equivalencia		
	Adaptation			Adaptation		
Degree of difficulty not specified	Amplification		secondary	Amplification	Recrescence	Amplification $A \rightarrow AB$
	Implicitation			Omission		Reduction $AB \rightarrow A$
	Compensation			Compensation		
	Explicitation			Explicitation	Repackaging	Diffusion $A \cap B \rightarrow A \mid B$
	Dilution					Condensation $A \mid B \rightarrow A \cap B$
	Particularization				Zigzagging	Divergence $A \rightarrow B/C$
	Generalization					Convergence $B/C \rightarrow A$

calques become far more frequent and acceptable ways to produce equivalence in those particular fields. One of the results is that, if, for instance, you are translating *from* Chinese into English in an international field, the source text seems to contain so many loans from English that it is hard to describe what you are doing with them – should we perhaps add a category for "loans returning to lender"? (Thanks are extended to students at the Monterey Institute of International Studies for all these observations.) The classical linguistic theories of equivalence require more work if they are to be extended beyond European languages.

2.4 TEXT-BASED EQUIVALENCE

We have noted that **John Catford** (1965) saw equivalence as being mostly "**rank-bound**," in the sense that it is not established on all linguistic levels at the same time. As the translator moves along the text, the level of equivalence can thus shift up or down, from function to phrase to term to morpheme, for example, in accordance with the various constraints ensuing from the source text. Vinay and Darbelnet's catalog of procedures (Table 2.1) does not contradict that view, since the procedures correspond to the same hierarchy of linguistic levels. Their preference is for movements downward in order to enhance naturalness, but another theorist could legitimately argue for movements upward, without breaking the theory.

One of the most developed theories of this kind is by the Swiss-German theorist **Werner Koller**, whose textbook on "translation science" went through four editions and many reprints between 1979 and 1992. Koller proposes five frames for equivalence relations: **denotative** (based on extra-linguistic factors), **connotative** (based on the way the source text is expressed), **text-normative** (respecting or changing textual and linguistic norms), **pragmatic** (with respect to the receiver of the target text) and **formal** (the formal-aesthetic qualities of the source text). These categories suggest that the translator selects the type of equivalence most appropriate to the dominant function of the source text. Although Koller allows that translators actively *produce* equivalence in the sense that equivalents need not exist prior to the translation, the implicit role that he allows to the source text should be enough to bring his approach under the umbrella of "natural equivalence." He does not really give us any other criterion for choosing between one level of equivalence or another, since the source text itself ultimately determines when "pragmatic" equivalence is necessary.

The German theorist **Katharina Reiss** (1971/2000) was voicing fairly similar claims during the same period. Her approach recognizes three basic **text types** (informative, expressive, and operative) and she then argues that each type requires that equivalence be sought on the level corresponding to it (giving appropriate weight to content, form or effect). Reiss's theory is traditionally classified as "functionalist," and we will go into its details in our chapter on German-language *Skopos* theory (4.2 below), but its basic approach is not entirely out of place here. For as much as some would oppose Koller and Reiss, their theories are both based on a mode of equivalence where the translation has to reproduce aspects of what is functional in the source text, and the decisive factor is held to be none other than the nature of the source text. To that extent, both have at least a foothold within the general theory of natural equivalence.

2.5 REFERENCE TO A *TERTIUM COMPARATIONIS* AND THE "THEORY OF SENSE"

The theories are rather vague about how natural equivalence works. They mostly assume that there is a piece of reality or thought (a referent, a function, a message) that stands outside all languages and to which two languages can refer. That thing would be a third element of comparison, a **tertium comparationis**, available to both sides. The translator thus goes from the source text to this thing, then from the thing to the corresponding target text. Non-natural translations will result when one goes straight from the source text to the target text, as in the case of *Slow* rendered as *Lentement.*

Perhaps the best-known account of this process is the one formulated by the Parisian theorist **Danica Seleskovitch**. For her, a translation can only be natural if the translator succeeds in forgetting entirely about the form of the source text. She recommends "listening to the sense," or "**deverbalizing**" the source text so that one is only aware of the sense, which can be expressed in all languages. This is the basis of what is known as the **theory of sense** (*théorie du sens*) (Seleskovich and Lederer 1984). From our perspective, it is a process model of natural equivalence.

The great difficulty of this theory is that if a "sense" is deverbalized, how can we ever know what it is? As soon as we indicate it to someone, we have given it a semiotic form of one kind or another, and there are no forms (not even the little pictures or diagrams sometimes used) that can be considered truly universal. So there is no real way of proving that such a thing as "deverbalized sense" exists. "Listening to the sense" metaphorically describes a mental state that simultaneous interpreters attain, but what they are hearing cannot be a sense without form. This theory remains a loose metaphor with serious pedagogical virtues.

One of the paradoxes here is that process models like Seleskovitch's encourage translators *not* to look at linguistic forms in great detail, whereas the comparative methods espoused by Vinay and Darbelnet and the like were based on close attention to linguistic forms in two languages. The process theories were breaking with **linguistics**, tending to draw more on **psychology** (Seleskovitch turned to the French psychologist Piaget). The comparative method, however, was entirely within linguistics. It would go on to compare not just isolated phrases and collocations, but also pragmatic discourse conventions and modes of text organization. Applied linguists like **Hatim and Mason** (1990, 1997) extend the level of comparison, generally remaining within the sub-paradigm of natural equivalence.

For the most idealistic natural equivalence, the ultimate aim is to find the pre-translational equivalent that reproduces all aspects of the thing to be expressed. Naturalistic approaches thus spend little time on defining translation; there is not much analysis of different types of translation; there is no real consideration of translators having different aims. Those things have somehow been decided by equivalence itself. Translation is simply translation. But that is not always so.

2.6 THE VIRTUES OF NATURAL EQUIVALENCE

Natural equivalence is the basic theory in terms of which all the other paradigms in this book will be defined. To that extent its role is foundational, at least within the narrative we are creating here (soon we will see how historical the idea of natural equivalence actually is). All the following paradigms will be able to say bad things about natural equivalence. To achieve something of a balance, let us quickly repeat a few of the good things that may be said about it.

In a period of structuralism that seemed to make translation theoretically impossible, the concept of natural equivalence defended the existence of translation as a vital social practice.

In a period of abstract speculation about structures, systems, and meaning, the theorists of natural equivalence adopted rather empirical standpoints. They went to see what could be done with language structures. If you look at Vinay and Darbelnet, Vázquez-Ayora, Catford,

Nida, or virtually any of the theorists mentioned here, the first thing you find is that their books are full of examples, to the extent that the illustrations are often more engaging and entertaining than the ideas being illustrated.

To give order to the data thus obtained, the theorists usually provided lists of procedures and techniques actually used by translators. These results have proved to be valuable in the training of translators, even when pedagogical applications were not the prime purpose of the theories.

No matter how naïve or idealistic notions such as "same value," "tertium comparationis," or "deverbalization" might be, their operational functions correspond to some very widespread ideas about what translation is (or should be). If there is a general consensus among professionals and clients that a translator should reproduce natural equivalence (no matter what the actual terms used), then a theory which expresses that expectation is serving a valuable social function. Only when we have terms for the consensus can we actually start to discuss it and test its viability. To that extent, natural equivalence was perhaps the necessary starting point for the paradigms that would come later.

2.7 FREQUENTLY HAD ARGUMENTS

Thanks to its foundational role, the concept of natural equivalence will be the subject of many arguments throughout this book. At this stage it is nevertheless useful to summarize the main debates that we have touched on so far.

2.7.1 "Natural equivalence presupposes a non-existent symmetry"

At the beginning of this chapter we saw Mary Snell-Hornby criticize equivalence as presenting "an illusion of symmetry between languages." We might now like to see her criticism as actually stating the position of all the structuralist linguists that see different languages dividing up the world in different ways. Does natural equivalence deny that fact? Probably not, at least not if we look at the range of procedures formulated by Vinay and Darbelnet, or if we follow the theories of "marked" vs. "unmarked," or if componential analysis is used to describe the differences as well as the similarities between languages. On the other hand, Snell-Hornby might be referring to supposed symmetries of functions, in which case her point appears valid: theorists of natural equivalence tend to assume that all languages have the same expressive capacity (see 2.8 below).

2.7.2 "The tests of equivalence have no psychological basis"

Methods like componential analysis or the identification of procedures can to some extent explain the equivalent pairs that we find, but they cannot claim to represent the way translators actually think. As argued by **Jean Delisle** (1988: 72–73), they are linguistic explanations without any reference to translators' cognitive processes. This means that their use in pedagogical situations could be misleading and even counter-productive. Similar questions should also be asked about the empirical status of "deverbalization" and the like.

2.7.3 "New information cannot be 'natural' "

If translations are supposed to bring in information that is *new* to a language or culture, then they cannot be expected to be "natural." That is, new ideas and techniques will eventually require new terms and expressions, so the translations are going to be marked in ways that their source texts are not. This argument usually becomes a question for terminology: should the translation use loans from the source text, or should new terms be invented from the resources considered "natural" in the target language? The ideology of natural equivalence would certainly prefer the latter, but the speed of technological change is pushing translators to the use of loans and the like, particularly from English. There is little evidence that languages are suffering directly as a result (as is occasionally claimed in the heat of debate). Languages tend to die when they receive no translations at all.

2.7.4 "Naturalness hides imperialism"

If a translation brings to a culture a new way of thought, any attempt to present that thought as being "natural" is fundamentally deceptive, and quite possibly imperialistic. Can Nida really pretend that the Christian God was already in the countless non-Christian cultures into whose languages the Bible is translated? When the "lamb of God" becomes a "seal of God" for Inuit readers, the New Testament quite simply ceases to refer to first-century Palestine. The nature of the source is thus concealed, the Inuit readers are deceived, and we have an ideological "illusion of symmetry" far stronger than anything Snell-Hornby was criticizing. At that point, translation has been reduced to the problem of marketing a product (for criticisms of Nida along these lines, see Meschonnic (1973, 2003) and Gutt (1991/2000)).

2.7.5 "Naturalness promotes parochialism"

Although equivalence could conceivably be based on the literalist level of the source text or on "functions" of some kind, the sub-paradigm of natural equivalence mostly favors translations that do not read like translations. **Ernst-August Gutt** (1991/2000), for instance, argues that "equivalent function" produces an illusory naturalness, which misleadingly presents the translation as if it were a non-translation. It is better, for him, to look for equivalents that make the reader work. One variant of the anti-domestication argument is found in the American translator and critic **Lawrence Venuti** (particularly 1998), who is concerned not so much with the ways minor cultures are deceived as with the effects that naturalness ("fluency") has on the way major cultures see the rest of the world. If all cultures are made to sound like contemporary fluent English, then Anglo-American culture will believe that the whole world is like itself. For Venuti, a non-natural ("resistant") translation should therefore use forms that are not frequent in the target language, whether or not those forms are equivalent to anything in the source text. At that point the argument concerns primarily how one should write, and only secondarily how one should translate.

Most of these points will be developed in future chapters.

2.8 NATURAL EQUIVALENCE AS A HISTORICAL SUB-PARADIGM

To close this chapter, we should insist that natural equivalence is a profoundly historical idea, even though it seems to express common sense. Notions of "equal value" presuppose that different languages do or can express values that can be compared in some itemized way. This need not mean that all languages look and sound the same; it need not involve the "illusion of symmetry" that Snell-Hornby claims to have seen, but it does assume that different languages are somehow on the same level.

That assumption is easily made with respect to our contemporary national languages: English, French, Russian, Arabic, Japanese, or Hindi are by no means symmetrical but they have roughly the same ranking in terms of expressive capacities. No one is seriously arguing that any of these languages are inherently inferior to the others. But if we did believe that a language was inferior, or perhaps systematically less developed in some area of technical terminology, how could we defend natural equivalence as an ideal for translations into that language?

Belief in the equal values of languages was quite rare in European theorizing prior to the Renaissance. Much of medieval thinking assumed a **hierarchy of languages**, where some were considered intrinsically better than others. At the top were the languages of divine inspiration (Biblical Hebrew, New Testament Greek, Arabic, sometimes Sanskrit), then the languages of divinely inspired translation (the Greek of the Septuagint, the Latin of the Vulgate), then the national vernaculars, then the patois or regional dialects. This usually meant that translation was seen as a way of **enriching the target language** with the values of a superior source language. Most translations went downward in the hierarchy, from Hebrew or Greek to Latin, or from Latin to the vernaculars. For as long as the hierarchy existed, claims to equivalence (certainly without the term) played little role in thought on translation.

For roughly parallel historical reasons, the basic idea of equivalence was difficult to maintain prior to the age of the **printing press**. Before printing, the source text was not a stable entity. Texts tended to undergo constant incremental changes in the process of **copying** (each copyist adapted and changed things), and those small changes followed the numerous variations of regional dialects, prior to the standardization of national vernaculars. There was usually not just one "source text" waiting to be translated. There would be a range of different manuscripts, with layer upon layer of different receptions inscribed in those manuscripts. Translation could be seen as an extension of that process. Why try to be equivalent if there is nothing stable to be equivalent to?

Printing and the rise of standardized vernaculars helped the conceptualization of equivalence. True, the term "equivalence" was not used. In its place we usually find talk of "fidelity," often to an author, but also to a sense, intention, or function that could be found in a fixed text.

In accordance with this same logic, the relative demise of equivalence as a concept could correspond to the electronic technologies by which contemporary texts are constantly evolving, primarily through updating (think of websites, software, and product documentation). Without a fixed text, to what should a translation be equivalent?

Seen in this historical light, natural equivalence cannot really provide any guarantee of a "true" or "valid" translation. Yet its power as a concept remains strong.

SUMMARY

This chapter started by defending the equivalence paradigm against those who misleadingly reduce it to a belief that all languages are structured the same way. The chapter nevertheless finishes with a rather negative assessment. We have indicated some of the things the sub-paradigm of natural equivalence tends to leave out; we have argued that the ideal of pre-existing equivalence is based on the historical conditions of print culture and national vernacular languages; we have seen that the commonsensical notion of "equal value" really only had intellectual validity in opposition to the structuralist belief in languages as world-views; we have noted how natural equivalence can be described as illusory and deceptive. Those critical evaluations certainly do not mean that the concept of natural equivalence can simply be forgotten. Perhaps the most important things to retain from it are the categories of translational procedures and modes of analysis. Terms like "modulation," "explicitation," "compensation," "markedness," and "componential analysis" form the basic metalanguage of linguistic approaches. They must be known and understood, even though different theories tend to use the same terms in slightly different ways. No matter how much we might personally believe that, in theory, equivalence does not exist, the sub-paradigm of natural equivalence brings together the central problems of translation theory, and does so in ways that are not always naïve. Once you have grasped the basic principles of this sub-paradigm, all the other paradigms can be seen as responses to it.

SOURCES AND FURTHER READING

The *Translation Studies Reader* (Venuti 2000/2004) has texts by Vinay and Darbelnet, Catford, and Nida (although Catford is not in the second edition). Munday (2001/2008) places Vinay and Darbelnet and Catford in the chapter on shifts ("product and process" in the second edition), which for us belongs to the descriptive paradigm. The basic theories of natural equivalence are well summarized in Peter Fawcett's *Translation and Language. Linguistic Theories Explained* (1997). The classical texts are often still available and remain very readable, thanks to the wealth of examples used within this sub-paradigm. A good library should have Catford (1965), Vinay and Darbelnet (1958 and subsequent editions; English translation published in 1995), and something of Nida (the general theory is in *Toward a Science of Translating*, 1964). Critics of natural equivalence are nowadays abundant. Very few of them, however, have taken the trouble to read the foundational texts in detail, or to understand the intellectual climate of the decades in which the sub-paradigm developed.

Suggested projects and activities

Here we list questions and tasks that should be taken as general suggestions for what can be done in the classroom. In some cases the tasks are aimed at consolidating awareness of the theories presented in this chapter. In other cases, however, we seek to raise awareness of problems that will be picked up in the next few chapters.

1   Consider this definition of translation: "Translating consists in *reproducing* in the receptor language the *closest natural equivalent* of the source-language message" (Nida and Taber 1969: 12). What should happen when the source text contains items that are not natural? Find examples in any passage from the Old Testament.

2   Consider the road signs in your language. Which of them result from natural equivalence? (Think about "Stop," for a start.)

3   The following is a Dominican friar giving orders in recently conquered Mexico:

> I hereby order that all friars in this house, whether in sermons, catechisms, private talk among themselves, with secular Spaniards or with Indians, shall refrain from using the name Cabahuil or Chi, or whatever else may be the case, but shall use the name Dios [God in Spanish] to explain to the natives the nature of the one true God.
>
> (cited by Remesal 1966: 2.277; our translation)

Which name *should* the missionaries have used for God?

4   Locate the automatic translation programs Babelfish and Google Translate. Use both to do back-translations several times (e.g. moving from English to German to English to German, for the one text). What happens to equivalence? What translation procedures are involved? What procedures are needed to improve the translations?

5   Select a problematic term and several possible translations of it. Now attempt a componential analysis of the term's function in its original context. How many components are found in the translations? How many have been lost? What gains have been made?

6   For the same term, select its most frequent equivalent and do a comparative analysis of both, as in the example of *key* vs. *llave* above. Does the comparative analysis reveal semantic components that were not clear when you just looked at the source language?

7   The Italian version of the game show *Who Wants to be a Millionaire?* was originally called *Chi vuol esser miliardario?* (Who Wants to be a Billionaire?) when it started in 1999, then became *Chi vuol esser milionario?* (Who Wants to be a Millionaire?). Why the change? What kind of equivalence is this?

8   Check the names of game shows in your languages-other-than-English. How many of them look natural? Do a web search to see how many of them are actually translations. What kind of equivalence can explain them?

9   Consider the terms used in your languages-other-than-English for websites, webpages, and Internet technology. How many of these terms are obviously translations? How many would count as "natural" translations? Can you describe the procedures by which they were produced (check the terms used in Table 2.1)? Is there a difference between the official terms and the ones that people commonly use?

10 Consider the terms used in your language for a "USB drive," "pen drive," "memory stick," or combinations of these. Is there a standard English term from which your language has translated? Is "natural equivalence" still working when there are several competing terms in the source language? Who did the translations?

CHAPTER 3

Directional equivalence

This chapter looks at a set of theories that are based on equivalence but do *not* assume that the relation is natural or reciprocal. For these theories, if you translate from language A into language B, and then back-translate from language B into language A, the result in language A need not be the point from where you started. This means that *directionality* is a key feature of translational equivalence, and that translations are thus the results of active *decisions* made by translators. Whereas the sub-paradigm of natural equivalence develops categories of translation procedures, the sub-paradigm of directional equivalence tends to have only two opposed poles, for two opposed ways of translating (usually "free" as opposed to "literal," although there are many versions of these concepts). Since translators must decide how they are going to translate, there is no guarantee that two translations of the same text will ever be the same. The logic of this view will be seen at work in theories of similarity, in Kade's typology of equivalence, and in the classical dichotomies of translation strategies. We close the chapter with a short presentation of relevance theory, which remains a theory of equivalence, and a consideration of equivalence as a functional social illusion. After all, what people believe about equivalence may be more important than any actual testing of its existence.

3.1 TWO KINDS OF SIMILARITY

The English theorist **Andrew Chesterman** (1996, 2005) argues that the relation between translations and their source texts may be understood in terms of **similarity**. He then points out that there are different kinds of similarity. We might say, for example, that although translations are commonly supposed to be "like" their source texts, those source texts are not always held to be "like" their translations. This is strange. The relation "to be like" may be thought of in two ways. On the one hand, the same quality is considered to be equally present on both sides, so that "Friday the thirteenth" in English is like "martes 13" in Spanish, and the same relation may be seen the other way round. On the other hand, we can say that a daughter is like her mother (in the sense that she "takes after" her mother), but we would not usually say that a mother is like her daughter (chronologically, it is unlikely that she would "take after" her daughter). In this second case, the relation is *asymmetric*, with different roles and expectations being placed on the two sides.

Chesterman sees these relations as two different kinds of similarity. He represents **"divergent similarity"** as:

$$A \rightarrow A', A'' \ldots$$

The main points covered in this chapter are:

■ Directional equivalence is an *asymmetric* relation where the creation of an equivalent by translating one way does not imply that the same equivalence will also be created when translating the other way.

■ Theories of directional equivalence allow that the translator has a choice between several translation strategies, and that those strategies are not dictated by the source text.

■ The strategies for directional equivalence tend to be expressed in terms of two opposed poles, where one pole is a strategy that stays close to the source-text form and the other pole is a strategy that departs from that form. For example, "formal equivalence" is opposed to "dynamic equivalence."

■ Although there are usually more than two ways of translating, the reduction to two is very much a part of the way translation has been seen in Western tradition. The two opposed strategies are based on the two sides of an assumed cultural and linguistic border.

■ Directional equivalence can describe the way a translation represents its source text. This concerns categories like "illusory" vs. "anti-illusory" translation (Levý), where an "illusory" translation is one that does not show itself to be a translation.

■ Relevance theory may be used to describe the beliefs people have about translations. Equivalence thus becomes a belief in "interpretative resemblance" (Gutt).

■ Directional equivalence may also be seen as a useful social fiction, a belief structure that has proved cost-effective in order to reduce doubts in cross-cultural communication.

This may be the way the translator sees the task of translating: a new text is produced, which is like its source in some respects, but it does not replace the source (texts continue to exist), and it is only one of many possible representations (alternative renditions are imaginable, and there may be other translations in the future). What is most obvious here is the *directionality* that leads from source to target, as from mother to daughter, and which does not have the same causal standing the other way round.

Chesterman then presents "**convergent similarity**" as:

$$A \leftrightarrow B$$

This may be the way a translation is seen by its receiver, in the expectation that what they seek in A is also in B. This is the case of "Friday the thirteenth" and "martes 13."

Chesterman suggests that these similarity relations may be able to replace theories of equivalence. We might also ask, however, if theories of equivalence have actually long had both of these kinds of relations, albeit without the names.

According to the ideals of what we have called "natural" equivalence, the relation between terms should work in the same way as "convergent similarity," operating equally well in both directions. You should be able to go from "Friday the thirteenth" to "martes 13" and then back exactly to "Friday the thirteenth," with full confidence in the legitimacy of each step. And yet there is surely another kind of equivalence that comes into play as soon as we allow that, under some circumstances, a translator could opt for "Tuesday the thirteenth" in English (perhaps to explain something about Hispanic culture). This might then be rendered back into Spanish as "martes 13" (Tuesday the thirteenth), but it could also conceivably lead to "viernes 13" (Friday the thirteenth). Whatever we put will be one of a series of possibilities. In this second set of circumstances, natural equivalence is no longer supplying the same measure of certitude. We have entered the world of asymmetric relations, where one-way movements look like Chesterman's "divergent similarity." We suspect there are many theories that see equivalence (not so much similarity) as being characterized by this same directionality.

Here we go in search of what we will call "directional equivalence." If natural equivalence forms one side of the equivalence paradigm, this would be the other.

3.2 DIRECTIONALITY IN DEFINITIONS OF EQUIVALENCE

From the late 1950s, many definitions of translation have referred to equivalence, especially within Applied Linguistics. We have already seen one of those definitions, where the term "natural" is what most interested us:

> Translating consists in *reproducing* in the receptor language the *closest natural equivalent* of the source-language message.
>
> (Nida and Taber 1969: 12; italics added)

Consider this definition in terms of **directionality**. Note that the term "equivalent" is only "of the source-language message," so there is no question of that original message being the equivalent of the translation. In that sense, the concept of equivalence would appear to be directional. At the same time, however, the verb "reproducing" suggests that the natural equivalent actually exists prior to the act of translation in the make-up of the languages or cultures themselves. To that extent, the definition retains some of the idealism of natural equivalence. In other words, the mode of thought seems to be both natural and directional at the same time.

We can try this kind of analysis on a few more of the early definitions (italics added):

> Interlingual translation can be defined as the *replacement* of elements of one language . . . by *equivalent elements* of another language.
>
> (Oettinger 1960: 110)

> Translation may be defined as follows: the *replacement* of textual material in one language (SL) by *equivalent material* in another language (TL).
>
> (Catford 1965: 20)

> [Translation] *leads* from a source-language text to a target-language text which is *as close an equivalent as possible* and presupposes an understanding of the content and style of the original.
>
> (Wilss 1982: 62)

Look closely at the definitions. In each case, the term "equivalent" describes one side only, the target side. The processes ("replace," "lead," and "reproduce" in the example from Nida and Taber) are profoundly directional: translation goes from one side to the other, but not back again. Many similar definitions may be found in the literature. So it seems that the directionality that Chesterman finds in relations of similarity may also be found in some theories of equivalence.

We will use the term "directional equivalence" to refer to all those cases where an equivalent is located on one side more than the other, at least to the extent that they forget to tell us about movements that could go either way. The term "natural equivalence" then refers to theories that assume the possibility of an equally balanced two-way movement. Both kinds of equivalence would seem to fall within the one paradigm since they are often blended, and we are aware of no major disputes between the two camps. For example, both naturalness and directionality have to be used if we are to cover all the things that happen to the names of game shows (check how often the term "millionaire" implicitly refers to English-language capitalism). Or again, when Vinay and Darbelnet present their list of translation strategies, the mode of thought goes from directional at one end to naturalness at the other (reading from top to bottom of their diagram). According to the criteria of both directionality and naturalness, you go from one language to the other, and the result is a translation if and when a relationship of equivalence is established on some level.

Now, if we take the above definitions and ask what the target-side equivalent is actually equivalent to, we find an interesting array of answers: "elements of a language," "textual material," "the message," "source-language text." The theories in this group would seem to agree on some things (target-side equivalents, directionality) but not on others (the nature of the thing to translate). Their debates are not about equivalence itself, but about the nature and location of value.

In any theory, look for the definition of translation and try to see what it is assuming, then what it is omitting. What you find usually indicates the strengths and weaknesses of the whole theory. In this case, the strength of the definitions, whether based on naturalness or directionality, is that they have the one term ("equivalent") that distinguishes translation from all the other things that can be done in interlingual communication (rewriting, commentary, summary, parody, etc.). The weakness is that they mostly do not explain why this relation should just be one-way in some cases, or two-way in others. Further, they are often in doubt as to whether the equivalent is equal to a position or value within a language, to a message, to a text with content and style, or to all those things but at different times.

Do relations of equivalence really have to be one-way? The question was raised many years ago in an elegant piece of theorizing by **Otto Kade**, who worked in what was then East Germany. Kade (1968) proposed that equivalence at the level of the word or phrase comes in four modes: "**one-to-one**," as in the case of stable technical terms; "**one-to-several**," when translators have to choose between alternatives (as in our "lifeline" example); "**one-to-part**," when the available equivalents are only partial matches, or "**one-to-none**," when translators have to create a new solution (coining neologisms or perhaps borrowing the foreign term, as in the upper part of Vinay and Darbelnet's table). Kade describes one-to-one relationships as "**total equivalence**" and considers the clearest examples to be technical terms. We might add that they involve a decision process pertinent to terminology and phraseology more than to translating as such. Those relationships are obviously two-way: we can go from language A to language B and then back to A. They fit in with the ideal of natural equivalence. The one-to-several and one-to-part cases, however, should be profoundly **directional** in practice, since there is no guarantee that the return will bring us back to the same place. Kade sees one-to-several equivalence as being "**choice-based**" (*facultativ* in German), while "one-to-part" equivalence is considered "**approximate**" (*approximativ*). As for the "one-to-none" kind of problem, it would appear to be even more directional.

In terms of Kade's categories, the directionality in the above definitions of translation would seem to imply the one-to-several scenario. Yet we suspect that Kade's whole theory is ultimately of the directional type, since he limits absolute reciprocity to technical terms (probably the least "natural" pieces of language to be found). In hindsight, Kade's is a remarkable piece of theorizing in that he managed to fit both the natural and directional sub-paradigms into the one frame, and he did so while incorporating some awareness of similarity ("approximate" equivalence).

Kade's types of equivalence

Otto Kade (1968) proposes four types of equivalence. The following are our terms for the types, with possible examples.

- *One-to-one* (*Eins-zu-Eins*): One source-language item corresponds to one target-language item. For example, English *Lion* corresponds to German *Löwe*, and this relation may be considered "total equivalence" for as long as neither culture has intimately different relations with lions. The surer examples are technical terms like the names of chemical elements.

- *One-to-several or several-to-one* (*Viele-zu-Eins*): An item in one language corresponds to several in the other language. There are two ways to understand this. For example, the English word *key* corresponds to *llave, tecla*, and *clave* in Spanish (see 2.2 above). In context, however, the translator will usually know what kind of key is being referred to and will have few real choices to make (which is why this example is from the sub-paradigm of natural equivalence). A different example would be the Spanish term *competencia* (domain of activity exclusive to a governmental or administrative organism), which could be rendered by "responsibility," "mandate," "domain," "competence," and so on. Unless a one-to-one equivalent has been established in a certain situation (e.g. *competencia* = *competence*), the translator will have to choose between the alternatives. The result will be "choice-based equivalence."

- *One-to-part* (*Eins-zu-Teil*): Only partial equivalents are available, resulting in "approximate equivalence." For example, the English term *brother* has no full equivalent in Chinese or Korean, since the corresponding terms have to specify whether it is an older or younger brother. Whichever choice is made, the equivalence will thus be only "approximate."

- *One-to-none* (*Eins-zu-Null*): No equivalent is available in the target language. For example, most languages did not have a term for a *computer* a century ago. When that term had to be translated, the translators could use a circumlocution (a phrase to describe the object), they could generate a term from within the target language (e.g. French *ordinateur* and Iberian Spanish *ordenador*), or they could borrow the form of the English term (e.g. German *Computer*, Danish *computer*, Bulgarian *компютър*, or Latin American Spanish *computadora*). Some cultures prefer to import or represent foreign terms; others prefer to generate new terms from their own existing resources.

3.3 BACK-TRANSLATION AS A TEST

To see whether an equivalent is natural or directional, the simplest test is back-translation. This means taking the translation and rendering it back into the source language, then comparing the two source-language versions. When natural equivalence prevails, we can go from *Friday* to *viernes* then back to *Friday*, and it makes no difference which term is the source and which the translation. This is because the correspondence existed in some way prior to the act of translation. More to the point, the transfer of the Judeo-Christian seven-day week occurred several millennia before our act of translation, so the original directionality has now come to appear natural. That **naturalness is certainly an illusion** (in historical terms, all equivalents are probably the result of as much force and authority as is assumed in Kade's one-to-one technical terms). Yet the illusion has had a strong ideological pull on many translation theories. On the level of bad luck, we can indeed go from "Friday the thirteenth" to "martes 13" and back again, and we can make people believe that the equivalence is somehow written into the nature of our cultural systems. The same kind of test might work for *Le juste prix*, and even for *Der Preis ist heiss*, if we define carefully the levels we are operating on. But the back-testing cannot be extended all the way; the mysteries of the "one-to-several" quickly appear. For example, why does the French apparently not have "Le prix juste" (with the adjective after the noun, as is frequent in the language)? And what about the "lifelines" that become "jokers" and "wild-cards" but could become many other things as well? Can they also be justified as being in any way natural? For that matter, what should we say about the "Friday the thirteenth" that is recognized in Taiwan (we are told) not because it was always in the culture but because it traveled there in the title of a horror film? Some kinds of equivalence refer to what is done in a language prior to the intervention of the translator (hence the illusion of the natural); others refer to what translators *can* do in the language (hence the directionality of the result). But one could also argue, historically, that all equivalence is in some way directional.

"Directional" and "natural" are the terms we are using here to describe the different concepts elaborated by theories of translation; they are not words used by the theories themselves. They nevertheless help to make some sense of a confusing terrain. As we have seen, most of the questions coming from structuralist linguistics concern strictly *natural* equivalence, or the search for it. When we mentioned Saussure's *sheep* and *mouton* example, we talked about the words "translating each other." The same would hold for Polish milk and universal bad-luck days. For that linguistic paradigm, it should make no difference which of the terms is the source and which is the target. For the above definitions of translation, on the other hand, equivalence is something that results from a directional movement.

Reference to directionality was perhaps the most profound way in which the problem of structuralist linguistics was solved.

3.4 POLARITIES OF DIRECTIONAL EQUIVALENCE

Most theories of directional equivalence do not list procedures or linguistic levels (as in theories based on natural equivalence) but instead separate different *kinds* of equivalence. They also talk about different kinds of translating, which amounts to much the same thing, since you translate quite differently depending on the level at which you want equivalence to work.

Many of the theories here are based on just two types of equivalence, sometimes presented as a straight dichotomy (you can translate one way *or* the other). That general approach goes as far back as **Cicero**, who conceptualized the one text as being translated from Greek into Latin in two different ways – *ut interpres* (like a literalist interpreter) or *ut orator* (like a public speaker) (Cicero 46CE/1996). That is, literally or freely. Note that the distinction need *not* map on to any profound difference between "natural" and "directional" equivalence. If anything, the freer translation is likely to be the most "natural" in the target language, whereas the more literal translation is the one most likely to give reciprocal directionality – but there is no guarantee. This is why we tend to see the dichotomy as part of a directional theory of translation, since Cicero was not particularly concerned with anyone translating speeches from Latin back into Greek. The important point is that the naming of those two different ways necessarily assumes there is some value that remains constant between them; they are different translations of the same thing. That was a fundamental conceptualization of equivalence, although without the term.

Dichotomies like Cicero's are found throughout Western translation theory. The early nineteenth-century German preacher and translator **Friedrich Schleiermacher** (1813/1963) argued that translations could be either **foreignizing** (*verfremdend*) or **domesticating** (*verdeutschend*, "Germanizing"). He famously described the two possible movements as follows: "Either the translator leaves the author in peace, as much as possible, and moves the reader toward that author, or the translator leaves the reader in peace, as much as possible, and moves the author toward that reader" (1813/1963: 63; our translation). Although Schleiermacher's preference was for the foreignizing option, just as Cicero's was for the *ut orator* or domesticating method, both approaches ultimately allow the translator to decide. The decision does not particularly depend on the nature of the source text.

Perhaps the best-known theory of equivalence formulated in this way is the one developed by the American linguist and Bible scholar **Eugene Nida**. This could seem paradoxical, since we have seen Nida's view of translation as incorporating naturalness. His wider argument, however, is that the Bible may be translated to achieve either "**formal equivalence**" (following the words and textual patterns closely) or "**dynamic equivalence**" (trying to re-create the *function* the words might have had in their original situation). As we have seen, the term *Agnes Dei* can become the "lamb of God" that we know in English-language Christianity, but it might also become the "seal of God" for an Inuit culture that knows a lot about seals but does not have many lambs. The latter translation would be an extreme case of "dynamic equivalence." On the other hand, the name "Bethlehem" means "House of Bread" in Hebrew, so it might be translated that way if we wanted to achieve dynamic equivalence on that level. In that case, our Bible translators traditionally opt for formal equivalence, even when they use dynamic equivalence elsewhere in the same text. (Of course, things are never quite that easy: the Arabic for Bethlehem, Beit Lahm, means "House of Meat" – so to whose name are we to be equivalent?)

We have noted that Nida's definitions claim to be seeking a "natural" equivalent, which would appear to be more on the dynamic than the formal side. That is indeed his general ideological preference, since dynamic equivalence, the illusion of the natural, is well suited to evangelical purposes. At one stage Nida toyed with Chomsky's idea of "kernel phrases" as the *tertium comparationis*, the underlying third thing to which the source and target segments should both be equivalent. Yet the general theory, particularly in its practical applications, remains remarkably directional. Nida was mostly talking about translating the Bible into the languages of cultures that are not traditionally Christian. What "natural" equivalent should one find for the name of Jesus or God in a language where they have never been mentioned? Most solutions actually concern a *directional* notion of equivalence, not a natural one.

A similar kind of dichotomy is found in the English translation critic **Peter Newmark** (1988), who distinguishes between "**semantic**" and "**communicative**" translation. The semantic kind of translation would look back to the formal values of the source text and retain them as much as possible; the communicative kind would look forward to the needs of the new addressee, adapting to those needs as much as necessary. Newmark's preferences tend to lie on the "semantic" side, especially with respect to what he terms "authoritative texts." In theory, however, translators have to choose whether to render one aspect or another of the source text. There is thus no necessary assumption of just one "natural" equivalent, and the result is a generally directional theory.

These theoretical dichotomies are mostly presented as the ways translators work. They are obviously not on the same level as the lists of procedures we find in theories of natural equivalence. Here the categories generally name approaches to *the text as a whole*, as opposed to the many linguistic procedures that naturalistic theories locate at sentence level or below.

Large directional dichotomies can also be based on the way a translation represents its source text. For example, the Czech theorist **Jiří Levý** (1969) distinguished between "**illusory**" and "**anti-illusory**" translations. When you read an "illusory" translation, you are not aware it is a translation; it has been so well adapted to the target culture that it might as well be a text written anew. This is an ideal for many common conceptions: a translation is successful when you do not know it is a translation. An "anti-illusory" translation, on the other hand, retains some features of the source text, letting the receiver know it is a translation. This basic opposition has been reformulated by a number of others. The German theorist **Juliane House** (1997) refers to "**overt**" and "**covert**" translations, where "overt" means that the receiver is aware they interact with a translation, and "covert" means they are not. **Christiane Nord** (1997: 47–52) prefers the terms "**documentary**" and "**instrumental**" to describe different translations, since the translation can either work as an explicit representation of the previous text (and thus as a "document") or it can re-enact the communicative function (as an "instrument"). The Israeli theorist **Gideon Toury** (1980, 1995a) talks about translations being "**adequate**" (to the source text) or "**acceptable**" (in terms of the norms of reception). The American theorist and translator **Lawrence Venuti** (1995), referring back to Schleiermacher, identifies "**fluent**" translations as the domesticating kind he generally finds being done into English, and opposes them to "**resistant**" translations, which show the reader the foreignness of the text. Again, in all these dichotomies, we are talking about a choice made by the translator, not necessarily determined by the nature of the source text.

All these oppositions could be regarded as operating within the equivalence paradigm. In all cases the two ways to translate can both lay claim to represent some aspect or function of the source. So have translation theorists been saying the same thing over and over, down through the centuries? Not really. The relations between the poles have been thought about in many different ways. To see this, try to apply the oppositions to the simple examples we have used. If we take "martes 13," we know that a formal-equivalence translation would refer to "Tuesday the thirteenth" and a dynamic-equivalence translation would give "Friday the thirteenth." Now, which of those two translations is foreignizing? Which is domesticating? Which is moving the reader? Which is moving the author? It seems impossible to say, at least until we have a little more information. Or rather, both translations could be domesticating

Polarities of directional equivalence

Many theories of directional equivalence are based on two opposed ways of translating, often allowing that there are possible modes between the two poles. The strategies they are talking about are not always the same, and some of the theorists have diametrically opposed preferences, but they are all thinking in twos. Here is a shortlist:

Cicero:	ut interpres	ut orator
Schleiermacher:	foreignizing	domesticating
Nida:	formal	dynamic
Newmark:	semantic	communicative
Levý:	anti-illusory	illusory
House:	overt	covert
Nord:	documentary	instrumental
Toury:	adequacy	acceptability
Venuti:	resistant	fluent

in their way. If we wanted something foreignizing (anti-illusory, overt, documentary, adequate, resistant) we would have to consider saying something like "bad-luck *martes* thirteenth," "Tuesday the thirteenth, bad-luck day," or even "Tuesday the thirteenth, bad-luck day in Spanish-speaking countries." Is this kind of translation equivalent? Certainly not on the level of form (in the last rendition we have added a whole phrase). Could we claim equivalence in terms of function? Hardly. After all, a simple referential phrase has become a whole cultural explanation, at a place where the source text need offer no explanation. Some would say that the explanation is not equivalent, since our version is too long to be a translation. Others might claim that this kind of expansion is merely taking implicit cultural knowledge and making it explicit, and since the cultural knowledge is the same, equivalence still reigns. Our version might then be a very good translation.

This is a point at which natural equivalence appears to break down. Directionality becomes more important; we could use it to justify quite significant textual expansion or reduction. The equivalence paradigm nevertheless tends to baulk at this frontier. How much explanatory information could we insert and still claim to be respecting equivalence? There is no clear agreement. The debate then concerns what is or is not a translation. That is a question that the equivalence paradigm was never really designed to address (it merely assumed an answer).

3.5 ONLY TWO CATEGORIES?

Is there any reason why so many directional theories of equivalence have just two categories? Surely most translation problems can be solved in *more* than two ways? Naturalistic approaches tend to have many more than two categories (Vinay and Darbelnet, for example, listed seven main procedures; Koller gives five types; Reiss works with three). How should we explain this profound binarism on the directional side? Let us suggest a few possibilities.

First, there may be something profoundly binary within equivalence-based translation itself. To grasp this, translate the following sentence into a language other than English (preferably not Dutch or German for this one!):

(1) The first word of this very sentence has three letters.

In French this would give:

(2) Le premier mot de cette phrase a trois lettres.

Here the word-level equivalence is fine, but functional equivalence has been lost (since the first word now has two letters, not three). A true self-reference has become a false self-reference (see the analysis of this example in Burge 1978). So how *should* the English sentence be translated? One might try the following:

(3) Le premier mot de cette phrase a deux lettres.

This tells us that the first word of the *French* sentence has *two* letters. We have lost word-level equivalence with the English, but we have maintained the truth of the self-reference. Our translation would seem to have moved from anti-illusory to illusory, documentary to instrumental, and so on. In this example there would seem to be only these two possibilities available: one kind of equivalence *or* the other. Or are there further possibilities?

A second reason for having just two categories may be found in the early nineteenth century. As we have seen, **Friedrich Schleiermacher** argued that there were only two basic strategies: either you move the author toward the reader, or you move the reader toward the author. Schleiermacher claimed it was not possible to mix the two. This is because "just as they must belong to *one* country, so people must adhere to *one* language or another, or they will wander untethered in an unhappy middle ground" (1813/1963: 63; our translation). Translators, it seems, cannot have it both ways; they must decide to situate their texts in one country or the other.

If we look at these two reasons, they are both saying much the same thing. Translation has two sides (source and target), and thus two possible ways of achieving self-reference, and two possible positions from which the translator can speak. This might suggest that directional equivalence is a particularly good mode of thought for certain kinds of translation, and that those kinds, with just two basic sides, are particularly good for keeping people on one side or the other, in separate languages and countries. Or could that be the ultimate purpose of all translation?

Are the dichotomies strictly necessary? It would certainly seem that the ideology of "one side or the other" is deeply anchored in Western thought. The practical problems of translating, however, are rarely quite so simple. Consider the difficulties of translating someone's résumé or curriculum vitae. Do you adapt the normal form of résumés in the target culture? Or do you just reproduce that of the source culture? The solution is usually a mix, since the first option means too much work, and the second option would mostly disadvantage the person whose résumé it is. These days, however, many résumés are in a database that can be printed out in several different formats and in several different languages (English, Spanish, and Catalan, in the case of our own university). The results are somehow equivalent to something; they certainly look like translations; but their production seems not to be in accordance with any of the directional parameters listed above. In those cases, technology would seem to have returned us to a "natural" equivalence of a particularly artificial kind.

3.6 RELEVANCE THEORY

The German linguist and translation consultant **Ernst-August Gutt** (1991/2000) proposes a very elegant theory that addresses the main problems of directional equivalence. Gutt looks at theories of natural equivalence (of the kind we have seen from Vinay and Darbelnet) and says that, in principle, there is no limit to the kinds of equivalence that they can establish. Every text, in fact every translation decision, may need its own theory of equivalence. So all these theories are seriously flawed since, in principle, a theory should have fewer terms than the object it accounts for.

To overcome this difficulty, Gutt looks closely not at language or translations as such, but at the kinds of things people believe about translations. Here he distinguishes between different kinds of translation, using two binary steps.

1   As in House (see above), "**overt translations**" are texts marked and received as translations, whereas "**covert translations**" would be things like the localization of a publicity campaign for a new audience, which may as well not be a translation. Receivers of a covert translation will not have any special beliefs about its equivalence or non-equivalence, so Gutt is not interested in those translations.
2   Within the category of "overt translations," considered to be translation proper, there are two kinds: "**indirect translation**" covers all the kinds of translations that may be done without referring to the original context of the source text; "**direct translation**" would then be the kind that does refer to that context. In Gutt's terms, direct translation "creates a presumption of complete interpretative resemblance" (1991: 186). When we receive a direct translation, we think we understand what receivers of the original understood, and that belief is not dependent on any comparison of the linguistic details.

Here the critique of natural equivalence (too many possible categories) brings us back to the two familiar categories ("direct" vs. "indirect"). Those two, we can now see, are very typical of directional equivalence. That alone could justify seeing Gutt as a theorist of equivalence.

What makes Gutt's approach especially interesting here is the way he explains directional equivalence as a belief in "**interpretative resemblance**." He regards language as a very weak representation of meaning, no more than a set of "communicative clues" that receivers have to interpret. When he sets out to explain how such interpretation is carried out, Gutt draws on the concept of **implicature**, formulated by the philosopher **H. Paul Grice** (1975). The basic idea here is that we do not communicate by language alone, but by the relation between language and context. Consider the following example analyzed by Gutt:

Source text: Mary: "The back door is open."
Source context: If the back door is open, thieves can get in.
Intended implicature: We should close the back door.

If we know about the context, we realize that the source text is a suggestion or instruction, not just an observation. What is being said (the actual words of the source text) is not what is being meant (the **implicature** produced by these words interacting with a specific context). Grice explains such implicatures as operating by breaking various maxims, here the maxim of "relevance." If we know about the context and the maxims, we can reach the implicature. If we do not, we will not understand what is being said. Note that Grice's maxims are *not*

Grice's maxims

The following are Grice's maxims, the breaking of which creates implicatures.

- *Maxim of quantity*: Give no more and no less information to your audience than is needed for a full understanding of the intended message.
- *Maxim of quality*: Do not misinform your audience; that is, say what you believe to be true and do not say something you do not believe to be true.
- *Maxim of relevance*: Be relevant. Do not say something that is not relevant to the conversation.
- *Maxim of manner*: Communicate your message in an orderly and clear manner without ambiguity and unnecessary wordiness.

These maxims may be quite culture-specific (they seem particularly English). However, the general idea that implicature comes from breaking maxims should not be culture-specific. Every culture is free to add the maxims it wants, then to break them.

rules for producing good utterances; they are more like norms that are regularly broken in order to produce implicatures. The actual maxims may thus vary enormously from culture to culture. This variability is something that the linguists **Dan Sperber and Deidre Wilson** (1988) tend to sidestep when they reduce Gricean analysis to the one maxim: "be relevant." They thus produce "relevance theory," saying in fact that all meaning is produced by the relation between language and context. It is from relevance theory that Gutt develops his account of translation.

Looking at the above example, if we were going to translate source text (1) we would have to know if the receiver of the translation has access to the context (2) and to the pragmatic maxim being broken. If we can be sure of both kinds of access, we might just translate the words of the text, producing something like formal equivalence. If not, we might prefer to translate the implicature, somehow rendering the "function," what the words apparently mean. The notion of implicature can thus give us two kinds of equivalence, in keeping with two kinds of translation. The fundamental dichotomy of directional equivalence persists.

Gutt, however, does not really want those two kinds of equivalence to be on the same footing. He asks how Mary's utterance should be reported (or translated). There are at least two possibilities:

Report 1: "The back door is open."
Report 2: "We should close the back door."

Gutt points out that either of these reports will be successful if the receiver has access to the source context; we can thus establish equivalence on either of those levels. What happens, though, when the new receiver does *not* have access to the source context? Let us say we do not know about the possibility of thieves; perhaps we are more interested in the children being able to get in when they come home from school. If the reporter is working in this new context, only the second report (5), the one that renders the implicature, is likely to be successful. It will tell us that the back door should still be closed, even if there remain doubts about the reason. Gutt, however, prefers direct translation to allow interpretation in terms of the *source* context only. He would opt for the first report (4). For him, something along the lines of the second report (5) would have no reason to be a translation.

Gutt's application of relevance theory might be considered idiosyncratic on this point. It could be attributed to his particular concern with Bible translation. In insisting that interpretation should be in terms of the source context, Gutt effectively discounts much of the "dynamic equivalence" that Nida wanted to use to make biblical texts relevant to new audiences. Gutt insists not only that the original context is the one that counts, but also that this "makes the explication of implicatures both unnecessary and undesirable" (1991: 166). In the end, "it is the audience's responsibility to make up for such differences" (ibid.). Make the receiver work! In terms of our example, the receiver of the second report (5) should perhaps be smart enough to think about the thieves. Only when there is a serious risk of misinterpretation should the translator inform the audience about contextual differences, perhaps by adding, "because there might be thieves."

At this point, the equivalence paradigm has become quite different from the comparing of languages or the counting of words in phrases. The application of relevance theory shows equivalence to be something that operates more on the level of beliefs, of fictions, or of possible thought processes activated in the reception of a translation. This is a very profound shift of focus. If we knew more about the way people actually receive translations, this new approach could rise above many of the problems equivalence had in the days of structuralist linguistics.

3.7 EQUIVALENCE AS AN ILLUSION

With respect to equivalence (regardless of his personal translation preferences), Gutt probably got it just about right. Translations, when they are accepted as such, do indeed create a "presumption of complete interpretative resemblance," and that presumption, no matter how erroneous, could be all there ever was to equivalence. There is then no need to go further; no need actually to test the pieces of language according to any linguistic yardstick. Equivalence is always "presumed" equivalence and nothing more.

In this, Gutt's position is deceptively close to Toury's (1980: 63–70, 1995a), where all translations manifest equivalence simply because they are translations. The work is then to analyze what the translations actually are (which is where equivalence becomes a non-issue for Toury). Gutt's location of equivalence is also very much in tune with Pym (1992a), except that Pym stresses that the belief in equivalence is historical, shared, and cost-effective in many situations: "The translator is an equivalence producer, a professional communicator working for people who pay to believe that, on whatever level is pertinent, B is equivalent to A" (1992a: 77).

Gutt, Toury, and Pym might agree that **equivalence is a belief structure**. Paradoxically, that kind of rough consensus also logically marks the end of equivalence as a central concept. If equivalence concerns no more than belief, linguists can venture into pragmatics, descriptive scholars can collect and analyze translation shifts, and historians might similarly shelve equivalence as an idea pertinent only to a particular conjuncture of social and technological factors. All those avenues take debate away from equivalence itself; they minimize the tussle between the natural and the directional, stifling the internal dynamics of the paradigm.

Equivalence might appear to be dead, except for the occasional deconstructionist who has read little translation theory and needs a straw man. Then again, history has not finished.

3.8 THE VIRTUES OF DIRECTIONAL EQUIVALENCE

Since directional equivalence is part of the general equivalence paradigm, it shares many of the virtues for natural equivalence we have listed in the previous chapter. We may nevertheless add the following positive points.

Directional equivalence does not make grand ideological assumptions about what is natural, or about the true nature of languages, or about translations being linguistically conservative (which tends to be the effect of natural equivalence). Its lighter ideological baggage means, for example, that it may be applied without contradiction to situations where there are hierarchical relations between languages.

This set of ideas generally casts its net wider than does natural equivalence, recognizing that translators have a broad range of renditions to choose from, and allowing that the factors influencing their choices are not restricted to those of the source text. After all, if there are different equivalents to choose from, the selection criteria must come from somewhere close to the translator. To this extent, directional equivalence becomes fairly compatible with the *Skopos* paradigm that we will meet in the next chapter.

Some theories of directional equivalence are clearly aware that translations create illusions, and they are prepared to analyze those illusions as such. This, however, may be a disadvantage for those theorists who believe that equivalence relations can be substantiated according to firm empirical criteria.

Directional equivalence definitively solves the apparent "impossibility of translation" posited by structuralist linguistics. Equivalence becomes so possible that there are many ways of achieving it.

In posing its great polarities, directional equivalence sets the stage for discussions of translators' ethics. This is why many of the theorists mentioned here have expressed strong opinions about how one should translate.

In some cases, the same great polarities open up a space where the translator has to decide between one kind of equivalence or another, and the theorist does not say which way the translator should go. In those cases (in Levý, House, or Toury, for example), the sub-paradigm opens up the way for further empirical investigation. Instead of telling translators how to translate, theorists can try to find out how they actually do translate, in different cultures and in different historical periods. This leads into the descriptive paradigm, which we will meet below (Chapter 5).

In general terms, directional equivalence imposes weaker constraints than does natural equivalence. These theories can thus become compatible with other paradigms: with *Skopos* theory on the one hand, and with descriptivism on the other. But we run ahead of ourselves.

3.9 FREQUENTLY HAD ARGUMENTS

Some of the historical problems with the equivalence paradigm will be dealt with in the next few chapters, since there were other paradigms at work at the same time and it was from within them that many debates were generated. Let us nevertheless consider a few of the arguments that have concerned directional equivalence as such.

3.9.1 "Equivalence presupposes symmetry between languages"

Mary Snell-Hornby, we noted in the last chapter, criticized the concept of equivalence as presenting "an illusion of symmetry between languages" (Snell-Hornby 1988: 22). We are now in a position to see that her criticism may be valid with respect to some aspects of natural equivalence (those that are tied to an ideology of common "natural" usage), but it hardly holds at all for theories of directional equivalence. The theories of natural equivalence were basically analyzing languages, battling within the paradigm of structuralist linguistics. Directional theories, on the other hand, apply very much at the level of creative language use, in keeping with attempts to analyze *parole* rather than *langue*. As for the promotion of an "illusion," the tables turn as soon as we accept that much of what users believe about translations is indeed illusory, and that the illusions can be analyzed as such. That is, the illusions come not from the theories, but from the domain of social usage itself.

3.9.2 "Theories of directional equivalence are unnecessarily binary"

We have seen that most of the theories in this camp operate on the basis of large polarities. The French theorist and translator **Henri Meschonnic** (1973, 2003) argues that these oppositions (particularly Nida's distinction between formal and dynamic equivalence) depend on a more primary opposition between form and content, or on the separation of the **signifier** and the **signified** as parts of the Saussurean sign. Meschonnic considers that these separations are not valid, since texts function on both levels at the same time, as discourses marked by rhythm: "a way of thinking [*une pensée*] does something to language, and what it does is what is to be translated. And there, the opposition between *source* and *target* is no longer pertinent" (Meschonnic 1999: 22). This critique seems not to take us beyond the equivalence paradigm. It simply stakes out a particularly demanding kind of constraint (the reproduction of discursive effects), well suited to the translation of sacred, philosophical, and literary texts.

3.9.3 "Theories of equivalence make the source text superior"

This is a criticism in the spirit of **Vermeer** (1989a, 1989b/2004), from the *Skopos* approach that we will meet in Chapter 4. If we ask what a translation is "equivalent to," the answer usually involves something in the source text. The source text would thus be the determining factor in the equivalence relation, and the equivalence paradigm thus tends to regard the source text as being superior to the translation. On the other hand, as soon as directional theories stress the *plurality* of possible equivalents, some further criteria are required if the translator is to make a guided choice between those equivalents. The equivalence paradigm names but does not investigate those further criteria, and to that extent it allows the source text to retain its apparent superiority.

3.9.4 "Equivalence is not efficient; similarity is enough"

This is the general position of **Andrew Chesterman**, whom we cited at the beginning of this chapter. Should we be talking about similarity or equivalence? Chesterman claims that "[a]dequate similarity is enough – adequate for a given purpose, in a given context . . . anything more would be an inefficient use of resources" (1996: 74). In other words, the equivalence paradigm makes translators work harder than they really have to. Then again, we have to ask exactly who is perceiving the equivalence (or the similarity). One of Chesterman's models ("divergent similarity," which we have assimilated into directional equivalence) seems to operate in the eyes of the translator (and presumably others able to adopt that position). The other model ("convergent similarity," our natural equivalence) is, for Chesterman, a relation established by anyone actually comparing the two texts. That comparison is a lot of work, hardly compatible with efficiency! In these terms, equivalence might be an assumption of similarity made by the end-user of the translation who has *no* direct access to the source. Now, for the translator, who is surely aware of directionality and plurality, similarity may indeed be enough, and there is no reason to work hard in order to attain some imaginary absolute equivalence (which seems to be the only kind that Chesterman allows for here: "perfect and total transfer of meaning" is associated with "the illusion of total equivalence"). For the user, however, equivalence may be a convenient fiction that allays suspicions of non-similarity. Since it would be too much work actually to check the validity of the decisions made by the translator, we simply accept the translation as equivalent, as an act of trust in the translator. The illusion of equivalence should actually *reduce* cognitive effort at the point of text use. Further, if translators are aware of the way equivalence works in reception, they can reduce and direct their efforts accordingly. In other words, the illusion of equivalence may well enable a very efficient use of resources.

Theorists working within the equivalence paradigm will probably not win all these debates. They should nevertheless be able to hold their own, and may even find quite a few blind spots in the paradigms that came later.

SUMMARY

This chapter started by pointing out the rather strange way that a relation of similarity can depend on directionality (since a mother is not normally considered "like" her daughter). This relation introduces a series of theories about the general ways translators make decisions about how to translate, since they constantly have to select between alternatives. For example, you can choose the path of "dynamic equivalence" or "formal equivalence" (in Nida's terminology). The history of translation theory gives many versions of this basic opposition, all of them introducing different considerations and often making different recommendations about which of the poles is superior. At the end of this chapter we have related the options to relevance theory, particularly as applied to translation by Gutt. The text-user's "belief in interpretative resemblance" may be seen as a concept operative within the sub-paradigm of directional equivalence, since it depends heavily on directionality. At the same time, Gutt's approach fits in with a handful of theories that emphasize the social function of equivalence as a shared illusion, a social fiction that becomes cost-effective in the practice of cross-cultural communication. Although very few of the theorists in this sub-paradigm would share that view (most believe they are describing social facts in the linguistic tradition), the idea of a functional illusion makes the concept of equivalence compatible with some of the other paradigms that we will deal with in the next few chapters. Those newer paradigms will actually pick up threads from directional equivalence. If the translator has to choose between strategies, and the reasons for the choice are not all in the source text, where might the reasons lie?

SOURCES AND FURTHER READING

The Translation Studies Reader (Venuti 2000/2004) includes fundamental texts by Jerome, Schleiermacher, and Nida. Munday (2001/2008) mentions the main polarities of directional equivalence in his chapter on "equivalence and equivalent effect," giving more examples than we do here. There are relatively few pedagogical texts presenting theories of directional equivalence, certainly as compared with the more linguistic theories of natural equivalence. Important texts like Kade's are also quite difficult to find. Key texts by Cicero, Schleiermacher, and so on are in the main anthologies. One might fruitfully tackle Gutt's *Translation and Relevance* (1991/2000), and the first chapter of Venuti's *The Translator's Invisibility* (1995) presents a rich mixture of argument and insinuation about the effects of equivalence. For an even more virulent debate, a selection of texts by Henri Meschonnic is available in English (2003).

Suggested projects and activities

1   If we go back in history, we find the Latin churchman and translator Hieronymus (Jerome) claiming that he translated sense-for-sense, except in the case of the Bible, where he worked word-for-word because "there is mystery in the very order of the words" (Letter to Pammachius). What theories of equivalence can this be related to? Should we have different theories for different texts? Check to see what Hieronymus, in the Latin Vulgate, put for the Hebrew term *'almah* in Isaiah 7:14. Compare this with other available equivalents.

2   The sentence "La primera palabra de esta misma frase tiene dos letras" could be rendered as "The first word of the sentence in Spanish has two letters." What kind of equivalence is this? Is the English sentence a translation? Give reasons.

3   Can "The first word of this sentence has three letters" be effectively translated into a language that does not have words, or does not have three-letter articles? What kind of equivalence is achieved by the following: "Les lettres du premier mot de cette phrase sont trois en nombre"?

4   Compare different translations (in the same language) of the one paragraph. Do the differences indicate different kinds of equivalence? Is there any evidence of different equivalence-maintaining strategies?

5   For the following sentences, state which of Grice's maxims (see 3.6 above) are being broken and propose at least two different translations of each sentence. You may want to check the examples we have taken from Gutt.

Text: "Juliette is the sun" (see Appiah 2000).
Context: The speaker loves Juliette.
Text: "Frequently had arguments."
Context: This book.

Text: "She was given a violin lesson for free, with no strings attached."
Context: A stand-up comic.

6   It has been suggested that Grice's maxims (see 3.6 above) are specific to English-language culture. For example, the "maxim of quantity" is coherent with the English recommendation to "keep it short and simple" (the KISS principle). A corresponding Italian principle might be "keep it long and complete" (KILC?). Which of the maxims do you think might not be operative in your culture? Remember that a maxim is operative when its transgression produces an implicature.

7   Find a poem that has been creatively translated into the students' first language (hopefully a translation that does not challenge the equivalence paradigm). Now present the translation as if it were the source text, and the source as if it were the translation. Ask the class to evaluate the translation. Why will they all find the "assumed translation" inferior to what they believe the source to be?

8   The whole class translates the same text into their mother tongue. Then they see in what places in the text they all agree on the one equivalent, and in what places there are many different equivalents (this is an application of the choice-network analysis proposed by Campbell 2001). Does it make sense to call one kind of equivalence "natural" and the other "directional"? Do the places with many equivalents necessarily correspond to what is hardest to translate?

9   Take the same source text as in Activity 7 (above). Now, as in Chapter 2, use the automatic translation programs Babelfish and Google Translate to do back-translations of it several times (e.g. moving from English to German to English to German, for the one text). At what points does equivalence cease to be directional (i.e. when do we enter the ping-pong relation of natural equivalence, where we go back and forth between the same things)? Why do we reach those points? Is there more directionality in human translation or machine translation? Why?

10 Each student writes a short text about a topic they are closely related to (the most wonderful moment in their life, or the moment they were most frightened) in their mother tongue. Other students then translate those texts (into *their* mother tongue, if the class group is mixed). The first students receive their translations back and are asked to evaluate them. How do they feel about being translated? Do theories of equivalence have any relation to their feelings? Usually, no matter how exact the translation, the experience will be felt to be most real in the source text. What might this say about the nature of equivalence? (Our thanks to Andrew Chesterman for this task.)

11 As an extension of Activity 10 (above), the translation is revised by a third student and by the author of the source text. Who will make the most changes to the translation? Why? What does this say about the nature of equivalence?

12 As suggested in the chapter on natural equivalence, consider the terms your language uses for websites (e.g. "site," "webpage," "browser," "navigate", "surf"). How did those terms come into your language? If they evolved from situations of one-to-none equivalence (see 3.2 above), were they borrowed from a foreign language or generated from within your language? Do the terms indicate a global hierarchy of languages? Which strategy does your culture prefer? Which strategy *should* it prefer?

CHAPTER 4

Purposes

This chapter looks at a group of theories that have generally been opposed to the equivalence paradigm. These theories all insist that a translation is designed to achieve a purpose. If that purpose is to repeat the function of the source text, as is the case in Reiss's theory of text types, then there should actually be little difference between the two paradigms: the relation between source-text function and target-text function is still one of equivalence. However, as soon as a theory accepts that the target-side purpose can be *different* from the source-side function, we are dealing with a new paradigm. For Vermeer, the target-side purpose (which he calls *Skopos*) is the dominant factor in a translation project. Vermeer thus claims to "dethrone" the source text and go beyond source-bound theories of equivalence. This approach accepts that the one source text can be translated in different ways in order to carry out different functions. The translator thus needs information about the specific goals each translation is supposed to achieve, and this requires extra-textual information of some kind, usually from the client. In this way, the linguistic frame of the equivalence paradigm becomes much wider, bringing in a series of professional relationships. Several different theories can be fitted into this extended interpersonal frame. Holz-Mänttäri focuses on the translator's status as an expert in cross-cultural communication, working alongside experts in other fields. Hönig and Kussmaul consider how much information the receiver of the translation really needs, and they advise the translator to adjust the text accordingly. These approaches deal with "purpose" in a sense that seems more general than the target-side *Skopos* conceptualized by Vermeer. This more general sense enables us to close the chapter with insights that come from much closer to the translation industry itself. For Daniel Gouadec, translation concerns not so much texts as *projects*, understood as sets of material and information. Gouadec proposes numerous categories for the way translation projects should be organized, including extensive information to be supplied by the client. His general approach is similarly based on the translator achieving communicative purposes. Like all the theories covered in this chapter, he picks up many factors that were overlooked or sidelined in the equivalence paradigm.

4.1 *SKOPOS* AS THE KEY TO A NEW PARADIGM

A paradigm shift in translation theory can be dated from 1984, at least as a symbolic point. That year saw the publication of two books in German: *Grundlegung einer allgemeinen Translationstheorie* (Foundation for a General Theory of Translation) by Katharina Reiss (also written Reiβ) and Hans Vermeer, and *Translatorisches Handeln. Theorie und Methode*

The **main points** covered in this chapter are:

- The *Skopos* theory developed by Hans Vermeer breaks with the equivalence paradigm by giving priority to the target-side purpose to be fulfilled by the translation.
- For *Skopos* theory, equivalence characterizes a "constant function" translation and is considered a special case.
- This theory allows that the one source text can be translated in different ways to achieve different purposes.
- Holz-Mänttäri's concept of "translatorial action" sees the translator as an expert in cross-cultural communication who may be called upon to do much more than translate.
- Hönig and Kussmaul's "principle of the necessary degree of precision" (the "good enough" theory) states that the translator should give the details that the reader needs, which may be more than those in the source text, or less.
- Gouadec's approach to project analysis is similarly based on purpose as defined by the client, but it assumes that complete information in the pre-translation phase will resolve most translation problems.
- Although the purpose paradigm is compatible with the equivalence paradigm at many points, the opposition between the two was largely institutional within the context of the 1980s and 1990s in Germany and Austria.

(Translatorial Action. Theory and Method) by Justa Holz-Mänttäri. Both books, in different ways, directly challenged the idea that a translation has to be equivalent to a source text. They both initiated a partial break with the equivalence paradigm.

Those books are not exactly world-famous. They were very slow to become known outside of German (the first was translated into Spanish in 1996; the second has not been rendered out of German as far as we know). General texts on translation theory do nevertheless carry frequent references to **Skopos theory**, the theory of *Skopos*, a Greek word for what we will more broadly call "purpose" (it could also be translated as "aim," "goal," or "intended function"). The basic idea is that the translator should work in order to achieve the *Skopos*, the communicative purpose of the translation, rather than just follow the source text. This "*Skopos* rule" appears to mean that the translator's decisions should be made, in the last instance, in accordance with the reasons why someone asked the translator to do the translation. Yet it could also mean that the dominant factor is what the end-user wants the translation for. Then again, the determining factor might be what the translator *thinks* the purpose should be. For the general paradigm, all these interpretations are possible and have proved mildly revolutionary, since none of them is on the side of the author or the source text. The theories thus invite the translator to look in a new direction.

The novelty of this approach thus lies in what it does *not* say. For this paradigm, the translator's choices need *not* be dominated by the source text, or by criteria of equivalence, unless of course the source text and equivalence happen to be stipulated as essential for the purpose. A legal agreement, for example, may be adapted to target-side textual norms

Vermeer's Skopos rule

Vermeer formulates the *Skopos* rules as follows:

> An action is determined by its goal [*Zweck*] (it is a function of its goal [*Zweck*]).
>
> (Reiss and Vermeer 1984: 100)

This would be a general principle of action theory. What it means for the translator is described in the following terms:

> The dominant factor of each translation is its purpose [*Zweck*].
>
> (Reiss and Vermeer 1984: 96)

Note that both of these formulations use the normal German term *Zweck* ("goal," "aim," or "purpose"), rather than the technical neologism *Skopos*. Why the Greek term is necessary remains unclear. It may be that the slight opacity of the Greek tells us that we do not know exactly what it refers to.

A more elaborate explanation may be found in Vermeer:

> Each text is produced for a given purpose and should serve this purpose. The *Skopos* rule thus reads as follows: translate/interpret/speak/write in a way that enables your text/translation to function in the situation in which it is used and with the people who want to use it and precisely in the way they want it to function.
>
> (Vermeer 1989a: 20; translation from Nord 1997: 29)

Here the end-user appears to call the shots, although we shall later ask "who decides?" (4.5 below). The important point at this stage is that when you consider these formulations, the *Skopos* rule does not actually say *how* a text should be translated. It simply tells the translator where to look for indications about the way to translate. In each case, you have to see what the intended purpose is. Vermeer is clear on this point:

> What the *Skopos* states is that one must translate, consciously and consistently, in accordance with some principle respecting the target text. The theory does not state what the principle is: this must be determined separately in each specific case.
>
> (Vermeer 1989b/2004: 234)

if and when it is to be governed by the laws operative in that culture, or it may be rendered with the source-text form if and when the translation is more for purposes of understanding, or again, it may be translated in an almost word-for-word way if, for instance, it is to be cited as evidence in court. The source text would be the same in all cases. What is different is the *purpose* that the translation has to serve. One source, many possible translations, and the key factor determining the actual translation is the purpose, the *Skopos*.

The idea is simple enough. It has led theorists into considerations of what purposes are, how they are defined in relation to clients (a dimension wholly absent from the equivalence paradigm), and how they turn translations from texts into projects. This paradigm shift, however, was complicated by several factors.

First, the *Skopos* idea was presented by Hans Vermeer in a book of which he was the co-author (although he had announced the idea in articles as early as 1978). The other co-author, Katharina Reiss, was working within a less radical paradigm, based on text types, in the same book.

Second, Reiss and Vermeer were in Heidelberg; Holz-Mänttäri was working in Tampere, Finland, where her work was published. So the two books published in 1984 came from distant contexts and have different approaches.

Third, Vermeer was undoubtedly the one who did his publicity best and made sure his term (*Skopos*) become the company logo. The German-language scholars who followed the general paradigm have nevertheless been quite free in selecting from the ideas of Reiss and Holz-Mänttäri, as well as from Vermeer.

So there is a rather more complicated story to tell.

4.2 REISS, VERMEER, AND THE ORIGINS OF THE *SKOPOS* APPROACH

As we have noted, the equivalence paradigm was prominently represented in German by Werner Koller's textbook *Einführung in die Übersetzungswissenschaft* (Introduction to Translation Science (1979 and many later reprints)). Koller had formulated a complex concept of equivalence in which there were five frames: denotative, connotative, text-normative, pragmatic, and formal. That amounted to saying that the way you translate (the kinds of equivalence you seek) depends on the function of the text or fragment you are translating. The five frames are basically names for things that language can do. If the text you are working on is mainly referring to things in the world, you should make sure those references are exact (and probably updated if necessary). If a poem is functioning primarily on the level

---

Some key terms

- **Skopos**: The purpose or aim of the translation; the function it is supposed to carry out in the situation of reception.
- **Skopos theory**: Here, the set of propositions based on the idea that the target-side *Skopos* or purpose has priority in the translator's decisions. This theory is only one part of the purpose paradigm, alongside other theories that also talk about purposes as functions without giving priority to the target side.
- **Brief**: The instructions the client gives to the translator; *Auftrag* in German; also called "commission" in English. In actual translation practice, the more normal terms would be "instructions" or "job description."
- **Translatorial**: Adjective to describe qualities of *translators*, as opposed to the adjective "translational," used to describe qualities of translations.
- **Translatorial action**: All the actions carried out by a translation, only one of which may be translating.
- **Translatory**: Here, adjective to describe the translation *process*.

of form, then you should primarily seek equivalence on the level of form, and so on. For Koller, and for most people at the time, the way you translate depends on the kind of text you are translating. That paradigm was pluralist, functionalist, and source-oriented. That view seems happily at home within the equivalence paradigm. It was about to be challenged.

Katharina Reiss was another theorist working more or less within the equivalence paradigm. Her fundamental theory had actually been published earlier than Koller's and was quite compatible with his concept of equivalence, the one we have outlined above. In her 1971 book *Möglichkeiten und Grenzen der Übersetzungskritik* (translated into English in 2000 as *Translation Criticism: Potential and Limitations*), Reiss had proposed that different text types require different translation strategies. She recognized three basic text types: expressive, appellative ("appeal-dominated," or "calling"), and representational (or "content-dominated"), with each text classified according to which of these functions is dominant (Table 4.1). These were actually based on the three linguistic persons (related to language functions by Bühler in 1934/1982). The "expressive-dominated" text is oriented by the first person ("I") and would cover such things as personal letters and many literary genres. The "appeal-dominated" text would involve genres like publicity, which have to have an effect on the second person ("you), the receiver, and should be rendered so as to have such effects. The "content-dominated" text would then be anything that refers to the external world, to third persons ("he," "she," "it," "they"), and thus requires a mode of translation where the references are exact. In 1976 Reiss revised her typology. The term "appellative" became "operative," which is easier to understand in English, but the basic idea remained the same: the communicative function of the source text tells you what strategies to use when translating it.

Reiss's work was actually more sophisticated than the triadic models, since she recognized mixed genres and considered the implications of communication media (for example, when a novel becomes a film, we would expect the translation strategies to change). The model is quite easily extended by recognizing additional language functions. Drawing on **Roman Jakobson** (1960) we could add the "metalinguistic," "phatic," and "poetic" functions, in fact adding a vertical axis to Bühler's three-person model. The basic idea nevertheless remains unchanged: whatever the function of the source text is, the translator should try to have it work in the translation. Reiss has remained faithful to that vision throughout, to the extent of appearing uncomfortable with a paradigm that would enable translators to stray from an ethical obligation to source-text function.

This is a point where misunderstandings abound. Reiss's position has been called "functionalist," which is fair enough. Her main idea, after all, is that the way we translate depends on the function of the text we are translating, the way it is to be used by people. Many other theorists have picked up that idea, and the banner of "**functionalism**" has been used as a general term for this approach. In **Christiane Nord** (1988/1991), for example, we find an extensive description of how texts should be analyzed prior to translation, so that

Table 4.1 Reiss's correlations of text types and translation methods (adapted from Nord 2002/2003)

Text types 1971	Text types 1976	Translation method
Content dominated	Informative text	Correctness of contents, acceptability of form
Form dominated	Expressive text	Correctness of contents, corresponding form
Appeal dominated	Operative text	Effect has priority over content and form

translators can then ascertain the function of those texts with exactitude (in very Germanic fashion, Nord's analysis comprises some 76 questions that students should be taught to answer before translating). The analysis, says Nord, should first be of the instructions for the target text, then of the source text, in order to locate the correspondences and differences between the two. Nord is also aware that in professional translation processes these analyses become largely automatic: no one really ever asks all 76 questions. On the level of theory, Nord certainly recognizes that translations can have functions different from their source texts, yet the main weight of her actual analyses has tended to fall on the source side. In her comments on her own co-translating of biblical texts, for example, Nord (2001) first isolates the "intended function" of problematic source-text passages and then considers how that function can be reproduced or modified in order to emphasis "otherness" with respect to modern-day readerships (which in this case is the "intended function" of the translation). **Mary Snell-Hornby**, at that time director of the large translation school in Vienna, placed a similar "functionalism" at the heart of her influential "integrated approach" (1988). The basic message underlying all these theorists was that one should translate the functions of texts, not the words or sentences on the page. Of course, that message can be traced back as far as Cicero, at least, since it is essential to the very concept of equivalence. This "functionalism" should have been nothing new.

What is strange is that both Nord and Snell-Hornby *opposed* their functionalism to the equivalence paradigm, especially as represented by Koller (cf. Nord 1988/1991: 23, 25–26; Snell-Hornby 1988: 22). In hindsight, that was rather ungenerous. These writers somehow equated equivalence with straight formal equivalence, or with literalism, whereas the concept of equivalence had been developed precisely so that the categories of "dynamic" equivalence could work alongside the possibilities of literalism. Nida's approach, and certainly Koller's model of equivalence, could also legitimately be called "functionalist." In fact, all the functionalist models of equivalence remain entirely compatible with Reiss's insistence on text types. And "functionalism," as we shall see in the following chapters, was a term that could also be extended to many of the theorists pursuing descriptive approaches. If "function" was the only game in town, the German-language theorists were having a debate about very little.

Consider a chestnut example like Adolf Hitler's **Mein Kampf**. What is the function of this text? In some parts it is certainly expressive, manifesting a strong first-person character, as befits an autobiography. In other aspects it gives a vision of history, and is thus referential. Finally, its overall function is undoubtedly to convert readers to the cause of National Socialism, so it should also be classified as "appelative," as a "call to action." How should we translate the text? The mixing of functions is not the real problem (functionalism never promised pure categories beyond its carefully selected examples). If we analyze the source text carefully, if we refer back to what we know about the author's intentions and the effects on the first readers, we should probably translate *Mein Kampf* in such a way as to convert even more readers to National Socialism. That could be the outcome of straight source-text functionalism. Unfortunately, many publishers and perhaps most translators would feel unhappy about that kind of goal. In most contemporary situations it would make better political sense to translate the text as a historical document, adding footnotes and references to historical events that happened after the source text was written. The translator might decide to tone down the most rabble-rousing prose, just in case the reader starts believing the text instead of regarding it as a partial explanation why others became Nazis. Alternatively, we might make the exclamations even more outrageously strident, to defuse the "call to action" by making it unbelievable. A few well-selected translation strategies could potentially direct readers down one path or the other, and there are serious ethical considerations at stake.

Source-text functionalism cannot really discuss the reasons why a translator might want to change the function of the source text. But **Vermeer's concept of** *Skopos* can. For Vermeer, the translator of *Mein Kampf* would have to give priority not to how the original German text functioned, but to **the function the text is supposed to have on the target reader**. Those two functions could be quite different, and in this particular case they probably should be very different. Even in instances of what Vermeer calls "constant function" (*Funktionskonstanz*), where the *Skopos* requires the source-text function to be maintained, significant changes may be required. In fact, maintenance of source-text function (which might be another term for one kind of equivalence) is probably the principle that requires the most textual shifts. The first right-wing translators of Hitler into English wanted to have him accepted by the new readership, and thus toned down the rhetoric and tried to make Mr. Hitler sound like a quite rational politician (cf. Baumgarten 2001).

Vermeer's concept of giving priority to the *Skopos* or purpose thus radicalized the functionalism that was already there, shifting its focus from the source to the target. It brought in pragmatic factors like attention to **the role of clients**, to the importance of the translator having **clear instructions** prior to translating, and to the general principle that the **one text can be translated in many different ways**, to suit many different purposes. Those were all good ideas. They were not particularly troubling in themselves, given that they called on common sense and a dash of existentialist liberalism (each translator has to decide for themselves). So why such a hoo-hah about the issue?

The problem could have been this. As long as you are analyzing modes of equivalence to the source, you are doing **linguistics** of one kind or another. But if you have to choose between one *purpose* and another (e.g. different reasons for translating *Mein Kampf*), linguistics will not be of much help to you. You are engaged in applied sociology, marketing, the ethics of communication, and a gamut of theoretical considerations that are only loosely held under the term "cultural studies." Theories of equivalence could be formulated in linguistic terms, and translators could thus be trained in faculties of language and linguistics. The more radical versions of target-side functionalism, on the other hand, justified the creation of a new academic discipline. They could remove translator training from the clutches of the more traditional language departments. Translation theory thus surreptitiously became a debate about **academic power**. Equivalence was on one side, "functionalism" on the other; and they were opposed, even when, as theories, they were basically compatible.

The **institutional context** was not ephemeral. Germany and Austria at that time had a handful of very large translation schools offering full degree programs. A survey (Caminade and Pym 1995) gave the following student numbers: Germersheim 2,900, Vienna 2,500, Innsbruck 1,800, Heidelberg 1,350, Graz 1,300, Saarbrücken 1,200, and Hildesheim 600. Those student numbers represent many academic jobs, a real demand for research, and consequent publication space. Those are the sources of academic power, and theorists can fight to get those things. Further, after the fall of the Berlin Wall in 1989, there was a struggle for the translator-training schools in Central and Eastern Europe, with **Mary Snell-Hornby** quite logically seeking an "integrated approach" in part by insisting that translation teachers in the East should "cut the umbilical cord with the departments of Modern Languages" (1994: 433). The new paradigm seemed set to create a small empire in Europe.

We can also follow the geography of the theorists themselves. **Koller** was at Heidelberg but moved to Bergen, Norway, in the late 1970s. **Reiss** was also at Heidelberg until 1969, when she moved to Würzburg; **Vermeer** was at nearby Germersheim, where he coincided with translation researchers including Hönig, Kussmaul, and Kupsch-Losereit. The Germersheim connection also enabled contact with the anthropologist Göhring, who provided significant support for the broader cultural view. Vermeer then moved to Heidelberg in the mid-1980s, where his approach influenced **Christiane Nord** (whom we thank for these details). Nord moved to Hildesheim and Vienna where, with **Snell-Hornby**, "functionalism" became the order of the day. Nord later moved to Magdeburg, in former East Germany. Saarbrücken, meanwhile, has long remained faithful to Applied Linguistics as its frame, as indeed have many scholars within all the institutions mentioned. The result, throughout the 1980s and into the 1990s, was a series of institutional tussles that are best not recounted here. In that context, translation theory was playing an active role in academic politics.

The thrust of the *Skopos* theory, with its various internal differences and debates, found a home in the Heidelberg journal *TextconText* from 1986, under Vermeer's editorship and initially with editorial input from Holz-Mänttäri. The group recruited many fellow travelers in those pages, publishing work from cultural anthropology, from growing areas like community interpreting, from translation history, and from deconstruction, which seemed to fit in with the critique of equivalence and the empowerment of the individual translator. As such, the journal became a highly fruitful meeting place, leaving a mark on German-language theorizing for several decades.

4.3 JUSTA HOLZ-MÄNTTÄRI AND THE THEORY OF THE TRANSLATOR'S EXPERTISE

While all of this was happening, Justa Holz-Mänttäri was a German working in Finland, relatively distanced from the feuds and working with considerable creative independence. Her project was quite simply to rewrite the entire translation process from the perspective of **action theory**, which was also of some importance to Vermeer. To do this, she felt the need to **change the terms** that are most commonly used to describe what translators do. Part of this was already happening in Germany: for example, the German loan word from English *Translation* had been adopted to cover both written translation (*Übersetzen*) and spoken interpreting (*Dolmetschen*). Holz-Mänttäri (1984) went much further, however. The notion of "text" became a *Botschaftsträger* (message-bearer); translators, who were called upon to do many things beyond translating, had their general profession described as *Texter* (on the model of a "writer," who writes, a "reader," who reads; so a "texter" is someone who "texts"); and so on. Coupled with impressive syntactic density, the neologisms make Holz-Mänttäri a monument to why translators say they cannot understand translation theory.

Holz-Mänttäri's guiding ideas are nevertheless not difficult to grasp. She starts from a functionalist view not only of texts but also of society (drawing on action theory and sources like Malinowski's theory of different social institutions fulfilling comparable social functions). Within this frame, **functions are manifested in actions, each of which is guided by its aim**. The communication of messages is an action like any other, ruled by the function the message is to fulfill. Different social groups, however, are expert in carrying out different kinds of actions, and indeed at communicating different kinds of messages. When a message has to cross into another culture, the people sending that message will require help from an **expert in cross-cultural communication**. That expert should be the translator, who may therefore be called on to do many different things, including giving advice on the other culture, or writing a new text on the basis of information provided by the client.

It is easy to see how Holz-Mänttäri's theory fitted in with the dominance of the target-side function. Taken individually, most of her ideas would seem unlikely to upset anyone. The idea of actions achieving aims was a mainstay of **pragmatics** and indeed of many kinds of **sociology**; it was working in the same way as Vermeer's *Skopos* rule. Holz-Mänttäri's arguments against the simple determinism of "when X in the source, then Y in the translation" amounted to a non-mechanical view that was common enough within the equivalence paradigm. What did rankle, however, was the idea that a translator could actually write a new text and still be called a translator. This was stretching definitions of "translation" a long way. Nonetheless, if we look at the terms closely, Holz-Mänttäri and others were talking about "**translatorial action**," the range of actions carried out by translators (and other "texters"); her interest was not limited to the physical facts of translations. We thus find schemas like Figure 4.1.

Here we see that "**translatorial action**" (where the adjective "translatorial" refers to the person, the "translator") can be categorized as "mediated cross-cultural communication." That action is properly "translational" (the adjective refers to the thing, the translation) when it is with respect to a source text, although there are many other kinds of translatorial actions that translators can be involved in. We can also see that the attempt to repeat the same function as the source text is just one possible aim of translating; translators can legitimately attempt to carry out new functions. One could try to extend the branches further at the bottom of the tree, asking which kinds of equivalence would fit under "new function" and "same function" ("new function" would be "directional"; "same function" might be "natural"), but that would be an adventure beyond the concerns of the purpose paradigm. For the theorists we are talking about here, the above terms form a loose geography in which the work of the translator may be located.

Seen in this way, both Holz-Mänttäri and Vermeer were producing radical critiques of traditional equivalence-based definitions of translation. They were also challenging the traditional role of linguistics in the training of translators. At the same time, they were quite possibly speaking on behalf of changes in the translation profession, at least to the extent that translators were increasingly being called on to do more than translate (terminology,

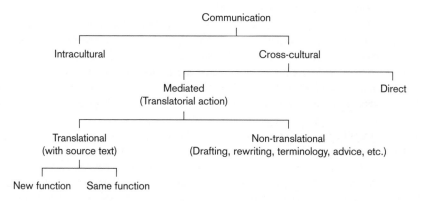

Figure 4.1   Translation as a form of mediated cross-cultural communication (adapted from Nord 1997: 18)

reviewing, desk-top publishing and project management all take translation work beyond the source text, and then there are logical career moves into international marketing and public relations). The theorists were, in a very broad sense, allowing the profession to erupt into theory.

That did not mean, however, that translators could do whatever they liked.

4.4 PURPOSE-BASED "GOOD ENOUGH" THEORY

An important consequence of the purpose paradigm is that, in terms of the general approach, the translator can presumably give *more* information than is in the source text if necessary, and *less* information if so required. That possibility was partly recognized within the equivalence paradigm, but never fully condoned. Nida, for example, talked about "addition" as something a translator could do with a text, but he immediately explained that "there has been no actual adding to the semantic content of the message, for these additions consist essentially in making explicit what is implicit in the source-language text" (1964: 230–231). Similarly, what Nida calls "subtraction" "does not substantially lessen the information carried by the communication" (1964: 233). The equivalence paradigm generally does not legitimize cases of outright addition or omission, where the translator need not point to something in the source text as the reason for what is in the target text (cf. Pym 1992a: 84). In fact, while an author like **Vázquez-Ayora** could certainly discuss the category of "paraphrase" as something that translators are occasionally called upon to do, he issues repeated warnings that such uses of reduction do not really belong to the domain of translation: "To translate does not mean to explain or comment on a text, or to write it as we see fit" (1977: 288; our translation). Lying beneath this general refusal to allow additions or omissions, we might find the biblical prohibitions of modifying the sacred text (cf. Deut. 4:2; 12:32; Rev. 22: 18–19). More generally, however, an age of strong authorship tends to respect the integrity of all texts and, for as long as the source text remains the measure and justification of translation strategies, the question of exactly how much the translator can add or take away need never be formulated as such. On the other hand, in an age where many texts are relatively authorless (brochures, webpages, and instructions usually do not carry the name of any one author), there seems to be greater translatorial liberty, the weight of the source can be diminished, and serious thought must be given to the question.

One answer to the problem was formulated by **Hans Hönig** and **Paul Kussmaul**, theorists and teachers working in Germersheim, a large translation school near Heidelberg. Influenced by *Skopos* theory in the 1980s, Hönig and Kussmaul (1982/1996) formulated what they term the "**principle of the necessary degree of precision**." The principle proposes that the appropriate degree of precision is determined by the required function of the translation. That would seem to be another formulation of the *Skopos* rule. Its illustration, however, is a little more challenging.

Hönig and Kussmaul discuss the question of how to render culture-specific terms like "Bachelor's" or "Master's" degrees, which tend to occur in relatively authorless texts like a curriculum vitae. They recognize that the translator cannot hope to tell the reader *everything* about studies and degrees in the foreign institution, nor is it fair simply to leave the reader totally unaware of the way basic terms and structures differ. As Hönig puts it in a later text (1997: 11), "there has to be a cut-off point where translators can safely say: 'This is all my readers have to know in this context'."

Where that point lies depends on the specific function of the translation, so there is not really any further general principle to be announced. What remains of interest, though, is the way this is explained. Here is Hönig's 1997 account of an example that has incited discussion and debate (cf. Hönig and Kussmaul 1982: 53):

> The principle of the necessary degree of precision is by no means limited to culture-specific terms, and indeed not to the meaning of words alone, but it can best be illustrated by this type of translation problem. For instance, the term "public school" implies such a large amount of culture-specific knowledge that it is impossible to render its meaning "completely" in a translation. Within a functionalist approach, however, the function of a word in its specific context determines to what degree the cultural meaning should be made explicit. In a sentence such as [emphasis added]:
>
> (2a) In Parliament he fought for equality, but he sent his son to *Eton*.
>
> the translation will have to be different from translating the identical term "Eton" in the sentence:
>
> (3a) When his father died his mother could not afford to send him to *Eton* any more.
>
> The following translations would be sufficiently detailed:
>
> (2b) Im Parlament kämpfte er für Chancengleichheit, aber seinen eigenen Sohn schickte er auf eine der englischen Eliteschulen.
>
> (. . . one of the English elite schools)
>
> (3b) Als sein Vater starb, konnte seine Mutter es sich nicht mehr leisten, ihn auf eine der teuren Privatschulen zu schicken.
>
> (. . . one of the expensive private schools).
>
> Of course, there is more factual knowledge implied in the terms "Eton" or "public school" than expressed in the translation, but the translation mentions everything that is important within the context of the sentence, in other words, the translation is semantically precise enough.

We note here that the translator has made certain assumptions about the readers' knowledge of English institutions, and has given information accordingly. To that extent, the solutions are determined by the target-side situation, and thus by the assumed purpose of the translation, as the *Skopos* rule would have it. There is no question of the translation being exact or perfect; there is no need for excessive work to go into any kind of strategic analysis or componential semantic; the rendition is simply "good enough" for the situation concerned. The translator may thus assume that "this is all my readers have to know," and no more need be said. For example, Hönig does not reproduce the translation offered in the earlier book (1982: 53):

> konnte es sich seine Mutter nicht mehr leisten, ihn nach Eton zu schicken, jene teure englische Privatschule, aus deren Absolventen auch heute noch ein Großteil des politischen und wirtschaftlichen Führungsnachwuchses hervorgeht.
>
> [his mother could not afford to send him to Eton, the expensive English private school that still today produces a large part of the political and economic elite.]

That amount of added information is now considered excessive. In the context of the mother's financial difficulties, the reader only "needs to know" that Eton is expensive.

Note that in the above citation Hönig does not really speak about the relation between the translation and the reader. He actually refers to "the function of a word in its specific context," and this is later glossed as "the context of the sentence." Further, the two different translations of the term "Eton" are not really presented as adding or taking away anything that is in the source. When all is said and done, those translations are *making explicit* a few semantic values that English-language readers of the source text are assumed to activate. Despite the best principles of target-side functionalism, the actual practice suggests that we are not too far removed from the basic principles of equivalence, in this case directional and dynamic.

At this point we return to one of the basic problems of the wider purpose paradigm. If the nature of the source text can determine one kind of function (as it seems to do in Hönig's example), are we always certain there are no other purposes to be respected?

4.5 WHO REALLY DECIDES?

Despite our doubts about how radically new some of the functionalist approaches were, Hans Vermeer saw his *Skopos* rule as effectively "dethroning" the source text. For him, the translator's decisions could no longer be based solely on what was in the source. Once you accept that principle seriously, a whole new dimension opens up. Suddenly there are numerous social actors involved: the paying client, the person actually giving the job (perhaps a translation company or agency), the translator, a series of experts potentially helping the translator, editors controlling the translator, and hopefully the final reader or user of the translation. German-language functionalist theories are full of diagrams connecting all those agents and describing their numerous possible roles. Together, however, all these people and factors somehow appear to converge in the one *Skopos* or purpose, the thing that the translation is supposed to achieve. We might say, for example, that a childlike suicide note is undoubtedly an expressive text (as Reiss's text typology might classify it), but when rendering it in a courtroom situation the translator should work with absolute philological exactitude, since the new purpose is to decide if the note was really written by the child (an authentic example, taken from Mayoral 2003). In this case, the function of the source text is quite different from that of the translation, and the change responds to a new purpose.

That kind of analysis works well for as long as everyone agrees on the purpose of the translation. But what happens when there is no clear agreement? Imagine, for example, that a neo-Nazi party has asked you to do a new "dynamic" equivalence translation of *Mein Kampf*, or the defense attorney insists that the suicide note be translated in a way that arouses no suspicion of forgery. How should the translator decide in these situations?

If we read the functionalist theories closely, we find remarkably little agreement on this question. The source may have been dethroned for some, so who is the new king?

For Holz-Mänttäri, **the properly trained translator is the expert** in things translational, and so should be left to decide such issues. Authors and clients, on the other hand, tend to be experts in their own respective fields, and so should be left to decide on such things as field-specific terminology and the desired effect on the reader. Holz-Mänttäri thus projects a world of complementary expertise, full of mutual respect, and with a prominent and well-defined place for the properly trained translator. The translator is thus sovereign in properly translational matters. Of course, the extent of those things still remains quite hard to define.

Vermeer's position is rather more difficult to pin down. We have seen him describe the translation process as making a text "function in the situation in which it is used and with the people who want to use it and precisely in the way they want it to function" (1989a: 20). This appears to make the end-user king. Yet we also find Vermeer describing the translator as a respected expert (1989a: 40), a professional who "acts translatorially" (*handelt translatorisch*) (1989a: 42), and whose ethical responsibility is to fulfill the goal of the translation as well as possible (1989a: 77). So who decides what that goal is? The answer must lie somewhere in the following: "The highest responsibility of the translator is to transmit the intended information in the optimal manner" (1989a: 68, our translation). So who then decides what information is really intended (intentions are not usually available to analysis), and who determines what "optimal" means here? On the second question, at least, Vermeer does give a clear answer: "optimal" is "*aus der Sicht des Translators*," in the eyes of the translator (1989a: 68). So here, as in Holz-Mänttäri, the well-trained translator is the one who ultimately decides.

Here we come up against one of the shortcomings of the whole paradigm. For some decisions, the theorists seem to say, we cannot really help translators, who must ultimately act in their own name in each specific situation. As in basic existentialism, this places huge responsibilities on the shoulders of translators, along with considerable liberties. According to Margret Ammann (1994), the old categories of equivalence and eternal binary choices had sought to **repress the translator's individuality**, whereas Vermeer's *Skopos* theory would emphasize precisely that individuality, at once **liberating** and **empowering** the translator.

Other theorists, however, have seemed less anxious to travel down that road. Reiss has never renounced the priority of source-text functions, and Hönig and Kussmaul's seminal principle, as we have seen, was far from ignoring the source text. In Nord and Snell-Hornby, on the other hand, one finds more emphasis on the **client's instructions** (brief, commission, *Auftrag*). For example, Nord states that the *Skopos* remains "subject to the initiator's decision and not to the discretion of the translator" (1991: 9); she consequently defines a "translation mistake" as a failure to comply with the client's instructions (1997: 75); and she later insists that "the translation purpose is defined by the translation brief, which (implicitly or explicitly) describes the situation for which the target text is needed" (2001: 201). For her, the *client* clearly has the final say, not the translator. So who are we to believe?

Much depends here on the words one uses to describe the indications the translator receives (or does not receive) from the client. Writing in English, Vermeer prefers the term "**commission**," which might call up the image of a portrait painter getting very broad instructions but basically being left to tackle a creative task. When editing Nord (1997), we opted for the imagery of the client's "**brief**," which conjures up a defense attorney who receives information from the client but is ultimately responsible for the success or failure of the case. Later we will see the French theorist Daniel Gouadec using the term "**job description**," in which as many technical details as possible are agreed upon in advance, as if the translator were helping the client to build a house. This is one of the many points where translation theory has had to rely on more or less explicit metaphors, selecting comparisons in accordance with the assumptions of the theorist. In all of this, it is rarely clear whether the theory describes what *always* happens, or merely what *should* happen in the best of possible worlds.

Christiane Nord has sought to add a prescriptive dimension to these relations. She claims that the translator has ethical obligations not only to texts (the traditional focus of "fidelity") but more importantly to people: to senders, clients, and receivers, all of whom merit the translator's "**loyalty**" (Nord 1997: 123ff.). Nord sees this interpersonal loyalty as a general relationship of solidarity that should somehow override any interpersonal conflicts: "If the client asks for a translation that entails being disloyal to either the author or the target readership or both, the translator should argue this point with the client or perhaps even refuse to produce the translation" (2001: 200). So who is calling the shots here: the individual translator or the overarching "loyalty principle"? Interestingly enough, when she herself was criticized as co-translator of New Testament documents (cf. Nord 2001), Nord's response was not particularly in terms of loyalty (why should she not have been loyal to the translation critics?) but in terms of *marked* functionality as a question of being honest. If the translators' preface says the purpose of the translation is to work in a certain way, then, says Nord, the translation cannot be criticized for working in that way. If you do what you promise to do, that is the purpose. Note that here the *Skopos* principle is not protected by the relatively hierarchical power structures of the translation class; Nord cannot use it to tell students to think beyond the surface of the text. In this more exposed situation, Nord ultimately claims that translators have the right and responsibility to do what they see fit. At that point, she would rejoin the sovereign translator of Holz-Mänttäri and Vermeer.

4.6 SOME VIRTUES OF THE PURPOSE PARADIGM

Let us now pull together these various strands. The following are principles to which most of the above theorists would agree, at least for the sake of an argument (of which there are many!):

- The translator's decisions are ultimately governed by the purpose of the translation.
- The purpose of what translators do ("translatorial action") can be to produce equivalence to various aspects of the source text, or to engage in rewriting, or to give advice, or anything in between.
- The one source text can be translated in different ways to suit different purposes.
- A key factor in defining the purpose of the translation is the job description given by the client or negotiated with the client.
- In the last analysis, the purpose of the translation is defined by the individual translator, working in relation with all the other social actors involved.

This general approach has several strong points that distinguish it from the equivalence paradigm:

- It recognizes that the translator works in a professional situation, with complex obligations to people as well as to texts.
- It liberates the translator from theories that would try to formulate linguistic rules governing every decision.
- It forces us to see translation as involving many factors, rather than as work on just one text.
- It can address ethical issues in terms of free choice.

These are all good things. In its day, this general approach was exciting, even revolutionary, apparently putting paid to the fundamental force of equivalence.

4.7 FREQUENTLY HAD ARGUMENTS

Although there have been several broad critiques of *Skopos* theory, few of them have received serious answers. When Vermeer responds to a series of objections (most accessibly in

Vermeer 1989b/2004), he does so at a rather banal straw-man level. One might argue, for example, that not all actions have aims or purposes (since we never know the complete outcome of an action prior to undertaking it), and Vermeer answers, quite correctly, that we nevertheless *orient* our actions in terms of intended aims and purposes, and that all actions have purposes by definition (since that is the way he defines "action"). The debates have stayed there, without scaling too many philosophical heights.

The following are some of the less portentous arguments that might be picked.

4.7.1   "We translate words, not functions"

All the theorists in this paradigm stress that one should translate what texts are supposed to do, their intended function, not the actual words on the page. Even when they disagree on who is "intending" the function, they all agree that the function has priority over the words. The British critic **Peter Newmark** (1988: 37), with typically phlegmatic pragmatism, retorts that words are "all that is there, on the page," so words are all that we can translate. This debate should serve to indicate that the sense or functions we translate are always as *constructed* by us on the basis of the information available (which usually goes well beyond the simple words on the page). "Intentions," no matter whom they belong to, are not immediately available. Contexts, of course, are also interpretative constructions, largely built on the basis of words. Indeed, language may be the only way we can conceptualize anything at all about a function or a situation.

4.7.2   "Purposes are identified in the source text"

A slightly more sophisticated version of Newmark's critique argues that there is no function or intention that is not expressed in words, so it is impossible to do without some kind of linguistic analysis of the source text. In this line, **Kirsten Malmkjær** (1997: 70) picks up **Hönig's "Eton" illustrations** and claims that, in Hönig's own analysis, "what is necessary depends far less on the function of a translation than on the linguistic context in which a problematic expression occurs." For example, if the main verb of a sentence is "afford" (as in "his mother could not afford to send him to Eton"), then the term "Eton," no matter what the language, is likely to be invested with the value "expensive," so there is really no need to spell this out for the foreign reader, and no reason for claiming "function" to be a new paradigm. This would seem to be a valid comment on Hönig and Kussmaul's general approach, but it cannot be applied to cases where the one source text can indeed be translated in several different ways (as in the case of the child's suicide note mentioned above).

4.7.3   "The concept of purpose (or *Skopos*) is an idealism"

This is a more philosophical version of the same critique. The importance of the objection will perhaps only become clear within the frame of the indeterminist paradigm that we will meet later. For the moment, let us simply note that if textual meaning is considered to be unstable and always open to interpretation, the same may be said of any assumed purposes or functions. The *Skopos* approach would thus want to undo the assumed stability of the source text, but somehow cannot see that the same critique may be applied to its own key terms. There is no reason why any greater stability should ensue from a shift of focus from the source to the target.

4.7.4 "The *Skopos* theory is unfalsifiable"

This is a rather simple piece of reasoning. If every translation is dominated by its purpose, then the purpose is what is achieved by every translation. To separate the two, we would have to look at "bad" translations where purposes are somehow *not* achieved, thus complicating the notion of what a translation is. However, if the purpose is ultimately defined by the translator, as Vermeer would suggest, then how can we consistently accuse translators of not fulfilling the purpose that they themselves have defined? Some appeal might be made to a principle of internal contradiction (one part of the translation goes one way, the other goes the other, so it is bad). But who said a translation only has to have one sole purpose? The longer one continues that line of argument, the less the *Skopos* rule seems to be saying.

4.7.5 "The theory does not address equivalence as an underlying default norm"

This argument posits that, in our societies, the dominant concept of translation requires that the translator aims to achieve as much equivalence as possible, on whatever level, unless there are special-case indications to the contrary. The analysis of purpose would then simply concern those special cases, and the linguistic analysis of equivalence can carry on regardless (our thanks to Basil Hatim for stating this position, although it could also be derived from Gutt's isolation of "direct translations," which would be those to which the default norm applies). A counter-argument may be that there are now many forms of translation, including dialogue interpreting and localization, where the default norm is now non-operative, to the extent that the profession has changed so much that equivalence itself has become the special case. No empirical studies, to our knowledge, have tested these claims either way. Indeed, there is only anecdotal evidence to support any of the propositions formulated within the purpose paradigm.

4.7.6 "Purpose analysis is mostly not cost-effective"

This kind of criticism focuses on the extreme rigor with which these theories are formulated, asking if translators really have to do so much theoretical work before they even begin to translate. We might think here of Nord's 76 questions to be asked of the source text (and potentially another 76 of the target text as well). Translators, it might be argued, mostly cut corners by adhering to the historical norms of their profession, without extensive thought about specific purposes. They are instinctively working in "good enough" mode anyway, with or without the theoretical back-up. The reply to this may be that a lot of translations would be much better if they were done in terms of specific purposes rather than by following endemic norms. That reply, however, would change the nature of the theory, taking it from a descriptive stance to an overtly prescriptive positioning. In fact, the critique brings out the very ambivalent status of the whole paradigm, which does have a strong pedagogical purpose beneath a thin veil of descriptivism.

4.7.7 "The well-trained translator is a self-serving notion"

As we have noted, the descriptive illusion is maintained by focusing only on the "good" translator, or on what translators do when they are properly trained experts. This enables the descriptive position to be prescriptive at the same time, particularly when one realizes that these theories have been used to modify training curricula, thus effectively helping to produce the "good" translators that they themselves define as "good." The ultimate risk is that we may be institutionalizing no more than the theorist's opinions.

4.7.8 "The theory cannot resolve cases of conflicting purposes"

This is in fact admitted to when one allows that individual translators have to make their own choices in many cases. What some might see as a failure to develop a guideline ethics thus becomes a moment of liberation and empowerment.

4.7.9 "The theory contradicts ethics of truth and accuracy"

Newmark (1997: 75) reduces Vermeer to the notion that "the end justifies the means," described as "a kind of brutalism that excludes factors of quality or accuracy." In thus opposing what he sees as "the ideal of the commercial *skopos*," Newmark affirms his belief that "translation is a noble, truth-seeking activity, and that it should normally be accurate" (1997: 77). In taking that stance, Newmark is certainly traditionalist and willfully unsophisticated, not to say technically wrong (Vermeer can define quality in terms of target-text function, and he allows that there should be as much accuracy as required – although he does indeed say that "the end justifies the means," in Reiss and Vermeer 1984: 101). Newmark nevertheless quite probably expresses the beliefs of most people who employ translators, not to mention the professional ethics of a great many translators themselves.

Further arguments may be found in Nord (1997: 109–122). As should be clear from the above, the paradigm shift from equivalence to purpose has been anything but smooth. Many of those debates are still working themselves out, and some will be continued in our next chapters.

4.8 AN EXTENSION INTO PROJECT ANALYSIS

We close this chapter with a brief look at an approach that extends the notion of purpose in a very practical way. The French translator-trainer **Daniel Gouadec** (2007) has virtually no intellectual association with the German-language theorists whom we have been considering; he is not really touched by the arguments we have just been looking at. Gouadec's thought has developed from the training of technical translators working in close relation with industry. In broad terms, Gouadec sees translation as concerning large-scale projects that involve not only clients and companies but also teams of translators, terminologists, and other communication specialists. He argues that special attention should be paid to clients' instructions, which he terms "**job specifications**." If the specifications are as complete as possible, the translator will know exactly how to translate. And if the specifications are not complete enough, the translator should be able to seek further details.

Gouadec has many versions of what the job specifications should look like. A description we use for our own teaching is shown in Table 4.2, where trainees are taught to ask the client for information on all the categories. The first column of Table 4.2 usefully reminds us that clients can provide much more material than the simple source text. If translators ask for them, clients can usually forward in-house glossaries, parallel texts (texts in the target language on the same subject matter), previous translations done in the same field, and perhaps the telephone number or email of an expert in the field. The client might express surprise that a translator could need all that material. But the material is often the best source of information for any translator in search of appropriate terminology and phraseology. Rather than guess or search the web, translators can reduce risk by using the material that their client already has.

The second column is very close to what the German theorists would call *Skopos*, the desired function of the translation. The third column concerns agreements on delivery arrangements and financial matters. Those are all aspects overlooked by most other approaches, yet are rarely overlooked by professional translators.

For Gouadec, if all the elements of the translation project can be adequately located and defined in this elaborate "**pre-translation**" phase through discussion and negotiation with the client, the actual translating will present relatively few problems. In fact, Gouadec goes a little further than this. For him, there remain many decisions for which translators are probably more competent than their clients, particularly concerning such things as text format and forms of address (polite or formal second person, for example). Translators should decide on these "optional" elements, but then present a list of proposed decisions to the client for their agreement. Pre-translation thus does as much as possible to remove all possible sources of doubt. It effectively establishes the equivalents prior to doing the job.

If we compare Gouadec's approach with German-language *Skopos* theory, several significant differences emerge. Most obviously, Gouadec sees the translator as a language

Table 4.2   Material and information in a complete job description for translators (cf. Gouadec 2007: 15)

Material	Function information	Task information
Source text	Desired function of	Deadlines (for delivery of raw
Source images, appendices, etc.	translation	translation, of revised translation)
Specialized glossaries	Readership profile	Format of translation (which CAT
Parallel texts	Quality required (for	tool)
Previous translations	information, for	Costing basis (by word, character,
Contacts with experts or	publication, revisions,	page, hour, day)
consultants	terminology)	Estimated cost
	Who revises?	Terms of payment
		Signed contract

technician able to follow explicit instructions as **part of a team**. Holz-Mänttäri and Vermeer, on the other hand, tend to see the translator as an expert individual trained to make decisions and to be responsible for them. Their ideal translator would be a consultant on cross-cultural communication, able to advise clients about how to present themselves in a different culture.

In terms of the theories we have surveyed thus far, we might say Gouadec does everything possible to establish agreement (possibly on equivalents) and thus reduce the margins in which the translators have to decide for themselves. Plurality is his enemy. For German-language *Skopos* theory, however, the variety of possible purposes is a liberation from equivalence, and thus presents an ethical confrontation with uncertainty. Not by chance, the pages of their journal *TextconText* have welcomed deconstructionists like Rosemary Arrojo. They have taken the idea of translation purposes in one direction, whereas Gouadec (and most of the profession with him) has taken it in another.

SUMMARY

This chapter has presented a paradigm that is based on one simple idea: a translation need not be equivalent to its source text. The various theories in the paradigm differ with respect to the degrees to which translations can break with equivalence, but they all focus on the target-side purpose that the translation is supposed to achieve. We have seen several aspects of this new focus. In theory, the one source text may be translated in different ways to achieve different purposes. This means that the translator needs information about the purpose, and that information should ideally be in the instructions provided by the client. The translator is thus placed in a social situation where they have to negotiate with all the parties involved, including the client, the reader or end-user, and the author. For Vermeer, the translator is the one who ultimately decides the target-side purpose (*Skopos*) of the translation. For Holz-Mänttäri, the translator's role in these relationships is as the expert in cross-cultural communication, which means that translators may rewrite or give advice, as well as translate. For Nord, the ethical component of these relationships is "loyalty," rather than the "faithfulness" that would characterize a relationship to a text in the equivalence paradigm. We have extended this general view of the translator's situation to include the work of Gouadec, who emphasizes the way technical translators work in teams, and who argues that complete information from the client in the pre-translation phase will determine many of the translator's decisions.

SOURCES AND FURTHER READING

The Translation Studies Reader (2000/2004) has good representative texts by Reiss and Vermeer. Chapter 5 of Munday (2001/2008) is on "functional theories," which includes the main ideas of the paradigm alongside the analyses of source texts. The best introduction is still Christiane Nord's *Translating as a Purposeful Activity* (1997), which contains the main citations, diagrams, and criticisms. Nord, however, tends to privilege the client's wishes more than the translator's freedom and she remains close to pedagogical considerations. Vermeer and Nord are to be preferred to some of the accounts that have not benefited from extensive readings of the German texts. The foundational texts, notably Reiss and Vermeer (1984) and Holz-Mänttäri (1984), have not been translated into English to our knowledge, and neither is particularly easy to read in German. Reiss's text-type theory of 1971, although on the fringes of this paradigm intellectually, remains an important statement and has been translated into English, after almost 20 years, as *Translation Criticism: Potential and Limitations. Categories and Criteria for Translation Quality Assessment* (2000). Gouadec's large compendium of recommendations and checklists for technical translators is available in English as *Translation as a Profession* (2007).

Suggested projects and activities

1 This is an activity in five parts, not all of which work every time. Some experimentation could be necessary:

   (a) In groups, select texts from three very different genres (say, contracts, advertising, or poetry, but also mixed genres like self-descriptions from Internet dating services, or the homepage of a computer company). Translate fragments of them in order to respect the different genres.

   (b) Once you have completed Task (a), find or invent names for the different translation strategies you have used. You may like to use the terms proposed by Vinay and Darbelnet, but any classification will do.

   (c) Once you have completed Tasks (a) and (b), try to apply the strategies you have used for one text to the other two, and vice versa. For example, you may try to translate a contract in the same way you have translated an advertisement, or you could translate an instruction manual using the strategies you have used for a novel.

   (d) Once you have completed Tasks (a), (b) and (c), try to imagine as many different situations as possible for which all the texts could be translated. Is it really true that the one text can be translated in many significantly different ways? Are there really so many different reception situations?

   (e) On the basis of this exercise, do you find that the main difference is the nature of the source texts or the nature of the purposes for which the translations are carried out?

2 Find or invent transcriptions of oral medical encounters (e.g. a conversation between a doctor and a patient via an interpreter) and delete the interpreter's renditions. Students then do written translations of what the interpreter had to interpret. They then act out the scenes, producing oral translations. Then compare the written translations with the spoken ones, and if possible with what the interpreter actually did. Which translations are most literal? Which are the closest to functions? Why?

3 Translate the two sentences: (a) "In Parliament he fought for equality, but he sent his son to Eton," and (b) "When his father died his mother could not afford to send him to Eton any more." Now consider Newmark's argument that "to translate 'Eton College' as 'one of (!) the English elite schools' or as 'one of the expensive private schools' suggests that the translator is unaware of Eton's importance as a British institution, and underrates or fails to enlighten the likely readership" (1997: 76). In what circumstances would you consider Newmark's criticism to be correct? Would it make you change your translation?

4   For the same two sentences, consider Malmkjaer's argument that "the presence in the [second] sentence of 'could not afford' effortlessly activates the EXPENSIVE sense of 'Eton' for the English reader. It would of course be possible for a German reader to attach the appropriate senses to 'Eton' by means of conscious inference and possibly some research, even if the place/school name had been left to fend for itself in the [target text]" (1997: 71). Can a similar argument be made for the first sentence (consider the function of "but")? Does this mean that linguistic analysis alone can identify text functions? Does it mean that cultural terms sometimes require no special translation strategy, since syntax tells the story?

5   Find three published translations (websites will do). Imagine you are the client who ordered the translations and write appropriate job specifications.

6   For philosophers: If all translations are dominated by their purpose, how can we define a bad translation?

7   Ask some professional translators about the kinds of instructions they actually receive from their clients. Which metaphor (order, commission, brief, job specification, etc.) best describes that communication (if indeed there is any communication)? If you find that professional translators receive no such instructions, is the theory therefore wrong, or should we change professional practice?

8   Vermeer proposes that translators should be trained to become "intercultural management assistants" or "consultants" (1998: 62). Is this a realistic aim? Or should translators be trained to become competent technicians able to carry out orders (as in Gouadec)? What happens when you only have a two-year training program and something has to be sacrificed? Could these different roles develop at different stages of a translator's professional career?

9   List the possible ways we could translate the German term *Skopostheorie* (literally "skopos theory") into English as a term to be listed in a glossary, paying attention to the use of italics and capitals (in German, all nouns begin with capitals). What different purposes could be associated with the selection of one translation or another? What purpose might lie behind our own preference for the term "*Skopostheorie*" (i.e. using the German term in an English text)?

CHAPTER 5

Descriptions

A simple description might seem to require no grand theory. In fact, it could be considered too simple to be taken seriously by scholars. Some of the most significant concepts in European translation theory have nevertheless come from what we will call a broad "descriptive paradigm." This paradigm can be traced back to the Russian Formalists at the beginning of the twentieth century, where we find the basic idea that scientific methods can be applied to cultural products. That idea connected with translation theorists in three broad regions. The first link was with the work done in Prague, Bratislava and, more loosely connected, Leipzig. The second link was with what is called the "Tel Aviv school" (Even-Zohar, Toury and the development of Descriptive Translation Studies). The third link was through Holland and Flanders. When literary scholars from those three areas met and discussed their projects at a series of conferences, Translation Studies started to take shape as an academic discipline. That history is extremely important – this particular paradigm does not come from the same roots as the others mentioned in this book. This chapter focuses on the main theoretical concepts derived from descriptive studies: translation shifts, systems and polysystems, "assumed translations," a focus on the target side, norms, universals, and some proposed laws of translation. In historical retrospect, descriptions have turned out to be anything but simple.

5.1 WHAT HAPPENED TO EQUIVALENCE?

Equivalence went out of style. German-language *Skopos* theory made it especially unfashionable by arguing that since "functional consistency" (the closest thing they had to equivalence) is no more than one of many possible skills a translator has to achieve, translation usually requires transformations of a rather more radical kind. For those theorists, equivalence became quite a small thing, a special case. At almost the same time, however, other theorists were dismantling equivalence in precisely the opposite way. For this second group, for what Gideon Toury would eventually construct as "Descriptive Translation Studies," **equivalence was a feature of *all* translations**, simply because they were thought to be translations, no matter what their linguistic or aesthetic quality (cf. Toury 1980: 63–70). That changed everything. If equivalence was suddenly everywhere in translations, or almost, it could no longer be used to support any linguistics that would help people create it. The theorizing of translation was thus moved into a realm that was relatively unprotected by any parent discipline; it had to found its own discipline. More than pure theory, however, the descriptive approach emphasized the need to carry out research on translation, mostly research of the

The main points covered in this chapter are:

- Rather than prescribe what a good translation should be like, descriptive approaches try to say what translations are like or could be like.
- Translation shifts are regular differences between translations and their source texts. They can be analyzed top-down or bottom-up.
- Translations play a role in the development of cultural systems.
- The innovative or conservative position of translations within a cultural system depends on the system's relation with other systems, and may correlate with the type of translation strategy used.
- When selecting texts to study, translations can be considered facts of target culture only, as opposed to the source-culture context that is predominant in the equivalence paradigm.
- Translators' performances are regulated by collective "norms," based on informal consensus about what is to be expected from a translator.
- Some proposed "universals of translation" describe the ways in which translations tend to differ from non-translations.
- Some tentative "laws of translation" describe how translations tend to correlate with relations between cultures.

kind done in structuralist literary studies. The theories associated with the research were thus positioned out of touch with the growing number of training institutions; they were in an institutional context quite different from that of *Skopos* theory. Here we will trace the adventures of that historical move.

5.2 THEORETICAL CONCEPTS WITHIN THE DESCRIPTIVE PARADIGM

The name "**Descriptive Translation Studies**" (note upper case) was never fully consecrated until Gideon Toury's book *Descriptive Translation Studies and Beyond* (1995a). It has since become a flag of convenience for a loose flotilla of innovative scholars. Around that particular name there is now a rather large body of thought and research. On the surface, this would seem to be a general paradigm in which scholars have set out to **describe** what translations actually are, rather than just **prescribe** how they should be. Those terms, though, are simplifications. If the aim were merely to describe, there would be little need for any grand theory. And yet what we find in this paradigm is a host of theoretical concepts: systems, shifts, norms, universals and laws, to name the most prominent, plus a long ongoing debate about how to define the term "translation" itself. Despite the emphasis on description, this remains very much a paradigm for theoretical activity.

In the following sections we will briefly describe the main concepts at work within the paradigm.

A shortlist of concepts in the development of the descriptive paradigm

Here we indicate some of the scholars who were instrumental in the development of the concepts. Many other names could also be listed and most names should be associated with far more than one idea:

■ The relations between source and target texts may be described in terms of "translation shifts" (Levý, Miko, Popovič).
■ The innovative or conservative position of translations within a cultural system depends on the system's relation with other systems, and correlates with the type of translation strategy used (Even-Zohar, Holmes, Toury).
■ Translation Studies should be an empirical descriptive discipline with a hierarchical organization and a structured research program (Holmes, Toury).
■ When selecting texts to study, translations should be considered facts of the target culture (Toury).
■ To understand not just translations but all kinds of "rewriting," we have to consider the social contexts, especially patronage (Lefevere).

5.2.1 Translation shifts and their analysis

The most obvious way to analyze translations is to view the source and target texts as sets of structures. We can compare the texts and see where the structures are different. We then have specific structures (the differences) that somehow belong to the field of translation. That idea is as simple to understand as it is difficult to apply.

The structural differences between translations and their sources may be described as "**translation shifts**," a term found in several different theories. For **Catford**, shifts are "departures from formal correspondence" (1965: 73), which sounds clear enough. If formal correspondence is what we find between "Friday the thirteenth" and "viernes y 13," then any other rendition will be a "shift" of some kind. The range of possible shifts might thus include all the things that Vinay and Darbelnet (1958/1972) found translations doing, or indeed anything detected by anyone within the equivalence paradigm. A shift might come from the translator's decision to render function rather than form, or to translate a semantic value on a different linguistic level, or to create the correspondence at a different place in the text (using a strategy of compensation), or perhaps to select different genre conventions. Much research can be carried out in this way: compare the texts, collect the differences, then try to organize the various kinds of shifts.

There are at least two ways of approaching this task: **bottom-up analysis** starts from the smaller units (usually terms, phrases or sentences) and works up to the larger ones (text, context, genre, culture); **top-down analysis** goes the other way, starting with the larger systemic factors (especially constructs such as the position of translations within a sociocultural system) and working down to the smaller ones (especially categories like translation strategies). In principle, it should make no difference which end you start at: all roads lead to Rome, and there are always dialectics of loops and jumps between levels. Yet, perhaps surprisingly, the difference between bottom-up and top-down has a lot to do with the role of theory in description. That is why we will spend some time on it here.

5.2.1.1   Bottom-up shift analysis

The range and complexity of bottom-up analysis is most completely seen in the comparative model developed by **Kitty van Leuven-Zwart** (1989, 1990). Here shifts are categorized on many levels from the micro (below sentence level) to the macro (in her case, text-scale narrative structures). A useful summary is in the first edition of Munday's *Introducing Translation Studies* (2001: 63–65) and in Hermans (1999: 58–63). Yet the model is omitted from the second edition of Munday (2008) since, as Munday states appropriately, it is rarely used any more. Here we are interested in the theoretical reasons why it is no longer used.

In Leuven-Zwart, the basic textual units entering into comparison are called "**transemes**." For example, the two corresponding units might be the English "she sat up suddenly" and the Spanish "se enderezó," which basically means that she sat up. What these two transemes have in common would be the "architranseme." Once you have identified that, you can start to look for shifts, which can then be categorized in much the same way as Vinay and Darbelnet proposed. For example, you might note that the two phrases occupy corresponding positions in the two texts but the English has a value (suddenness) that seems to be absent in the Spanish. So we write down "absence of aspect of action," and we call this absence a shift. Eventually we will have compiled a notebook full of such shifts, which we hope will form patterns that can tell us something about the translation. What could be wrong with that?

Since this "sit up" example is presented as being relatively uncomplicated in both Munday and Hermans, it is worth looking into the difficulties it might actually involve. To follow this discussion, you might first translate "she sat up" into your favorite languages-other-than-English:

For a start, how can we be sure that the value of "suddenly" is not in the Spanish? The verb "enderezó" is in the preterit tense (actually the *pretérito indefinido*), which in Spanish has a value in opposition to the past imperfect (the *pretérito imperfecto*, giving the form "enderezaba"), a tense that does not exist as such in English. That is, both languages can say, "she was in the process of sitting up," but English does not have a simple past tense for such drawn-out actions; Spanish does. One could thus argue, in pure structuralist mode, that the selection of the Spanish preterit in itself represents the value "suddenness." The shift would then be from the English adverbial to the Spanish tense, and it would be regulated by the differences between the two tense systems.

Alternatively (although possibly for similar reasons), we might check large corpora of general English and Spanish and note that the English verb "sit" is associated with adverbials and phrasal particles far more than is the case for the Spanish verb "enderezarse" (not the least because "sit up" and "sit down" have no formal equivalents in Romance languages). In that case, the translator may have omitted the value "suddenly" (which could be expressed as "de repente," for example) simply because it did not sound right in Spanish; it would have been an unusual collocation. Comparative frequencies may thus give an alternative justification for the translator's decision, although without denying the underlying logic of structures.

More worryingly, if we try to apply this type of analysis to our "Friday the thirteenth" example, how can we be sure that the non-shift involves the form or the function? In a context framed by superstition, surely "martes 13" (Tuesday the thirteenth) would be the expected translation, the normal one, the non-shift? What right do we have to pick one rendition and call it the "proper" or "expected" translation, and thereby relegate all the other possible renditions to the category of "shifts"?

Finally, there are many cases where formal correspondence itself implies some kind of shift. For example, the American English term *democracy* certainly corresponds formally to the East German term *Demokratie* (as in the Deutsche Demokratische Republik), but with a remarkable shift of ideological content (the example is used by Arrojo in Chesterman and Arrojo 2000). So why should the formal correspondence itself not represent a shift?

In all these ways, we find that bottom-up shift analysis presupposes far too quickly that the meanings of language are clear and stable (i.e. not subject to interpretation), and that there is thus one stable common core (the "architranseme") in relation to which all the rest would represent "shifts." On that score, the approach has far more to do with the equivalence paradigm than with description. Even without questioning the ultimately arbitrary way in which transemes are identified, there must remain some doubt about the identification of the shift and of its causation. The bottom-up accumulation of shifts tends to be methodologically murky, and the long lists of differences only rarely congeal into firm findings at the higher level of analysis. This approach can produce much doubt and even more data. At the end of the day, it requires orientation from a few reductive theories. That is one of the reasons why the descriptive paradigm is actually full of theories.

5.2.1.2 Top-down shift analysis

The descriptive work in Central Europe tended to be much more theoretical than the kind of bottom-up description given above. In Leipzig, **Otto Kade** (1968) explicitly argued that a bottom-up approach ("induction") had to be accompanied by top-down analysis (a "hypothetico-deductive" approach) if theoretical results were to be achieved. In Bratislava and Nitra, the analysis of "**shifts of expression**" was also happening in about the same period as Catford (cf. Popovič 1968/1970; Miko 1970), but the approach did not assume any simple desire to maintain equivalence. Shifts could thus be approached in a top-down way, starting from major hypotheses about why they might exist and how they could form tendencies.

Anton Popovič, for instance, claimed that there are "two stylistic norms in the translator's work: the norm of the original and the norm of the translation" (1968/1970: 82). This seems so simple as to be obvious. Yet consider the consequence: as soon as the two "**stylistic norms**" are announced, the multiplicity of shifts is already theorized in terms of coherent patterns. This kind of approach connects with the study of literary style, where one might see the two interacting "norms" as the voices of author and translator. On another level, shifts could be patterned differently owing to historical factors (the nature of the receiving system, patronage, new text purpose, different ideas about what translation is, etc.). Or again, some shifts might come about simply as a result of the translation process as such (these would later be dubbed "universals"). On all those levels, the top-down approach seeks **causal factors** (the reasons for the shifts) that are quite different from those of the equivalence paradigm. These descriptive approaches could obviously join forces with the bottom-up analyses carried out by linguists, but their theoretical frame was fundamentally different. In effect, despite the misnomer "descriptive," these were theories about the possible causes (personal, institutional, historical) explaining why people translate differently.

As an example of top-down analysis, consider the basic problem of what to do with a **source text that is in verse**. This is analyzed in a seminal paper by **James S Holmes** (1970). We know that in some target cultures (notably in French), foreign verse forms can consistently be rendered in prose. So the problem is solved: translators know what to do (translate into prose), and readers know what to expect (verse is only for texts originally written in French). That would be one huge kind of shift, and it has remarkably little to do with equivalence of the linguistic kind. In other cultural situations, however, alternative shifts may be deemed appropriate. Holmes formalizes these in terms of four available options (in addition to the blanket rendering of verse as prose): translators can use a form that looks like the source-text form ("mimetic form"); they can select a form that fulfils a similar function ("analogical form"); they can develop a new form on the basis of the text's content ("organic form"); or they can come up with their own individual solution ("extraneous form").

Holmes sees these options as being appropriate to **different historical situations**. Mimetic form tends to come to the fore "in a period when genre concepts are weak, literary norms are being called into question, and the target culture as a whole stands open to outside impulses" (Holmes 1970: 98). This might be the case of German in the first half of the nineteenth century. On the other hand, "the analogical form is the choice to be expected in a period that is in-turned and exclusive" (Holmes 1970: 97), such as the neoclassical eighteenth century in France. As for the use of "organic" form, Holmes sees it as being "fundamentally pessimistic regarding the possibilities of cross-cultural transference" (1970: 98) and he associates it with twentieth-century Modernism. "Extraneous" form is then regarded, not very convincingly, as having "a tenacious life as a kind of underground, minority

A model of options for the translation of verse (from Holmes 1970)

- *Verse as prose*: All foreign verse is rendered as prose, as has been the norm in translations into French.
- *Mimetic form*: The translator chooses a form in the target language that is as close as possible as the one used in the source language. For example, an English sonnet can be rendered as a Spanish sonnet well enough, even though the metrics of feet in English will not correspond to the syllabic metrics of Spanish. Often this involves introducing a new form into the target culture, as was done when English *terza rima* was modeled on the Italian verse form.
- *Analogical form*: The translator identifies the function of the form in the source-language tradition, then finds the corresponding function in the target-language tradition: "Since the *Iliad* and *Gerusalemme liberata* are epics, the argument of this school goes, an English translation should be in a verse form appropriate to the epic in English: blank verse or the heroic couplet" (Holmes 1970: 95). This option may be an application of the equivalence paradigm at a high textual level. It is to be distinguished from the blanket "verse to prose" option to the degree that it requires identification of the way the specific source-text form functions in the source culture.
- *Organic or content-derivative form*: The translator refuses to look solely at the form of the source text (as is done in the above options) and instead focuses on the content, "allowing it to take on its own unique poetic shape as the translation develops" (Holmes 1970: 96).
- *Extraneous form*: In some situations, the translator may adopt a form that is totally unconnected with the form or content of the source text, and that is not dictated by any blanket form for translations in the target culture. In other words, anything can happen.

form . . . resorted to particularly by metapoets who lean in the direction of the imitation"
(1970: 99).

Holmes's analysis here suggests that translators' decisions are always culture-bound,
give or take a few unruly "metapoets." When asked how any decision should be made, the
descriptivist will thus always be able to say, "it depends on the situation." But then, how
many different things can a decision actually depend on? Is there any way to model the
huge range of variables covered by phrases like "the translator's situation"? Descriptivists
have made use of at least three concepts that are of some help here: systems, norms, and
(for want of a better term) target-sidedness.

5.2.2 Systems

What Holmes does in his brief study is systematic: he identifies and classifies the available
options, and he gives them a certain logical symmetry, largely thanks to some blunt distinctions
between form, function and content. One must be careful, though, about the status of this
systematization. What Holmes does here is **systematic** (ordered, thorough, complete), but
not necessarily **systemic**.

If we were talking about a **language system**, we would see the speaker producing a
string of words such that at each point there is a *restricted* set of what words can follow. The
language system limits the choices that can be made. The same is true of the translator as
a language producer, since the target language imposes limited sets of choices, which vary
as we go about doing the translation. However, does the same kind of decision-making concern
how to render a foreign verse form? The translator can certainly select one of Holmes's five
options, and that choice may have meaning in terms of the overall history of European verse
forms, but is it a decision like those where we are obliged to select a certain kind of verb or
adverbial? Is it properly systemic? To a certain extent, yes: all receiving cultures have literary
genres, and they mostly maintain structural relations between themselves. Then again, no:
those sets of genres need bear no resemblance at all to the five alternatives outlined by
Holmes. The receiving culture is one thing; the sets of theoretical alternatives are something
quite different. In this case, the kind of choice outlined by Holmes surely cannot be considered
a psychological reality. If the translator was working into German at the beginning of the
nineteenth century, all kinds of social and cultural factors would not only make the use of
mimetic form appropriate, but would also make Holmes's alternatives relatively unthinkable.
Germanic culture, without a state, was prepared to draw on other cultures in order to develop.
Translations of Homer brought hexameters into German, and translations of Shakespeare
brought in blank verse. Indeed, speaking in 1813, Schleiermacher saw this capacity to draw
from other cultures as the key to foreignizing translations, regarded as being a particularly
Germanic strategy. A literary translator trained in that cultural environment would then see
"mimetic form" or "foreignizing" as the *normal* way to go about translation. The translator might
even see it as the true or correct way in which all translations should be done, in all sociocultural
environments. Prescriptive theorizing may result ("All translations should use mimetic form!");
some structural oppositions might be proclaimed in theory ("German mimetic form is better
than French translations into prose!"); but the choices are not made within an abstract system
comprising purely translational options.

As **Toury** would later clarify (1995a: 15–16), the kind of system elaborated by Holmes
belongs to the level of the theorist (the options *theoretically* available), which is to be

distinguished from the alternatives actually available to the translator at the time of translating, which are in turn quite different from what the translator actually does. Toury distinguishes between three levels of analysis: "all that translation . . . CAN involve," "what it DOES involve, under various sets of circumstances," and "what it is LIKELY to involve, under one or another array of specified conditions" (1995a: 15)

The top-down thinking is fairly clear (although, once again, one could work upward at the same time). Note, though, that the term "system" is used here only in the sense of "theoretical possibilities." This is quite different from the kind of social or cultural system presented as the context in which translations function. The relative importance of this second, more general sense of "system" varies from theorist to theorist. The problem then becomes: Can the levels of "should be" and "is" be properly systemic in any strong sense?

When **Holmes** tries to explain why a particular option is associated with a particular period, he cites a range of quite profound phenomena: "genre concepts," "literary norms," "cultural openness/closure," "pessimism/optimism about cross-cultural transfer," and so on. These are all placed in the target culture. Holmes mentions them in a fairly offhand way; they seem to be quite separate, isolated phenomena. However, it is possible to see such things as being bound together to some extent, as different aspects of the one culture. In other theorists, particularly those more closely in touch with the legacy of Russian Formalism, cultural systems can impose quite strong logics. Lotman and Uspenski (1971/1979: 82), for example, talk about entire cultures being "expression-oriented" or "content-oriented" (along with various more complex classifications). The stronger the logic by which the system

Three levels of analysis in Descriptive Translation Studies

Delabastita (2008: 234) elaborates on Toury's three levels of analysis as follows, relating them to the notion of norms:

1 Level of system: theoretical possibilities ("can be")

For each translation problem or source text, it is possible to envisage a whole range of possible or theoretical solutions or target texts [as does Holmes].

2 Level of norms: culture-bound constraints ("should be")

On the intermediate level of norms, some of these possible relationships will be recommended or even required as being the only ones that can generate "genuine" translations, whereas others will be dismissed or even simply ignored.

3 Level of performance: empirical discursive practice ("is")

We can then observe which relationships have actually materialized in a given cultural setting. By definition, these empirical relationships constitute a subset of the possible relationships; their degree of frequency in a given cultural situation is a crucial indication that certain norms have been at work.

is presumed to operate (i.e. the more *systemic* it is seen to be), the more that system may be seen as determining the nature of translations.

When the Israeli scholar **Itamar Even-Zohar** analyzes the relation between translations and cultures, he uses the term "**polysystems**." The "poly-" part means "many" or "plural," indicating that a culture is a system made up of many other systems (linguistic, literary, economic, political, military, culinary). Thanks to this plurality, the internal logics of something like the literary system need not be determined by everything that can be done within that culture; there is a relative freedom within cultures. For Even-Zohar, translated literature may be seen as a subsystem occupying a position within the literary polysystem that hosts it. The translations can become a key element in the literature (and thus "innovative" and "central" in position); they may be secondary or unimportant ("conservative" and "peripheral"); or they can occupy positions in between. In these terms, translation is seen as one of the ways in which one polysystem "interferes" with another, where the verb "to interfere" does not carry any pejorative sense. Even-Zohar (1978: 47) proposes that translations play an innovative or central role when

> (a) a polysystem has not yet been crystallized, that is to say, when a literature is "young," in the process of being established; (b) when a literature is either "peripheral" (within a large group of correlated literatures) or "weak," or both; and (c) when there are turning points, crises, or literary vacuums in a literature.

These three types of situation are described as "basically manifestations of the same law" (1978: 47), the nature of which we will explore below.

Even-Zohar's mode of thought goes well beyond Holmes's attempt to explain why translations are the way they are. The view of systems as dynamic and plural allows him to ask what translations can actually *do* within their target cultures, and how they evolve from relations between cultures. Even-Zohar's general finding is nevertheless rather negative, since he concludes that "the 'normal' position assumed by translated literature tends to be the peripheral one" (1978: 50); that is, that translations tend to have a conservative, reinforcing effect rather than a revolutionary, innovative one. That kind of finding is unlikely to be popular within a discipline nowadays disposed to see translations as a hidden and maligned cause of change. Even-Zohar stresses nevertheless that translation is an essential element to the understanding of *any* cultural system (since no culture is an entirely independent entity) and that translational processes occur within polysystems as well as between them.

The term "system" thus varies in meaning and importance from theorist to theorist. In each case, it pays to read the descriptions closely, paying particular attention to the verbs and the agents of the verbs (who is supposed to be doing what). In strong systems theory, you will find that the systems themselves do things, as if they were people. In other approaches, people are portrayed as doing things within systems of constraints. That is a big difference, bearing on fundamental issues such as human liberty, the determinist logics of history, and the role and nature of translations.

While on the terminological difficulties, we should note a related problem with the term "**function**." For descriptive studies, the "function" of a translation is generally correlated with its **position within its corresponding system**, in accordance with an extended spatial metaphor. When we say that, within a given cultural system, a translation is relatively "**central**" or "**peripheral**," we effectively mean that its function is either to change or to reinforce the receiving language, culture, or literature. The function here is what the text does in the system.

For the purpose paradigm, on the other hand, the "function" of a translation is generally conflated into the *Skopos*, the action that the translation is supposed to enable in a specific situation, just as the function of a source text is assumed to be the action in which the text is used (to teach, to express, to sell, etc.). Although both paradigms would claim to be "functionalist," the term "function" means one thing in relation to systems theory (a position and role within a large-scale set of relations) and something else in relation to action theory (an action within a situation comprising various agents). There obviously must be common ground between the two usages, yet few theorists have actually sought it. One attempt to bridge the gap might be **André Lefevere's** view of systems (1992) that includes factors very close to the translator (who pays for the translation?, what do editors and publishers do?). Another attempt in recent years has been the use of **network theory** to study the same close relations sociologically (we will meet this in our chapter on cultural translation). A third avenue would be the concept of **translation culture** (Prunč 1997), which would basically be the system of interrelations between all participants in the production of translations. The broadest and most basic bridge has nevertheless been the concept of translation norms.

5.3 NORMS

In his three-level schema (the one we have reproduced above), after the level of what "can be," **Toury** opens a space for what "should be," which he describes in terms of "norms." Norms are thus positioned somewhere between abstract possibilities (such as Holmes's alternatives) and what translators actually do (the kinds of pragmatic considerations that *Skopos* theory deals with). For Toury, norms are

> the translation of general values or ideas shared by a community . . . into performance instructions appropriate for and applicable to particular situations, specifying what is prescribed and forbidden as well as what is tolerated and permitted in a certain behavioural dimension.
>
> (Toury 1995a: 55)

The term "performance instructions" here might suggest that a norm is the same thing as a client's job description. It could also misleadingly be associated with a set of rules or official regulations. In the descriptive paradigm, however, the term *norm* usually operates at a wider, more social level. For example, we could say that in the nineteenth century the norm for translating foreign verse into French was to render it into prose. There was no official rule stating that this *had* to be done, but there was an informal collective agreement. When translators approached the foreign text, they would accept as a matter of course that their work was not to imitate what the text looked or sounded like. When publishers hired translators, that is what they expected them to do, and when readers approached a literary translation, they would similarly accept that foreign poetry simply had to be in prose. Of course, the norm was not respected by all translators; norms are not laws that everyone has to follow. Norms are more like a common standard practice in terms of which all other types of practice are marked.

Why did the norm of "verse into prose" exist? On several different levels, it no doubt embodied the general idea that French culture was superior to other cultures. In Toury's terms, it conveyed at least that much of the society's "general values and ideas." Given this assumed superiority, there was no reason to accept any foreign influence on the existing system of neoclassical literary genres. In Even-Zohar's terms, we would say the perceived prestige of the target system allocated translation a peripheral role and hence a very conservative range of acceptable forms. Further, if we follow Toury, there would be some kind of social (though not juridical) penalization involved whenever a translator did not adhere to the norm. For instance, a text that differed radically from the established genres might be considered peculiar, ugly, or simply not worth buying. In every culture, the nature of a good translation is determined by such norms, since "bad translations" are penalized in some way, even if only by hurling adjectives like "bad."

The concept of norms thus covers quite a few related but different things. Toury (1995a: 58) makes a basic distinction between "**preliminary norms**," which concern the selection of the kind of text and the mode of translation (direct/indirect, etc.), and "**operational norms**," which would cover all the decisions made in the act of translating. However, as our "verse into prose" example shows, norms also have different social and epistemological dimensions. They concern what translators think they are supposed to do, what clients think translators ought to do, what text users think a translation should be like, and what kinds of translations are considered reprehensible or especially laudable within the system. **Chesterman** (1997) organizes these various aspects by distinguishing between "**professional norms**," which would cover everything related to the translation process, from "**expectancy norms**," which are what people expect of the translation product. If translators in a given society usually add numerous explanatory footnotes, that might be a professional norm. If readers are frustrated when such notes do not appear, or if the notes are in an unusual place, then that frustration will be in relation to expectancy norms. Ideally, the different types of norms reinforce one another, so that translators tend to do what clients and readers expect of them. In times of cultural change, the various types of norms might nevertheless be thrown out of kilter, and considerable tension can result. Indeed, in systems of self-induced change, a logic of the avant-garde may mean that all text producers, including translators, set about breaking norms, and text users thus expect norms to be broken. That is, norm-breaking can become the norm.

The idea of norms and norm-breaking has been important for the way descriptive research relates to the other paradigms of translation theory. If we apply the concept of norms seriously, we should probably give up the idea of defining once and for all what a good translation is supposed to be (although it is perhaps still possible to say what a good or bad social effect might look like, and thus evaluate the way norms work). In fact, the very notion of what a translation is must become very relative. This **relativism** would be a major point of compatibility with the *Skopos* paradigm (and indeed with the paradigm of uncertainty that we will meet in Chapter 6). However, relativism runs counter to much of the linguistic work done in the equivalence paradigm. When a linguist analyzes a source text to see how it can or should be translated, the basic assumption is not only that the answers will come from the nature of that source text, but more importantly that the nature of translation is a very clear thing; there is not much relativism involved. In the *Skopos* paradigm, the answers will come from the situation in which the translation is carried out, to the extent that it matters little whether a text is a translation or a liberal rewrite. In the descriptive paradigm, however, any questions about the borders between translations and non-translations can be answered in terms of norms, which in turn express values from the wider system within which the translator is working. In this sense, the theory of norms positions translation somewhere between the relative certainty of equivalence and the relative indifference of *Skopos* theory.

Such comparisons of paradigms were made in the 1980s, when the various approaches were starting to congeal into a discipline called Translation Studies. Scholars working in the descriptive paradigm, usually with a background in literary studies, could legitimately criticize the narrow "prescriptive" work being done in the equivalence paradigm. How could a theory set out to tell someone how to translate, when the very notion of translation varied so much from epoch to epoch and from culture to culture? The call for descriptions was thus initially a negation of the kind of **prescription** associated with the equivalence paradigm. Similarly, whereas the equivalence paradigm invited analysis to start from the *source* text and its role in the source situation, the descriptive paradigm tended to favor the *target* text and its position in the *target* system. Toury (1995a) explicitly recommends **starting analysis from the translation** rather than from the source text; he thus creates space for research that takes no account of the source text at all. For example, you can simply compare different translations, or compare translations with non-translations within the target system. That kind of full-frontal opposition helped to make Toury the *enfant terrible* of his day.

The notion of norms, however, allows a kind of prescriptivism to be introduced into descriptive studies, almost through the back door. Even if the role of theory is not to tell translators how to translate, a descriptive approach can identify the norms by which a translation may be considered good by people in a certain place and time. This has allowed for a certain application of descriptive studies in the **training of translators and interpreters**. Toury (1992) has suggested, for example, that trainees be asked to render the same text according to different norms (e.g. translate as one might have done in nineteenth-century Germany, or under conditions of censorship). The trainee will thus become aware that there are many different ways to translate, each with certain advantages and disadvantages. Of course, the same kind of exercise can be recommended within the purpose-based paradigm: translate the one text in different ways in order to achieve different purposes. The different paradigms can lead to the same kind of training activity.

Another kind of compatibility is proposed by Chesterman (1999), who suggests that the study of norms will enable the teacher and learner to predict the **relative success of one strategy or another**. No teacher can tell any student there is only one way to translate (since many norms are available), but empirical research can make it possible to predict success or failure when dominant norms are violated. Chesterman (1999: 14) formulates his position as follows:

> Statements like "In principle, in authoritative and expressive texts [original metaphors] should be translated literally" (Newmark 1988: 112), or "translations should aim to have the same effect on their target readers as the source texts had on the source readers," or "translators should translate transgressively, not fluently" can be paraphrased approximately like this: "I predict that if translators do *not* translate in the way I prescribe, the effect will be that readers will not like their translations/that the publisher will reject the text/that intercultural relations will deteriorate" or the like.

In all these ways, the concept of norms has helped bridge some of the gaps between descriptivism and prescriptivism.

The concept of norms has thus helped bring several approaches closer together, at the same time as the empirical discovery of norms has increased our historical understanding of the way translations operate. The fundamental concept, however, is not as clear-cut as it may seem. Consider, for example, the way the German sociologist **Niklas Luhmann**

(1985: 33) describes legal norms as "**counterfactual expectations**," in the sense that they do not take account of the way people actually behave. When these expectations are defeated (we find that there are criminals), the legal norms do *not* adapt accordingly (criminals must still be punished, no matter how many criminals there are). Many expectancy norms concerning translations could be of this counterfactual kind. For example, no matter how often we find that translations are domesticating (or foreignizing, or explanatory, or full of shifts, etc.), users of translations might still insist that they should *not* be. If some norms are working like this, then the bottom-up counting of facts and frequencies will never connect with the social pronouncements of what is acceptable or unacceptable. This is another reason why a descriptive approach requires theoretical concepts.

Whenever theorists tell us about norms, we should ask exactly how they have discovered those norms. If bottom-up, the empirical patterns may not all have equal status as psychological or social facts. If top-down, we should ask where the theorist found the categories of analysis, and why.

5.4 "ASSUMED" TRANSLATIONS

Here is a theoretical problem that cuts to the heart of empirical methodologies. If we set out to discover the historical and cultural diversity of translation norms, can we pretend to be sure from the outset what is meant by the term "translation"? If so, exactly what criteria should we use for collecting a set of things called "translations"? And if not, how can we possibly avoid imposing our own translation norms on other cultures and periods? This is one of the classical aporias that tend to worry researchers in dominant Western cultures.

Toury's initial solution to the problem has been to leave the defining to the people we study. For him, "a 'translation' will be taken to be any target-language utterance which is presented or regarded as such [i.e. as a 'translation'], on whatever grounds" (Toury 1995a: 20). In other words, we wait to see what each culture and each period has to say about what is or is not a translation. The solution is the operative concept of "assumed translations," which simply means that **a translation is a translation only for as long as someone assumes it is one**. A **pseudotranslation** (a non-translation that is presented as a translation) might then be held to be a translation only for as long as the trick works, and it becomes a non-translation for those aware of the false pretense.

That solution remains fraught with logical difficulties. For example, if each language has different words for "translation," how do we know those words are translations of each other? In order to select the words, we would surely need our own concept of translation, if not some clear ideas about what good and bad translations are. The debate over that issue has been one of the most fundamental but recondite activities in Translation Studies (cf. among others Gutt 1991/2000; Toury 1995b; Hermans 1997, 1999; Halverson 2007; Pym 1998, 2007a). For some, the problem is basically without solution, since if we use our normal terms to describe another culture's term "we naturally translate that other term according to our concept of translation, and into our concept of translation; and in domesticating it, we inevitably reduce it" (Hermans 1997: 19). At the other extreme, we might argue that the empirical data are so diverse and so unruly that we have to make some initial selection, simply in order to get research moving (cf. Pym 2007a). We should then be honest and self-critical about our initial principles and criteria, and open to the discovery of new concepts in the course of the research process. As different as these two options may appear, they both accept that concepts of translation are culturally and historically relative and may be described in explicit terms. They are thus both within the descriptive paradigm.

Compare these three features with a brief summary of what Stecconi (2004) considers necessary (as a foundation) if semiosis is to be counted as translation:

1   *Similarity*: A translation is like a previous text.
2   *Difference*: A translation is different from that previous text, if only because it is in a different language or variety of language.
3   *Mediation*: There is a translator between the two sides, mediating between them.

Chesterman (2006) finds these three features in the words that many languages have for "translation," but he claims that modern Indo-European languages give more weight to the "similarity" dimension. He suggests that this may be why so much is made of "equivalence" in European theories.

Pym (2004b) proposes two "maxims" held to operate when translations are received as translations.

1   *The maxim of translational quantity* holds that a translation represents an anterior text quantitatively.
2   *The maxim of first-person displacement* holds that the discursive first person of the text ("I") is the same first person as the anterior text, even when the two texts are at the same time held to have been produced by different subjects.

The first maxim is broken when the receiver thinks the translation is too short or too long; the second is broken when the receiver thinks the first person of the text is the translator. In both cases, the breaking of the maxim produces meanings about the limits of translation.

What makes a translation a translation?

One of the features of the descriptive paradigm is that theorists try to be as explicit as possible about their procedures. You cannot simply accept that "everyone knows what a translation is." This is where the paradigm enters a clearly theoretical mode. For example, Toury (1995a) posits that we will recognize an "assumed translation" because three things are held to be true about it:

1   *The source text postulate*, which holds that "there is another text, in another culture/language, which has both chronological and logical priority over [the translation] and is presumed to have served as the departure point and basis for it" (Toury 1995a: 33–34).
2   *The transfer postulate*, "the process whereby the assumed translation came into being involved the transference from the assumed source text of certain features that the two now share" (1995a: 34).
3   *The relationship postulate*: "there are accountable relationships which tie [the assumed translation] to its assumed original" (1995a: 35). Thanks to these relationships we can talk about translations being more or less literal, function, adaptive, and so on.

There are many similar attempts to define translation in a careful way, particularly as a version of reported speech (Bigelow 1978; Folkart 1991). Almost all this work is overlooked by theories of "cultural translation."

5.5 TARGET-SIDE PRIORITY

As we have noted, **Toury** upset linguistics-based studies of translation not only by opposing prescriptivism, but more profoundly by insisting that translations should be studied in terms of their *target* contexts rather than in relation to their sources (see Toury 1995b: 136). This led to an extreme position: in Toury's words, "translations should be regarded as facts of target cultures" (1995b: 139; cf. 1995a: 29). This proposition should be understood as part of a specific research methodology; it does not mean that translations somehow never have source texts (which would absurdly imply that all translations are actually pseudotranslations). Toury's argument is that the factors needed to describe the specificity of how translations work may all be found within the target system. This is based on the assumption that translators "operate first and foremost in the interest of the culture into which they are translating" (1995a: 12), either in order to reinforce the norms of the target culture or to fill in perceived "gaps."

The principle of target-side priority has been contested. The researchers working on literary translation at **Göttingen** in the 1990s generally preferred a **"transfer" model**, which explicitly traced movements between particular source and target cultures. Others have objected to the separation of the two cultures, arguing that translators tend to work in an **"intercultural"** space in the overlap of cultures (cf. Pym 1998). More generally, as with the problem of defining translations, the binary opposition of source and target has been increasingly criticized from indeterminist perspectives, as we shall see later.

5.6 UNIVERSALS OF TRANSLATION

If the fundamental tenet of the descriptive paradigm is that translations can be studied scientifically, then the aim of such study could be like that of all science. We thus find various proclamations that the aim of research is to discover "universals" or "laws" of translation. That is an area for research, for Translation Studies, rather than for translation theory as such. But what the terms "universals" and "laws" mean is by no means clear, and that is where some theorization has been necessary.

At the simplest level, a "universal of translation" would be **a feature that is found in translations and in no other kind of text**. A universal, however, should not be something too obvious or tautological: it should not simply ensue from the way we decide to define what a translation is. For example, if we say "a translation presupposes a previous text," the proposition might be interesting as part of a universal definition but it is rather too obvious to be a universal in the sense we are discussing here. The term "universals" is thus generally used to refer not to the semiotic functions of translations (the relations people assume or activate when they approach a translation) but to linguistic features that can actually be measured.

A universalist proposition might be something like "translations tend to be longer than their source texts." Many people believe this to be true, but could it be true of all translations? There is a minor problem with the different ways in which text length can be measured in different languages, but that can be solved (for example, we might do an experiment where a text is rendered from language A into language B, then back into A, and so on, hypothesizing that the texts will become longer with each translation). For many genres, languages, directions and groups of translators, there will indeed be some expansion, at least in the first few directions. But the "universal" will probably not hold for all genres and languages. For example, it seems not to hold for technical reports rendered from Spanish into English, basically because experienced translators tend to eliminate many of the Spanish circumstantials. It could hardly hold for translated subtitles, which generally have to be much shorter than the spoken language they render. And it could scarcely describe the realities of simultaneous or consecutive interpreting, which are presumably to be included as modes of translation. Further, even if the proposition were found to be true for all languages, all genres, and all modes, could this kind of research tell us why that might be so? The search for universals is not an easy affair.

The early research on potential universals was mostly carried out by scholars associated with the Tel Aviv school in the 1980s. Here are some of the proposed universals, dug up and arranged in very rough chronological order.

5.6.1 Lexical simplification

Lexical simplification may be defined as "the process and/or result of making do with *less* words" (Blum-Kulka and Levenston 1983: 119). This means that translations tend to have a narrower range of lexical items than do non-translations, and they tend to have a higher proportion of high-frequency lexical items. The language is usually flatter, less structured, less ambiguous, less specific to a given text, more habitual, and so on (we take these adjectives from Toury 1995a: 268–273). In statistical terms, for each 1,000 words used (tokens), a translation would have fewer individually different words (types); it will thus have a lower type/token ratio. Table 5.1 gives a very simple example from Munday (1998), from well beyond the Tel Aviv school.

Table 5.1   Example of the way translations tend to have lower type-token ratios than non-translations (from Munday 1998)

	Different words (types)	Words used (tokens)	Type/token ratio (%)
Spanish original	1452	4498	32.3
English translation	1387	4561	30.4

5.6.2 Explicitation

Explicitation was defined by Blum-Kulka (1986/2004) as a particular kind of simplification found in the greater "redundancy" of translations. The hypothesis is as follows:

> The process of interpretations performed by the translator on the source text might lead to a TL [target language] text which is more redundant than the source text. This redundancy can be expressed by a rise in the level of cohesive explicitness in the TL

text. This argument may be stated as "*the explicitation hypothesis*", which postulates an observed cohesive explicitness from SL [source language] to TL texts regardless of the increase traceable to differences between the two linguistic and textual systems involved. It follows that explicitation is viewed here as inherent in the process of translation.

(Blum-Kulka 1986/2004: 292)

In practice, this means that translations tend to use more syntactic markers than do non-translations. In one of the clearest examples, Olohan and Baker (2000) find that the optional English reporting *that* (as in "She said [that] she would come") is more frequent in a corpus of English translations than in a comparable corpus of English non-translations. Translations may thus be said to be more explicit than non-translations.

5.6.3 Adaptation

Adaptation is a term for what Zellermayer (1987) found in her study of translations between English and Hebrew, where the translations into Hebrew were consistently more informal and spoken in character than the translations going the other way. Zellermayer attributes this to the more oral nature of Hebrew written texts in general. The general proposition is that translations tend to adapt to the norms of the target language and culture.

5.6.4 Equalizing

Equalizing is the term used by Shlesinger (1989) for the way simultaneous interpreting reduces both extremes of the oral–literate continuum (where texts at one end have many of the qualities of spoken language, and those at the other end have all the qualities of written language):

> Simultaneous interpretation exerts an equalizing effect on the position of a text on the oral–literate continuum; i.e., it diminishes the orality of markedly oral texts and the literateness of markedly literate ones. Thus, the range of the oral–literate continuum is reduced in simultaneous interpreting.
>
> (Shlesinger 1989: 2–3; see also Pym 2007b)

The mediation process thus brings the features toward a mid-point. Shlesinger found the tendency toward equalizing to be more powerful than the evidence of Zellermayer's "adaptation" and Blum-Kulka's "explicitation." Although formulated only for interpreting, the hypothesis might also hold for written translations. Then again, it might only be true for interpreting, which would suggest that the other supposed universals are not in fact universal to all modes of translation.

5.6.5 Unique items

Unique items are the basis for a hypothesis formulated by the Finnish researcher Sonja Tirkkonen-Condit (2004), well beyond the Tel Aviv school. The claim is that linguistic elements found in the target language but not in the source language tend *not* to appear in translations. Or better, such "unique items" are less frequent in translations than in non-translations, since "they do not readily suggest themselves as translation equivalents" (2004: 177–178). This has been tested on linguistic structures in Finnish and Swedish, but it might also apply to something like the structure "to be done" in English (as in "they are to be married"). If the hypothesis holds, such structures should be less frequent in translations than in non-translations in those languages. The hypothesis is compatible with the general thrust of simplification, although not reducible to it.

The study of translation universals has developed significantly thanks to **corpus studies** (for the frequencies of elements) and **think-aloud protocols, Translog, screen recording** and **eye tracking** (for the translation processes). However, although there is now a considerable body of research, we are not in a position to proclaim that any of the above hypotheses hold in all cases. Explicitation, for example, has been shown to prevail in a number of studies, but translations also exhibit **implication** (the reverse of implication), and in some cases there is more implicitation than explicitation (Kamenická 2007).

On the level of theory, the whole issue of universals becomes more nebulous the more you look at it. It is not clear, for example, if simplification, explicitation and equalizing are separate things or just different manifestations of the same underlying phenomenon. It is not obvious whether a universal has to be true in all cases studied, or just generally true when a lot of translations are put into one corpus and a lot of non-translations are put into another. No one is sure if the tendencies discovered are really specific to translation, whether they occur with similar frequencies in all interlingual mediation, whether they may also be found in processes of "retelling" within the one language, or whether the frequencies of linguistic items have any automatic correspondence with social or psychological importance. In all, the notion of universals is a very long way from the conceptual clarity with which the concept is used in Chomsky's linguistics. Here, it seems, researchers are merely counting things on the surface level of language. This means they have no way of saying why a potential universal should be universal.

We note that many of the more empirical studies on universals have been on non-literary texts, in contradistinction to the early history of the descriptive paradigm. Perhaps, for this reason, the researchers tend to forget about the radical options available to translators throughout history: researchers collect texts and translations from a newspaper, or from contemporary English, in the belief that the samples will eventually represent all languages and all translation practices. They thus overlook schemata like Holmes's four options for the rendition of form. "Simplification" could be a necessary consequence of strategies adopted in a "mimetic form" approach; something like "adaptation" may appear to be universal in a situation where "analogical form" is the norm, and so on. That is, the apparent universals could be dependent on specific kinds of social contexts. Alternatively, something like "explicitation" may be found to hold throughout all four of Holmes's large-scale historical contexts, including the free-shooters of "extraneous form." At the present state of play, no one is really sure.

5.7 LAWS

The search for universals attempts to identify linguistic features that are specific to translations. The quest for laws, on the other hand, aims to state *why* such features should be found in translations. In other words, the universals locate the linguistic tendencies, and the laws relate those tendencies to something in the society, culture or psychology of the translator. There is no good reason why the terms "universal" and "law" should differ in this way, but that seems to be what has happened.

Why we should consider causes is fairly obvious from the theoretical shortcomings of some of the research on universals. Work based on "**comparable corpora**," in particular, may compare translations done into English with non-translations originally written in English. This method is certainly economical (no need to waste time learning languages, cultures, or about otherness), but it is fundamentally unable to say why shifts occur. In the study we have cited on the high frequency of optional reporting *that* in translations in English, the researchers suggest that the phenomenon has a psychological cause, "subconscious explicitation" (Olohan and Baker 2000). However, since the corresponding connectors in the *source* languages must have been overwhelmingly non-optional (English is special in this regard), the cause might also have been straight interference from the source texts. Or it could be the effect of "equalizing," removing the orality of implicit *that.* Or it could be the avoidance of optional reporting *that* as a relatively unique item, as a special case of interference. On the level of universals, it is impossible to say. On the level of laws, however, one might at least hazard a guess.

The term "laws" is associated with **Even-Zohar** (1986 and elsewhere) and especially with **Toury** (1995a), from within the same school where the early notions of universals were hammered out. A law of translation would ideally be one of the principles underlying the way translation norms come about, which might in turn explain the linguistic manifestations on the level of universals. That, however, is very much on the level of ideal theory.

The general nature of these laws would be like what we have already seen in Even-Zohar (1978) when he proposes that translations tend to play an innovative cultural role when the target literature (or culture) feels itself to be inferior to the source literature (or culture). We could see this "innovative" function as a certain set of translation norms: translators might use Holmes's "mimetic" form; they would adopt foreignizing options, importing elements from the source text. On the linguistic level, they might indeed use less simplification, explicitation, adaptation, and equalizing than would be the case otherwise. The law then proposes that what happens in the process of translating is related to a certain context of production, specifically involving an intercultural relation of asymmetric prestige. Note, however, that the relation between the norms and the context is not one of automatic correspondence. These are generally "laws of tendency," a term that may be understood in two senses: (1) in the long run, the tendency is for factors on the two levels to correlate to a significant degree, and (2) the relation is such that the more the prestige is asymmetric on the context level, the more the translations will have an innovative role.

Toury proposes two laws of translation. The first is a general "**law of growing standardization**" (1995a: 267ff.), which brings together many of the tendencies we have seen on the level of universals. Toury proposes that, when compared with non-translations, translations are simpler, flatter, less structured, less ambiguous, less specific to a given text, and more habitual. The explanatory part of the law is then formulated as follows: "the more peripheral [the status of the translation], the more translation will accommodate itself to established models and repertoires" (Toury 1995a: 271). This could mean that the apparent "universals" are especially present when translations are not particularly important or active within a culture. That should beg the question of how "universal" a universal can be.

Toury's second law is the **"law of interference"** (1995a: 274–279). This basically says that translators tend to bring across structures that are in the source text, even when those structures are not normal in the target language. That seems to be nothing to get excited about. However, Toury makes two interesting claims about the tendencies involved. He posits, first, that **interferences tend to be on the macrostructural level** (text organization, paragraphing, etc.) rather than on the smaller levels of the sentence or the phrase. That is, translators tend to work on equivalents for the small things but forget about the big things. He then posits that "tolerance of interference . . . tend[s] to increase when translation is carried out from a 'major' or highly prestigious language/culture" (1995a: 278). This would seem to be a new formulation of the law first proposed by Even-Zohar. We might think, for example, that English-language cultures feel themselves to be so superior that they tolerate no interference from any other culture. We might then look at a few translations of French cultural theory, where there are all kinds of tell-tale syntactic interferences such as sentences beginning "For X cannot be held to be . . .," or high proportions of cleft sentences. Since the source culture ("French theory") is held to be prestigious, the interferences are tolerated. This makes sense: you only imitate people whom you admire.

The research on laws, on the possible causation of translation shifts, has not evolved with the same enthusiasm as the investigation of universals. This may be because causation is complex in any sociocultural field. In a more recent formulation, Toury recognizes the impossibility of discovering any complete causation: "There seems to be no single factor which cannot be enhanced, mitigated, maybe even offset by the presence of another" (2004: 15). This amounts to saying that contexts are multiple and irreducible; there can be no simple laws.

The relative lack of interest in laws may also point to a certain stagnation in descriptive theory. For many translation scholars with a literary background, the writing of literary or cultural history is probably enough of a goal. Theorists like Lambert, Lefevere or Hermans seem unlikely to share the passion of a collective search for universals or laws. Indeed, they and many others represent positions where the relativity of the descriptive paradigm, the plurality it reveals, precludes high-level abstraction. For some, history is not only enough but is also predominant: in the humanities, one might argue, any apparent law or universal must ultimately be dependent on context, and we have no real right to theorize beyond our own context.

5.8 FREQUENTLY HAD ARGUMENTS

We will now gather together a few general observations concerning the descriptive paradigm. The following points would generally be considered positive:

- The historical variety and vitality of translation has been revealed.
- The paradigm has played a central role in the development of Translation Studies as an academic discipline.
- It has created knowledge that is potentially useful for all aspects of Translation Studies, including the prescriptive approaches it originally opposed.
- It breaks with many of the prescriptive opinions of the equivalence paradigm, albeit at the expense of creating its own illusions of objectivity.

The counterweight to these positive points is a series of arguments about the apparent failings of the paradigm.

5.8.1 "Descriptions do not help train translators"

The basic argument here is that translation theory should help people learn about translation, and for this we need rules about what should be done. That is, we need prescriptions (for good translations), not descriptions (of just any old translations). Various scholars have responded on this point. Toury (1992) points out the usefulness of descriptions in the training situation, since one can always present alternative ways of translating, none of which is ideal or perfect (in Toury's words, "everything has its price"). We have noted above how Chesterman (1999) also argues that empirical research should reinforce training, since it may be used to predict the success or failure of certain strategies.

5.8.2 "The target side cannot explain all relations"

This is a common critique even within the descriptive paradigm. By no means everyone would agree with Toury (and Even-Zohar) that "translations should be regarded as facts of target cultures." The target-side focus certainly cannot explain the ways translations work in postcolonial frames where the distinctions between cultures are increasingly blurred, or wherever power asymmetries are so great that the source side is actively sending translations to the target culture. As we have noted, many researchers retain the importance of the source side, and many more are prepared to question whether there are just two cultures at stake. For that matter, one might point to the role of cross-cultural relations in the explanatory parts of Toury's laws. If translations are ultimately explained by relations between cultures, they cannot be facts of just one culture only.

5.8.3 "The models all concern texts and systems, not people"

This is a general critique that might be made of virtually all scientific approaches to cultural products in the twentieth century, including the equivalence and purpose paradigms. On the other hand, Toury's abstract concepts of norms and laws are offset by serious interest in how translators become translators (1995a: 241–258), and recent moves within the descriptivist project have been toward the incorporation of sociological models, particularly **Bourdieu**'s concept of "habitus" (Simeoni 1998; Hermans 1999). This would meet up with moves to write the history of translation as a **history of translators** (cf. Delisle and Woodsworth 1995; Pym 1998). It also connects with the many translation scholars who have been engaged in writing literary history, often in a humanist mode where translators play leading roles.

5.8.4 "The focus on norms promotes conservative positions"

This argument supposes that descriptions of norms can only help to reproduce those norms, without attempting to improve translational practices. The basic response is clear enough: you have to understand a situation before you can set about improving it (if and when it is possible to believe in disinterested understanding). A slightly better response is invested in the idea that norms may be taught as a series of viable alternatives (as in Toury and

Chesterman above), so the discovery of norms becomes a way to empower translators by enhancing their repertoires of solutions. As for the apparent promotion of conservatism, Toury proposes that we train students how to *break* norms, as indeed he himself has done within Translation Studies. The problem is thus not in the descriptions themselves, but in the way they are used.

5.8.5 "The definition of 'assumed translations' is circular"

This is a classical argument for theorists who are drinking beer. As we have seen, Toury refuses initially to define what a "translation" is, saying that the definition is made by the people who produce and use translations. We noted that this raises the technical problem of how the different terms for "translation" are assumed to be translations of each other. This means that, in the end, the researcher needs criteria for the selection of those terms, and those criteria must effectively constitute a theoretical definition of translation. So who is doing the assuming and/or the defining? What is most worrying is that many researchers in this paradigm seem not to want to take responsibility for their definitions. They want to pretend that everything comes from the object of study. This leads to a more serious critique.

5.8.6 "Descriptivist theory is unaware of its own historical position"

This argument basically sees the descriptive paradigm as an exercise in positivism. The paradigm would require belief in a neutral, transparent, objective knowledge about translation, and that progress will come by accumulating that knowledge. A great deal of conceptual armor is built around that belief. However, the armor cracks at several of the points we have seen: in the problem of defining translations, in the problem of how to use descriptions of norms, in the possibility that the various levels of description are themselves translations of a kind (check the way Toury uses the term "translation" to describe norms), and in the general emphasis on the role of context (if translations depend on context, why should this not be true of the way one describes translation?). At all these points, some attention is required to the role of the observer, the person doing the describing. The descriptive paradigm has not really been able to rise to that challenge. The role of subjectivity in the constitution of knowledge is better handled by the theories of uncertainty, and the wider senses of "translation" would be better developed by the paradigm known as "cultural translation." We will meet both of those paradigms below.

5.9 THE FUTURE OF THE DESCRIPTIVE PARADIGM

Where will the descriptive paradigm go from here? Recent calls have been for a "**sociological turn**," for some kind of alliance with a discipline better equipped to handle contextual variables. **Theo Hermans** (1999), for example, closes his account of the paradigm by pointing the way to the sociologies of **Bourdieu** and **Luhmann**. And so one turns that corner; but what do we find? Usually a plethora of data, on numerous levels, with very few categories able to organize the data in terms of cross-cultural communication. The great Modernist sociologies are based on the same structuralism that helped shape the descriptive paradigm itself, albeit now with more scope for self-reflexivity (the sociologist can do the sociology of sociologists). More problematic, these sociologies are overwhelmingly of single societies only, of systems in the "one side or the other" sense that has reigned within the descriptive paradigm. They fit in so well with the target-side orientation of descriptive approaches that they risk bringing in little that is new. Indeed, the descriptive literary studies of the 1970s and 1980s were already doing systemic sociology of a kind. A new "sociological turn" could risk bringing us back full-circle.

A great deal of research has been carried out within the descriptive frame. We could mention countless studies on literary translations, linguistic analyses of shifts, a growing body of research that integrates the various social actors, plus all the empirical work using corpora, think-aloud protocols, key-stroke recording, and eye tracking. We could add all the empirical work done on interpreting, classically studying the cognitive dimensions of conference interpreting, and more recently bringing in the social and political dimensions of community interpreting. Along the way, we have a great deal of work on translation and gender studies, translation and postcolonial studies, translation and censorship, translation and minorities, translation and languages of limited diffusion, and so on, all of which could be placed more or less within the descriptive frame. The worrying thing, though, is that none of these numerous avenues of investigation seems to have come up with any major new statement on the level of translation theory. There is no new translation theory coming from corpora studies, or from gender studies, or from any of the rest. There is certainly a lot of theorizing, but most of the concepts come from other disciplines and are *applied* to translation, making translation theory an importer rather than exporter of ideas.

In this respect, the potential of the descriptive paradigm, which once seemed to be leading to the most powerful theorizing of translation, has not been realized. Other modes of thought have taken the lead.

SUMMARY

This chapter has outlined a set of descriptive theories that oppose the equivalence paradigm in that they aim to be non-prescriptive, their prime focus is on "shifts" rather than types of equivalence, and they do not undertake extensive analysis of the source text. They tend to be like purpose-based *Skopos* approaches in that they emphasize the target-culture context and the *function* of translations within that context. They nevertheless differ from purpose-based approaches in that they see functions in terms of the positions occupied by translations within the target *systems*, rather than with respect to a client or a job description. Descriptive theories also tend to concern what translations are *usually* like in a particular context, rather than the ways in which particular translations might differ. They are thus able to talk about the "norms" that guide the way translations are produced and received. The paradigm is thus relativistic in that it is very aware that what is considered a good translation in one historical context may not be rated so highly in a different context. The research based on those concepts has done much to reveal the diversity of translation practices in different historical periods, different cultures, and different types of communication. It has been accompanied by high-level theorizing of the possible universals and laws of translation, although the paradigm has not seemed to be able to maintain a strong relation between the discovery of diversity and the development of new concepts.

SOURCES AND FURTHER READING

The Translation Studies Reader (Venuti 2000/2004) contains texts by Holmes, Toury, Even-Zohar, and Lefevere. Munday (2001/2008) deals with the paradigm in two chapters: one on "discourse and register," the other on "systems theories" (for us, they are all systemic). A good historical account of systems-based theories may be found in Theo Hermans's *Translation in Systems* (1999). The proceedings of the various conferences in Bratislava in 1968 (ed. Holmes et al. 1970) and Leuven in 1976 (ed. Holmes et al. 1978) are full of ad hoc insights into the development of the paradigm, although the books are hard to find. The same could be said of the seminal collection *The Manipulation of Literature* (ed. Hermans 1985), which is rather more profound than its misleading title. Anyone undertaking empirical research on translations should have tackled Gideon Toury's *Descriptive Translation Studies and Beyond* (1995a), if only to use it as a point of reference. Numerous papers on various aspects of methodology are available online at the sites of Itamar Even-Zohar (http://www.tau.ac.il/~itamarez/) and Gideon Toury (http://www.tau.ac.il/~toury/). A more entertaining and descriptive approach to literary translation is André Lefevere's *Translation, Rewriting, and the Manipulation of Literary Fame* (1992). For insights on the various sociocultural aspects of descriptive studies, see the selection of José Lambert's articles in *Functional Approaches to Culture and Translation* (ed. Delabastita et al. 2006). For a critical account of systems and norms, see Pym (1998). A broad update on recent work in the descriptive paradigm may be gleaned from the volume *Beyond Descriptive Translation Studies* (ed. Pym et al. 2008).

Suggested projects and activities

1 Consider all the language situations you participate in on a typical day, not only in newspapers, television and websites but also in shops, banks and public services. How much of this linguistic material must have been translated in one way or another? (Consider news events that have happened outside of your languages.) How much of that material is actually marked as translational?

2 Where do translators and interpreters work in your town or city? What laws or policies orient their work?

3 Look up translations in your language of John 1 that are similar to the following (taken from Nord 2001):

a) In the beginning was the Word, and the Word was with God, and the Word was God.

b) Au commencement était le Logos; et le Logos était près de Dieu, et le Logos était dieu.

c) En el principio existía el Verbo, y el Verbo estaba con Dios, y el Verbo era Dios.

d) Al principio era el Verbo, y el Verbo estaba en Dios, y el Verbo era Dios.

e) No principio era o Verbo, e o Verbo estaba com Deus, e o Verbo era Deus.

f) In principio era il Verbo, e il Verbo era presso Dio e il Verbo era Dio.

g)   Im Anfang war das Wort, und das Wort war bei Gott, und Gott war das Wort.

h)   Zuerst war das Wort da, Gott nahe und von Gottes Art.

Which translations make sense, and which do not? Could these differences be described in terms of norms?

The German translation (h) is from Berger and Nord (1999). It could be translated into English as something like "First the Word was there, near God and of God's kind." This radically changes the widely memorized phrases of the Lutheran version (g), which might be rendered as "In the beginning was the Word, and the Word was with God, and God was the Word." What might be the reasons for such a change? Could those reasons be described in terms of norms? Why was Luther the only one to make God the subject?

4   Use the Internet to find out about the Mexican interpreter La Malinche (also called Malineli Tenepatl or Doña Marina). What systems would she have been operating within? What was her relation with the systems? What norms would have regulated her work? Are these systems and norms different depending on whether her story is told by feminists, or by Mexican nationalists? (The same exercise may be done for any number of high-profile translators, preferably working in situations of conflict.)

5   Find a code of ethics for translators. Could any of the principles be described as norms? If so, what kinds of norms are they? How would they relate to an empirical study of what translators actually do? (For a critical analysis of codes of ethics, see Pym 1992a; Chesterman 1997.)

6   Find an authoritative history of your favorite national literature (e.g. French literature, Russian literature). Are translations part of the history? Are they mentioned in a separate chapter? In the index? Should they be? Would the inclusion of translations make any sense in the case of minor literatures in major languages (e.g. Australian literature)? Can periods of great change, such as the Italian Renaissance, really be written without reference to translations?

7   Select one page of a literary text and a professional translation of it. Try to divide the texts into paired segments (one source-text unit corresponds to one target-text unit) and identify the translation shifts. Are the shifts easily categorized? Can they all be described in terms of equivalence? For how many of the shifts could we say there are social or political factors involved? Should we talk about "shifts" or "variations," or perhaps "deviations," or even "errors"?

8   Find out about *The Poems of Ossian* (1773). Could this text be described as a translation? If not, what is it? Should it be analyzed within the field of Translation Studies?

9   Check the definition of pseudotranslations. Can you find any pseudotranslations in the literatures of your languages? What would their cultural function be? Why were they presented as translations?

10 Use a concordancer (or even the Readability tools in Word) to analyze the frequency of linguistic features in two different translations of the same text. Do the quantitative differences indicate some kinds of different norms?

11 Use the same tools to compare a translation with its source text, as in the example from Munday above. Do your findings support any of the proposed universals?

12 Find some way to listen to translators talking about their work, perhaps as they are translating (you might ask them to talk about everything they are doing, thus producing Think Aloud Protocols), or when they are discussing a translation they have done, or when they are disagreeing, perhaps on one of the many Internet discussion lists for translators. What terms seem to indicate the existence of norms? If you can identify a norm, can you also identify the punishment for non-compliance (in theory, norms are defined by the existence of such sanctions)?

CHAPTER 6

Uncertainty

This chapter deals with some theories that can be difficult to understand. The basic idea here is that we can never be entirely sure of the meanings that we translate. We thus have to admit we are uncertain about what we translate, and yet we must try to translate nevertheless. In the first part of this chapter we find that there are two groups of theories here: some express uncertainly about translations, since different renditions are always possible, while others express uncertainty about all meanings, whether in translations or in source texts. A reading from Plato's dialogue *Cratylus* will help explain the difference. We then run through a few ideas about how translation is possible even when we are uncertain about meanings. The last part of the chapter presents some ideas that come under the label of "deconstruction," where uncertainty becomes a basis for seeing translation as transformation.

The **main points** covered in this chapter are:

■ There are good reasons for doubting any cause–effect relationship between source texts and target texts.

■ The same reasons can be extended to uncertainty about communicating meanings in general.

■ Some theories do not question the meaningfulness of source texts (they are "determinist" with respect to language), but they do not accept that sources fully cause translations (they are "indeterminist" with respect to translations).

■ Other theories are more completely indeterminist because they question meaningfulness both in source texts and in translation.

■ There are several ways to explain how translation is still possible in a world of uncertainty. Illumination, consensus-oriented dialogue, hermeneutics, social constructivism, and game theory are some of the approaches that may be used to resolve this problem.

■ Deconstruction is an indeterminist approach which resolves the problem of uncertainty by accepting that all translation involves transformation.

6.1 WHY UNCERTAINTY?

The equivalence paradigm had a certain heyday in the 1960s and 1970s. Why exactly did it then diminish? One might say, on the basis of Chapters 4 and 5, that equivalence was undermined by two new kinds of theory: German-language *Skopos* theory and scientific descriptivism. That, however, would be only partly correct. Notions of function and purpose were already within the equivalence paradigm; all *Skopos* theory did was to restrict equivalence to special cases. As for descriptive studies, they owed their intellectual heritage to much the same structuralism that enabled the equivalence paradigm to gain currency; they were extending those same models into wider social fields. As we have noted, the newer paradigms did not do away with equivalence: they just made it narrower (in *Skopos* theory) or wider (in Toury's Descriptive Translation Studies).

Seen in this light, the basic tenets of the equivalence paradigm still underlie much of the work done on translation today. It is still the dominant paradigm in most linguistic approaches, especially when it comes to terminology and phraseology. Indeed, the concept of equivalence might be expected to gain a new lease of life in sectors like software localization, where many source and target phrases mostly have to match in both function and approximate length (see 7.5.4 below). Equivalence is by no means dead, but it has certainly been questioned.

There are at least two underlying reasons for the increasing dissatisfaction with equivalence:

1   ***Instability of the "source"***: Descriptive research has shown that what translators do varies considerably according to their cultural and historical position. For example, in the pre-print age "source texts" were often manuscripts that were constantly being copied, modified, and rewritten, as well as translated (in this, they were rather like our websites and software programs of today). They were not stable points of departure to which any translation could be considered equivalent. So the concept of equivalence was not something that medieval translators really argued about; the paradigm was simply not in place because there were few stable source texts around. Similar doubts about equivalence occur in our own technocratic age, where the success of a text tends to be measured in terms of the user pushing the right button or clicking on the right link, rather than by strict comparison with any anterior text. Since the source texts themselves are constantly evolving, to what should the translation be equivalent?

2   ***Epistemological skepticism***: Alongside the growing awareness of variability, the intellectual climate of the humanities was changing quite dramatically from the 1970s. The various forms of structuralism had assumed that scientific study could produce stable scientific knowledge in a world of relations between objects. However, philosophers had long been questioning that certainty. The relations between things could not be separated from how we think about these relations, and we have to do that thinking in some kind of language. The problem is then that different languages picture the relations in different ways, so no language can be assumed to be transparent to the world – we might be seeing only what our language enables us to see. In literary studies and cultural philosophy, structuralism gave way to post-structuralism and deconstruction. Those movements asked serious questions about equivalence. If a piece of language was supposed to be equivalent to some other piece of language, who had the right to say so? How could we ever be certain we had located the thing in common?

What was equivalent to what, exactly, for whom, and with what authority? Those questions concern **epistemology** (the study of the ways knowledge is produced), and they are asked from a position of **skepticism** (whatever knowledge is produced, we are not entirely sure about it). The challenge to equivalence thus comes from the general position we might call **epistemological skepticism**: the knowledge provided by equivalence may not be wrong, but we are not entirely sure about it.

So we see two reasons for the questioning of equivalence: technological changes in what people are translating from, and a general intellectual climate. In this chapter we will be concerned with the various ways epistemological skepticism has affected translation theory. We will see that there is more than one current at work: some theories express doubts about how translations represent their sources, and others are skeptical about *all* meanings. To grasp these theories in at least part of their complexity, we will meet a few ideas that go beyond traditional translation theory. Along the way we will meet some of the major European thinkers of the past century or so. This may be difficult to follow, but for some readers it will hopefully stimulate thought.

Some key terms

- **Epistemology**: The study of the ways in which knowledge is produced, in this case knowledge about the text to be translated, or the purpose to be achieved.
- **Skepticism**: The general attitude of having doubts about something.
- **Epistemological skepticism**: The general attitude of having doubts about how we get knowledge. In this case, we might be skeptical or uncertain about what we know about the source text or of the purpose the translator has to achieve.
- **Determinism**: The belief that an event is caused by a previous events or set of events that we can know about. For example, we might believe that a translation is caused ("determined") by what is in the source text, or by the instructions received from the client.
- **Indeterminism**: The belief that not all events are wholly caused ("determined") by previous events. If the one source text can cause many different translations, then none of the translations can be wholly "determined" by that source text. Indeterminism would generally allow for some freewill on the part of the translator.
- **Indeterminacy**: Here, an instance of indeterminism is believed to occur in a particular phenomenon. A belief in general indeterminism might thus make us believe in the particular indeterminacy of translation.
- **Determinist theory**: Here, a theory which assumes that, in a communication act, what is understood is determined by what is said or meant. Applied to translation, we would say that the correct translation is the one that corresponds to the source-text author's ideas, intentions, message, or words.
- **Indeterminist theory**: Here, a theory that does *not* assume determinacy. An indeterminist theory would accept that translation does not involve a transfer of ideas, intentions, meanings, or words. Most indeterminist theories would accept that a translation is based on an active interpretation of previous texts.

6.2 THE UNCERTAINTY PRINCIPLE

If you are told that "Friday the thirteenth" is equivalent to "martes 13" (Tuesday the thirteenth), you might accept the fact. Most professional translators would probably say the two are equivalent just because they are equivalent. The translators would perhaps then refer to some kind of **authority**: perhaps a dictionary, a passably bilingual person, or probably themselves. Alternatively, we might remain skeptical, no matter what the apparent authority. "**Skepticism**" means that we are unsure about something, but there are several ways of having doubts. You might sit there and stare at the unknown word and get nervous about how little you really know, or you might decide to adopt a more active kind of skepticism. You would then want to ask more questions about the word. Even if you believe you will never be certain about the matter, you can still try to get more knowledge. You could send translators mad by asking precisely what situations the equivalence holds in, or when the equivalence started to be produced, or why some formal difference persists, or how long the difference will remain (surely we should get the Spanish to adopt English superstitions about Friday, or vice versa?). Those kinds of questions will not help our translators at all. But they do lead to important questions about the kinds of authorities upon which the whole equivalence paradigm ultimately rests.

If we adopt this active kind of epistemological skepticism, we need not ask annoying questions just for the fun of it. Even if we believe the questions can *never* be answered in any final way, or that we will ever reach any final truth, we might still consider it our duty to express doubt about all those authorities (teachers, dictionaries, experts, translators) that stop others asking questions.

Epistemological skepticism has been a functional part of Western science since the early years of the twentieth century, at least. It is most conveniently attached to the physicist **Werner Heisenberg**, whose work on quantum mechanics (the relations between sub-atomic particles) famously reached the conclusion that it was impossible simultaneously to observe the speed and position of a particle: "The more precisely the position is determined, the less precisely the momentum is known in this instant, and vice versa" (1927: 172). This is Heisenberg's **uncertainty principle**, also known as the **principle of indeterminacy**. It has come to influence all kinds of science.

In the humanities, the point generally made is a weaker one called the **observer effect**, but that is sufficiently problematic for our purposes: each observation, we accept, is affected by the position of the observer. Something happens – let us say a car accident – and each observer's account of the event will be different. Each person was standing in a different position; they have different backgrounds and thus different interests in the accident, particularly when it comes to laying the blame. The element of uncertainty is simple enough in such cases, as is the epistemological skepticism of someone trying to investigate the accident. We can never trust any one observation absolutely. We might thus say that the thing observed – the car accident in this example – never fully causes (explains, justifies, or accounts for) the person's actual observation. Here we will say that the accident never fully **determines** the observations. **Indeterminism** is the general belief that events and observations are related in this way, and it is a consequence of epistemological skepticism. In the same way, we could say that a text never fully determines (causes, explains, justifies, or accounts for) what a receiver understands of it. Each receiver brings a set of conceptual frames to the text, and the reception process is thus an interaction between the text and those frames. The same would then hold for translation: no source text fully determines a translation of that text, if only because translations rely on observations and interpretations.

The idea of indeterminism does not suit theories of equivalence. If we say that Text A is equivalent to Text B, we assume there is a stable understanding of both texts, at least to the extent that they can be judged to have the same function or value. Indeterminism, as part of the general uncertainty principle, means that stable understanding can never be simply assumed.

6.2.1 Quine's principle of the indeterminacy of translation

In the late 1950s the American philosopher **Willard Van Orman Quine** set out to discover to what extent indeterminacy could affect language and meaning. To do this, he proposed a thought experiment involving translation. Here is a summary.

Imagine a "jungle linguist" who arrives in a village where people speak a completely unknown language. The linguist sets out to describe the language. They witness an event: a rabbit runs past, a native points to the rabbit and exclaims, "Gavagai!" The linguist writes down "*gavagai* = rabbit." An equivalent translation is thus produced.

Now, asks Quine, how can we be sure that *gavagai* really means "rabbit"? It could mean, "Look there, a rabbit!," or perhaps, "A rabbit with long legs," or even, "There is a flea on the rabbit's left ear," and so on. Quine argues that numerous interpretations are possible, and that no amount of subsequent questioning will ever produce absolute certainty that *gavagai* means "rabbit." Even if the linguist spends years with the tribe learning their language, there will always remain the possibility that each speaker's use of the word carries unseen individual values.

Quine actually argues that there are degrees of certainty for different kinds of propositions. As far as translation is concerned, however, the message seems to be that **indeterminacy will never completely go away**. Quine posits that the one source (*gavagai*) can give rise to many different renditions ("rabbit," "flea on rabbit," etc.), all of which may be legitimate and yet "stand to each other in no plausible sort of equivalence relation however loose" (1960: 27). Whatever relation there may be between the translations, it is not certain, and that idealized, impossible certainty was what Quine associated with "equivalence." But if not equivalence, what then is the relation?

In a later formulation of this indeterminacy principle (1969), Quine claims that **different translators will produce different translations**, all of which may be correct, and none of the translators will agree with the others' renditions. If the previous example of the jungle linguist seemed abstract and far-fetched (after all, there are no untouched tribes left in the world, and ethnolinguists have far more subtle modes of conducting fieldwork), the claim that different translators translate differently sounds familiar enough. And the claim that translators disagree with each others' translations seems uncomfortably close to home, especially when there is an element of authority or prestige at stake.

Indeterminacy accounts for those differences and disagreements; the concept of equivalence does not. That is one good reason for incorporating indeterminacy into a theory of translation. Indeterminacy, however, is not a term used in many translation theories, at least not beyond Quine and the tradition of analytical philosophy. For the most part, its nagging doubts have worked their way into translation theory through a variety of intermediary disciplines and movements. Here we will outline a few of those connections.

Quine's principle of the indeterminacy of translation

Manuals for translating one language into another can be set up in divergent ways, all compatible with the totality of speech disposition, yet incompatible with one another. In countless places they will diverge in giving, as their respective translations of a sentence of one language, sentences of the other language which stand to each other in no plausible sort of equivalence however loose.

(Quine 1960: 27)

6.2.3 Indeterminism in theories of language

The basic idea of indeterminacy might be considered to be obvious. The American linguist **Noam Chomsky** regarded Quine's principle as simply saying that "theories are under-determined by evidence," in the sense that a phenomenon may be accounted for by more than one theory (since a theory is ultimately like an observation, or like a reading, or like a translation). This, says, Chomsky, is "true and uninteresting" (1980: 14, 16). That is, **so what?** In Chomsky's own field there is little doubt that different grammars may be written to describe the same language, and all of them will be adequate to some degree and yet different from each other. In literary theory, texts are accounted for by a succession of paradigms (philology, New Criticism, structuralism, Marxism, deconstruction, psychoanalysis, gender studies, etc.), none of which may be said to be wrong. In fact, in all the sciences, both natural and human, the twentieth century saw a general divergence between the production of theories and the gathering of evidence; in all fields of enquiry, you can come up with a new theory on the basis of old facts (or a new translation of an old text). The study of translation is obviously no different in this respect (which, by the way, is how this book can address many different paradigms, all of them correct). Indeterminacy is the very basis for a plurality of theories.

Of course, **indeterminacy can be seen in all communication**, across the board. Although its workings are clearer when illustrated between languages, it also applies *within* languages. Whatever we say will be only one of many possible variations on what we think we mean, and what others make of our words will be only one of many possible interpretations. Here, our words ultimately operate like theories, or translations. Indeterminism says we cannot be sure of communicating anything, at least not in any exact sense. We cannot assume there is a meaning that is encoded on one side and then decoded on the other. The opposite of indeterminism might then be a theory that assumes "**codes**," or "**transmission**," or "**meaning transfer**," or a source-to-target "**conduit**" (all those metaphors have been used) that is somehow able to guarantee equivalence.

The general idea of indeterminacy may be used to divide translation theories into those that assume the possibility of exact communication of some kind (**determinist**: what X means is what Y understands) and those that do not (**indeterminist**: we can never be sure that the two sides share the same meaning). All students in the humanities should spend at least a few sleepless nights worrying that they will never be fully understood, and a few more nights concerned that they will never fully understand anyone else; then some five minutes accepting that they do not understand themselves either. Students of translation should probably invest some supplementary afternoons in existential preoccupation, since indeterminacy is even more of a problem when different languages and cultures are involved.

As we shall soon see, most indeterminist theories of translation simplify the division between themselves and the determinist theories, especially when it comes to equivalence. They make it look like there are just two camps, us and them, and a revolutionary battle to be fought, dethroning the illusions of equivalence. The problem, however, is that the indeterminist troops are actually far from united. More specifically, **many determinist theories of language become indeterminist when applied to translation**. Things are complicated. Let us look at a few classical examples, since the problem has been around for a very long time.

6.3 DETERMINIST VIEWS OF LANGUAGE WITH INDETERMINIST THEORIES OF TRANSLATION

Here we approach translation from the perspective of some ancient stories about language.

Plato's dialogue *Cratylus* is based on two characters who hold opposed views about the way words have meanings. They present their views, and Socrates asks them questions. The character Hermogenes argues that words are just arbitrary labels for things (i.e. encodings). The character Cratylus, on the other hand, argues that each thing has its proper word (i.e. the shape of the word fits the thing, as in onomatopoeia):

> Cratylus says that everything has a right name of its own, which comes by nature, and that a name is not whatever people call a thing by agreement, just as a piece of their own voice applied to the thing, but that there is a kind of inherent correctness in names, which is the same for all people, both Greeks and non-Greeks.
>
> (383A, trans. Fowler)

For most of us, Hermogenes's position would seem to be the more correct. Give or take a few onomatopoeias, **words would seem to have an arbitrary relation to their referents**. That is what **Saussure** posited as one of the very foundations of systemic linguistics. It is also a way of explaining why words vary enormously from language to language, and why translation is thus necessary.

In Plato's dialogue we nevertheless find Socrates spending a lot of time and effort defending Cratylus's position. He argues that the Greek words actually do tell us something about the nature of things. For example, the word for truth, *aletheia*, is decomposed into *theia*, meaning "divine," and *ale*, meaning "wandering." Truth, it seems, is a "divine wandering" (421B). That whole section of the dialogue is a farrago of insightful and playful etymology, brilliant enough to make one half-believe the theory. It reaches the level of syllables and rhythms, which are found to be particularly suited to what they express. Name-givers would use them the way painters use different colors. For example, the sound O is the chief element of the word *gogguloon* (meaning "round") (427C), and we might add that the mouth makes more or less the same shape when we say *round, rund, rond, redondo*, etc., which are perhaps correct names. The theory even assumes some kind of infallibility. Socrates recognizes that if there is a word that cannot be analyzed in this way (the word *pyr*, for "fire," is an example), it "is probably foreign; for it is difficult to connect it with the Greek language" (409E). That fails to explain why Greek alone should have all the good names, but let us proceed.

In the second part of the dialogue, Socrates starts to pull apart this same theory. Some of the weak points should be clear already. If the words are to be understood in terms of semantics within the Greek language, how could their apparent correctness be for all people "both Greeks and non-Greeks" (the latter are actually the "barbarians" in Greek, those who do not speak)? Further, within the Greek language, Socrates finds words for "intellect" or "memory" that do *not* reflect movement. They would thus contradict the wonderful "divine wandering" theory found in the word *aletheia* ("truth") (437B). These, apparently, are names that have been badly given. If it is possible to give a name badly, and yet those names are used, then there must be some degree of social convention in the names for things. Language is thus to some extent arbitrary.

If we look at these two theories, which one would be the less deterministic? Hermogenes' position is actually saying that the assigning of words to things or concepts is arbitrary, and thus undetermined by anything except convention. That theory makes translation easy (we just encode and decode). In fact, it makes equivalence quite possible. This means that **an indeterminist theory of naming can produce an equivalence-based theory of translation**. Think about it.

On the other hand, Cratylus's theory, which is highly deterministic (the nature of the thing determines the correct name), would make equivalence virtually impossible, and perhaps translation as well. How could we translate *aletheia* as truth if the Greek term really means "divine wandering"? This deterministic view says that Greek can only be properly understood in terms of Greek. So **no full equivalence is possible** beyond that language. Welcome to the paradoxes of theory.

6.3.1 Cratylistic determinacy in translation

Cratylus is not about translation theory, but it does illustrate a paradox to be found in many contemporary theories of translation. Indeed, the paradox of a **determinist theory of expression underlying an indeterminist theory of translation** is so widespread that we might label all these theories "Cratylistic." Here are a few examples.

As we mentioned in Chapter 2 on equivalence (see 2.2), **Wilhelm von Humboldt** saw different languages as building different views of the world, an idea that was further developed by the American linguists **Sapir** and **Whorf**. The idea may be found in a number of approaches. For example, the Russian linguist **Roman Jakobson** (1959/2004: 142) claimed that Germans see death as a man (*der Tot*, masculine gender) whereas the Russians see it as a woman (смертъ, feminine gender) because the languages attribute those genders. Similarly, says Jakobson, "the Russian painter Repin was baffled as to why Sin had been depicted as a woman by German artists: he did not realize that 'sin' is feminine in German (*die Sünde*), but masculine in Russian (rpex)" (1959/2004: 142). So our languages would shape the way we perceive the world. The masculine sins of Russian cannot really be a full equivalent of the feminine sins of German, and their rewards in death are similarly non-equivalent. Does each language really determine the way these things are seen?

The **"world-view" theory** would be a modern version of Cratylistic determinism. For Cratylus, the nature of the thing determines its correct name; for linguistic relativism, **the nature of the language system determines perception of the thing**. Either way, there is a strong deterministic link between expression and concept. In fact, strict "world-view" linguistics would be deterministic in an even stronger sense, since they see each piece of knowledge as being determined by the entire language, not just by a few creative name-givers. In its extreme form, this systemic determinism means that knowledge cannot be conveyed beyond the language in which it is formulated. Translation could at best give us an idea of what we are missing.

Modernist aesthetics, which in Europe we would date from the late nineteenth century, has followed similar paths. In the work of art, we are told, form and content are inseparable. Each set of words, or of sounds, has meaning precisely because of what they are and the way they have been put together: "that which is to be communicated is the poem itself," said the Modernist poet **T. S. Eliot** (1933/1975: 80); the poem would not convey any "meaning" that existed prior to the poem. This whole tradition has been traced back to Cratylus by Gérard Genette (1976). For most of the thinkers concerned, translation cannot be governed by equivalence, at least not on any aesthetic level.

The clearest formulation of this tradition is perhaps to be found in the Italian theorist **Benedetto Croce** (1902/1922: 73) when he describes:

> the *relative* possibility of translations; not as reproductions of the same original expressions (which it would be vain to attempt) but as productions of *similar* expressions more or less nearly resembling the originals. The translation called good is an approximation which has original value as work of art and can stand by itself.

Croce significantly describes the "**similarity**" or "approximation" as a "**family likeness**." Of course, that metaphor was to become rather better known through **Wittgenstein** (e.g. 1958: 32), who talked about "family likenesses" (Anscombe translates it as "family resemblances") to describe the relations between the elements of semantic sets. From there, the metaphor has been used within the equivalence paradigm to describe different ways translations relate to their sources: (see 3.1 and 3.9.4 above). It has also served in the descriptivist paradigm to portray the way translations are different yet belong to the same set (cf. Toury 1980; Halverson 1998). However, for the Modernist aesthetic, where form cannot be separated from content, the sense of "family likeness" was more radically negative: a likeness was the best that translation *should* hope to achieve, since there could be no absolute equivalence. **Translations are all very well, but they will never replace originals**. That is one way determinist theories of language, or of expression in general, have sought to retain the possibility of translation. It is a way that actually meets up with the concept of directional equivalence. Yet there are other ways as well.

6.3.2 Using Cratylistic determinacy as a way of translating

The German philosopher **Martin Heidegger** used something like Cratylistic method as a way of developing thought. For instance, he saw the Greek word for truth, *aletheia*, as configuring *Unverborgenheit* ("unhiddenness," "disclosedness") (1927/1953: 33, 219 and in several other places), based on its particles *a-* (absence of) and *-lethe* (deception). This is clearly quite unlike the "divine wandering" that Cratylus found by analyzing the word as *ale-theia*. Heidegger generally postulates that words convey knowledge within their own language, and that etymology conceals that knowledge. He nevertheless exploits the differences between languages in order to develop knowledge, and this is where we find his main reflections on translation. To take one of his more elaborate examples, the Latin philosophical term *ratio* would have as its normal equivalent the German term *Grund* (ground, or reason, or cause). That equivalent, however, suppresses many other possible interpretations. *Ratio* could also be rendered as *Vernunft* (reason), or indeed as *Ursache* (cause). In Latin, we are told, *ratio* also means "reckoning," "calculation," and it works as a translation of the Greek term *logos*. "*Grund* is the translation of *ratio*," says Heidegger,

> but this statement is a commonplace [*Gemeinplatz*], and will remain as such for as long as we do not think about what translation actually means in this and similar cases. Translation is one thing with respect to a business letter, and something quite different with respect to a poem. The letter is translatable; the poem is not.
>
> (1957: 163; our translation, here and throughout)

Given his implicit disdain of anything as banal as a business letter – just as **Freidrich Schleiermacher** (1813/1963: 62) had looked down on commercial translating or interpreting (*Dolmetschen*), where "the object is present" – Heidegger's attention is devoted to precisely what is **"not translatable," the "remainders," the non-equivalents** that are somehow covered over by the "commonplaces" of official equivalence. Rather than valuing family likenesses (similarities are supposed to be nice, as are families), Heidegger values the productive conflict of differences.

Heidegger's use of translation in this example cannot really be attributed to indeterminism in Quine's sense, since there is no epistemic doubt about the intentions of any speaker. The differences have more to do with **history**, with a mode of historical knowledge that is stronger than any individual:

> A word will have multiple references, therefore, not primarily because in talking and writing we mean different things by it at different times. The multiplicity of referents is historical in a more fundamental sense: it stems from the fact that in the speaking of language we ourselves, in accordance with the destiny of all beings' Being, are at different times differently "meant" or "spoken."
>
> (1957: 161)

We do not speak a language, **the language speaks us**. We become vehicles for the words and concepts that have been handed down to us across the centuries; the ideas of our cultural ancestors pass through us. This idea is rather like what biological evolutionists say about our being vehicles for the transmission of genes, rather than the genes being ways in which we transmit ourselves. In this context, Heidegger insists that a translation (*Übersetzung*) is not just an interpretation of a previous text but also **a handing-down, a question of legacy** (*Überlieferung*) (1957: 164). Heidegger gives the past more value than the present, and the task of translation – like that of philosophy itself – would be to recuperate lost or suppressed knowledge.

A similar placing of value in the past is at stake in the work of the German Jewish thinker **Walter Benjamin**. His 1923 essay "The Task of the Translator" plays with the millennial idea of the "true" or "pure" language (*reine Sprache*), of which the current languages would be partial representations. Here is Zohn's translation:

> All suprahistorical kinship of languages rests in the intention underlying each language as a whole – an intention, however, which no single language can attain by itself but which is realized only by the totality of their intentions supplementing each other: pure language. While all individual elements of foreign languages – words, sentences,

structures – are mutually exclusive, these languages supplement each other in their intentions. . . . the words *Brot* ["bread" in German] and *pain* ["bread" in French] "intend" the same object, but the modes of this intention are not the same. It is owing to these modes that the word *Brot* means something different to a German than the word *pain* to a Frenchman, that these words are not interchangeable for them. . . . As to the intended object, however, the two words mean the very same thing.

(Benjamin 1923/2004: 78)

From this it follows that the texts we find in different languages are parts of what the pure language could express. They are like "**fragments of a broken vessel**," as Benjamin puts it, and to translate them into each other would be to help reveal their fragmentary nature. Much has been written on Benjamin's essay and its translations in English, particularly about the way these "broken fragments" are supposed to connect with each other, perhaps ideally in the past, perhaps even more ideally in the future, or most probably not at all (see Jakobs 1975; de Man 1986; Andrew Benjamin 1989; Gentzler 1993/2001; Bhabha 1994/2004; Vermeer 1996; Rendall 1997). What interests us here is the way Benjamin effectively **turns the indeterminacy of translation from a problem into a virtue**. Although there is apparently no way that the words *Brot* and *pain* can be full equivalents, the attempt to translate them into each other, either way, must produce some knowledge not only about the thing they signify, but also about the different modes of signification. Translation thus reveals the difference between languages, rather than jumping over it; translation creates its own passing knowledge of that difference. Benjamin makes the interesting claim that **translations themselves are untranslatable**, "not because they are difficult or heavy with meaning, but because meaning adheres to them too lightly, with all too great fleetingness" (our translation from Benjamin 1923/1977: 61; cf. Rendall 1997: 199–200). The act of translation would be like quickly opening a window on differential signification, then seeing that window close as the subjectivity of the translator disappears and history moves on. This is not quite like Cratylus finding the "correct" names in Greek (as indeed Heidegger tends to). Benjamin does not actually say if the correct names exist in *any* language, past or present. Translation would be more like the space created by the debates in *Cratylus* itself, a space of critical and sometimes playful exchange. If there is a "family likeness," as Croce would put it, it is not because the source *text* is the parent, nor is it because one of the contemporary terms is better than the other. It has more to do with the way the passage from one term to the other, the brief jump across languages, enables a glimpse of similarities and differences that are otherwise hidden. Translators would have their own special hermeneutics.

What this means for actual translating is far from clear. Within this tradition of ideas, particularly as it dates from von Humboldt and German Romanticism, Benjamin would perhaps be seeking translations that are very close to their source texts, so that the reader is made aware of the differences between the two. Benjamin's text was written as a preface to his renditions of Baudelaire's *Tableaux parisiens* (a section of *Les Fleurs du mal*), the study of which might entertain a bilingual reader and could possibly suggest interstices awaiting a fuller language, but there is little to qualify it as a perfect or perfectionist translation (cf. Rose 1997: 41–49). To bring things down to earth: the text is so firmly set in Paris that the French *pain* might fairly be rendered as *baguette* (as an English word) or even *French bread*, allowing few glimpses of any pure meaning of bread. As it happens, the only bread in Baudelaire's *Les fleurs du mal* comes from Christian tradition ("bread and wine" in the poem *La Bénédiction* and "to earn your daily bread" in *La Muse vénale*), and that common

Christian tradition gives French and German shared expressions (yes, equivalents) at both those points. Benjamin's theoretical text has nevertheless been much more successful than his example, and we will return to it when discussing "cultural translation" (8.1 below).

All these theories, like Cratylus, posit a strong, almost mystical relation between expression and meaning. They thus do away with the idea of encoding something in one language and decoding it in the other. As we have seen, some of these theories would deny the possibility of translation altogether, while others accept it as a mode of transformation, or similarity, or knowledge-production, or insight, somehow beyond the boundaries of equivalence.

6.4 THEORIES OF HOW TO LIVE WITH UNCERTAINTY

These theories of indeterminacy are not of the kind where we can say "so what?," as Chomsky might have said to Quine. The theories question the possibility of translation, and thus the very thing we are supposed to be studying. Perhaps we can now understand why equivalence theory originally had to oppose much of structuralist linguistics. Following Saussure, structuralists were saying that meaning was formed within an entire language system, and that translation was not possible in any strong sense. Now we can see that they had some basic support from Modernist aesthetics and twentieth-century philosophy. And yet, the fact of translation as a social practice, its mere existence as something that people use and trust, would suggest that the theories were overstating the case.

Is it possible to accept indeterminism and still recognize the viability of translation? Let us suggest a few historical theories that can propose some kind of compatibility.

6.4.1 Theories of illumination

The first theory comes from the fourth/fifth-century theologian **Augustine of Hippo** (Aurelius Augustinus). In *De catechizandis rudibus* (2.3. 1–6). Augustine offers an intriguing analogy that would explain why translations can be different and yet talk about the same thing. Here the process of communication goes from ideas to "traces" or "vestiges" (*uestigia*), and only then to language. Augustine argues that language conveys thought very imperfectly:

> [T]he idea erupts in my mind like a rapid illumination, whereas my speech is long and delayed and not at all like the idea, and while I speak, the thought has hidden in its secret place. The idea has left no more than a few vestiges imprinted in my memory, and these vestiges linger throughout the slowness of my words. From those vestiges we construe sounds, and we speak Latin, or Greek, or Hebrew, or any other language. But the vestiges are not Latin, nor Greek, nor Hebrew, nor of any other community. They are formed in the mind, just as a facial expression is formed in the body.
>
> (c.400/1969; our translation)

What is happening here? The indeterminacy of language is clear enough. Ideas come as light, and language is like no more than a weak trace of that light, as when you close your eyes immediately after seeing a bright object. Yet Augustine does not abandon communication altogether. What is communicated is here anterior to language, and thus potentially available to all. Our words will have sense for someone who has experienced the same light. Thus our texts do not communicate messages as such; they help receivers to recall the **illuminations** that they have previously found for themselves.

Parts of this theory live on in the **translation of religious texts**. The legend of the Septuagint, the translation of the Hebrew Bible into Greek, says that 72 translators worked in isolated cells and all produced identical translations, in clear defiance of anything like Quine's problem with *gavagai*. How was it possible for them to overcome linguistic indeterminacy so miraculously? Presumably because they were not just any old translators: they were rabbis, with faith, and divine spirit thus oriented their words. Others have also seen faith as some kind of guarantor against indeterminacy. **Martin Luther** stated that "a false Christian or a person with a sectarian spirit cannot faithfully translate the Scriptures" (in Nida 1964: 16, 152), and in the preface to most versions of the Bible you will find some passage saying that the translators were "united in their faith." In effect, these translators all claim to be able to overcome indeterminacy through a shared experience that is somehow prior to language. **Revelation** or **faith** would be pre-linguistic experiences of which words need be no more than vestiges.

Augustine's general idea need not be restricted to religious messages. As we shall soon see, contemporary **theories of education** stress that we learn through experience, by actually doing things and discovering knowledge for ourselves, rather than by understanding someone else's words. Further, contemporary theories of reading see the text's schemata as interacting with the reader's schemata, such that meaning is actively created from what readers bring to the text. And again, relevance theory of the kind **Ernst-August Gutt** (1991/2000) applies to translation can accept that language is hugely indeterminate (meaning is created by breaking maxims) but that there is still some kind of mystic access to intention, as a pre-linguistic experience of the communicative situation. All these ideas could be seen as handling indeterminacy in a rather Augustinian way. The **real communication lies in shared experience**, and this can overcome the indeterminacy of language.

6.4.2 Theories of consensus

A second way of living with indeterminacy emphasizes the role of **dialogue** and **consensus**. The seventeenth-century philosopher **John Locke** certainly had a transmissionist model of communication, based on encoding and decoding:

> When a Man speaks to another, it is, that he may be understood; and the end of Speech is, that those Sounds, as Marks, may make known his Ideas to the Hearer.
> (1690/1841: 281, section 3.2.1)

This formulation is so fundamental that the corresponding view of language is sometimes called "Lockean." However, if we read Locke's text we find examples like the following:

> I was at meeting of very learned and ingenious Physicians, where by chance there arose a Question, whether any Liquor passed through the Filaments of the Nerves. The Debate having been managed a good while, by a variety of arguments on both sides, I (who had been used to suspect, that the greatest part of Disputes were more about the signification of words, than a real difference in the Conception of Things) desired, That

before they went any farther on this dispute, they would first examine, and establish amongst them, what the word Liquor signified. . . . They were pleased to comply with my Motion, and upon Examination found, that the signification of that Word, was not so settled and certain, as they had all imagined; but that each of them made it a sign of a different complex Idea. This made them perceive, that the Main of their Dispute was about the signification of that Term; and that they differed very little in their Opinions, concerning some fluid and subtle Matter, passing through the Conduits of the Nerves; though it was not so easy to agree whether it be called Liquor, or no, a thing which when each considered, they thought it not worth the contending about.

(Locke 1690/1841: 343, section 3.9.16 "On the imperfection of words")

Here we find a case where language is not fully determined by its referent, nor by concepts (the word "Liquor" only produces confusion). However, that indeterminacy is overcome through dialogue and consensus. The point of indeterminacy is ultimately avoided or considered "not the worth." A similar argument was formulated by the linguistic philosopher **Jerrold Katz** (1978: 234) with respect to **Quine**, arguing that if two different translations are both correct, then their differences must be insignificant and not worth bothering about. In the end, does it really matter if we use "Liquor" or some other word? The important point is that language enables us to keep talking about language (Locke's anecdote has probably justified some three centuries of philology), and it is through those exchanges that some sense of understanding is reached.

Seen in this way, a Lockean theory need not exclude initial indeterminacy. It might even teach us how to live with it. Keep the dialogues going, and consensus might ensue. But does that solution really help translators? Few intermediaries are allowed time to conduct long dialogues about language. And even though it has been proposed (in Brislin 1981: 213) that **conference interpreters** should be allowed to stop debates when there are misunderstandings based on words, not many job profiles actually give them that power.

We now move on to some of the theories that have been applied to translation closer to our own age.

6.4.3 Hermeneutics

Benjamin and Heidegger, along with many others, were writing in the tradition of German Romanticism and post-Romanticism. One line of that tradition has been particularly concerned with the idea that texts are not immediately meaningful and need to be **actively interpreted**. This general field is known as **hermeneutics**, from the Greek *hermeneuō*, meaning "to interpret" or indeed "to translate." The nineteenth-century development of hermeneutics was closely linked to ways of making sense of the Bible, especially in view of the growing scientific knowledge that contested literal readings of what was supposed to be God's word. The way you interpret a text is obviously connected with the way you would translate it, so it is not surprising to find thinkers like Schleiermacher intimately concerned with both hermeneutics and translation.

In the twentieth century, hermeneutics became more general in its application, especially through to the work of **Husserl, Heidegger,** and especially **Hans Georg Gadamer**. Although these thinkers have relatively little to say about translation, their progressive insistence on the active nature of interpretation has become part of the general intellectual climate. In **Gadamer** (1960/1972) we find a positive value given to the interpreter's subjective involvement in the text, described as a necessary kind of **"prejudice"** (*Vorwurf*). Instead of trying to be scientific and objective about the text to translate, here translators should seek to recognize the ways they are personally positioned with respect to the text, and what particular desires and aims they have in carrying out their task. Subjective prejudice need not be a bad thing; here it becomes a source of motivation for work, with implications about which the translator should be as aware as possible. This personal involvement is also something that we should not seek to explain in an objective or analytical way.

The development of hermeneutics fed into deconstruction, which we will meet later in this chapter. It also connected what might be called the **"philosophy of dialogue,"** a set of ideas about the way human relationships should be formed. Writings by **Buber, Marcel**, and **Levinas** deal with the way the relation between the self and the "other" (here the person we are communicating with) should be open, dialogic, and respectful of difference, without just imposing our own desires. Applying this mode of thought to translation, **Arnaud Laygues** (2006) insists that the translator should not ask "What does this text mean?", as the classical hermeneutic tradition would have us ask, but **"What does this person mean?"** The uncertainty remains, but here the doubts about texts are turned into an ongoing dialogue with a person. The problem of indeterminacy is humanized. We are no more certain of what a text means than we are of the absolute nature of the people around us, and yet we continue to interact with those people, and we do not try to make those people sound like ourselves. The practical message here would be that we should keep interacting with the text, without domesticating it. Of course, the notion of extended dialogue runs into the same problems we have just mentioned with respect to Locke.

The general view of translation as a mode of interpersonal dialogue underlies much of the work of the French translator **Antoine Berman** (1984/1992, 1985, 1995). Particularly in his study of German Romantic and hermeneutic approaches to translation, Berman (1984/1992) maintains constant awareness of the difficulties of great literary and philosophical works. He insists that the ethical translator should *not* adapt the foreign text to the target culture but should respect and maintain the specificity of its foreignness. If we try to "make sense" of the foreign text, we turn it into *our* sense, *our* culture, which could only lead to **ethnocentric translation**. For Berman, "the ethical act consists in recognizing and receiving the Other as Other" (1999: 74). This particular hermeneutic approach thus

---

What hermeneutics has to say

Chau (1984) summarizes the main points that hermeneutics has to make with respect to translation:

1   There is no truly "objective" understanding.
2   "Prejudices" are unavoidable and can be positive.
3   There is no final or definitive reading.
4   The translator cannot but change the meaning of the source text.
5   No translation can represent its source text fully.
6   Understanding is not always explicable.

meets up with the "foreignizing" side of the dichotomies we met in our discussion of directional equivalence.

Perhaps the best-known French theorist in the hermeneutic tradition is **Paul Ricœur**, who has written with subtlety on how relations between the self and the other construe identity. When he comes to translation, Ricœur (2004) is keenly aware that there is no encoding-decoding at stake, and that great texts will always retain their untranslatable secrets. His findings sound provocative: "one must conclude," writes Ricœur, "that misunderstanding is allowed, that translation is theoretically impossible, and that bilinguals must be schizophrenic" (2004: 29). When we look closely, though, these dichotomies really belong to the paradigm of natural equivalence, where structuralist theories had long ago posited that translation was impossible simply because they could not explain it. Ricœur is perhaps not the most profound translation theorist that hermeneutics has to offer.

6.4.4 Constructivism

Hermeneutics started from the problems of interpreting texts, in a situation usually involving just one reader or translator. However, some compatible ideas have come from quite different areas of the sciences, where the problem is not so much how an individual makes sense of a text as how social groups make sense of the world.

The fundamental idea of constructivism is that our knowledge of the world is not simply given or passively perceived. Long-standing experiments in the **psychology of perception** show that we actively "construct" what we see and know of the world. We have all seen the picture of the vase that is also an image of two faces, depending on how your brain wants to construct the image. Any interpretative process is thus a constant interaction between both the objective (the world beyond the person) and the subjective (the person's own mental frames). These basic tenets are highly compatible with the uncertainty principle. Constructivism may be seen as a general epistemology, and it has informed areas of psychology, sociology, and philosophy. Yet constructivism has built its fiefdom within the psychology of education, particularly in the American tradition, and it is from there that it reaches translation theory.

What does constructivism have to do with translation? The American theorist **Donald Kiraly** (2000) argues that constructivism should be opposed to the entire "transmissionist" paradigm of encoding and decoding. According to the latter, knowledge would be something that can be moved from one passive receptacle to another, like water being dished out into buckets. Some knowledge would go into one text and is then transmitted to another (others talk about the "conduit" metaphor, where meaning flows through some kind of tube from one language to another). Translation would be nothing but one kind of such transmission. Indeed, one of the Latin verbs for translation is *vertere*, to pour, which gives the idea of equivalence as the same amount of water occupying vessels of different shapes. For Kiraly, the same transmissionism is at the base of the way many translators are trained. A teacher, like a source text, possesses knowledge that can then be poured into the minds of passive students, who are lined up like so many empty vessels. Constructivism says that knowledge simply does not work that way. Translators actively construct the text they produce, just as students actively participate in their learning process. Kiraly's main concern is with the consequences of constructivism for **translator training**. His ideas connect with a string of movements like learner-centered education, autonomous learning, and action research. What is interesting for us here is that his views are compatible with indeterminism, and they incorporate a view of translation based on that principle.

The correlative, of course, is that the equivalence paradigm is made to appear transmissionist. For Kiraly, the way equivalence assumes stable knowledge would reinforce a **teacher-centered mode of transfer**. We would thus face a choice between just two enormous paradigms: transmissionism (equivalence) or constructivism (active creation). This reduction to one-or-the-other is too simple. In the first place, transmissionism would only apply to what we have termed "natural" theories of equivalence; "directional" theories, on the other hand, stress that the translator actively produces equivalence, so there is no passive transmission at stake. Second, Kiraly's own position does not exclude the values of knowledge through **practical experience, discussion**, and **consensual understanding**. His classroom methodology is explicitly based on practice, on students finding their own illumination, and on group work, on students getting together to talk about what they are doing. In this, Kiraly correctly identifies his approach as "**social constructivism**." We might also see it as having elements of Augustine and Locke, in the senses described above. Here there is no drastic uncertainty that would destroy all attempts at communication. Social constructivism might teach us to live with indeterminacy.

6.4.5 Game theory

Let us now try to model uncertainty in terms of someone actually translating. Here we are using the model explained in our introduction to this book. A source text can be rendered as any one of several target texts. From the perspective of indeterminacy, there can be **no absolute rule for deciding between those various translations**. Someone might claim that "the translation has to have exactly the same cultural function as the source," but that is not universally true. Not only are there many cases in which translations are more determined by the *form* of the source (think of lip synchronization in film dubbing), but different people will see the source "function" as being different things. So translators will decide, and their decisions are only partly determined by the source text.

One result of this situation is that most of the translator's decisions cannot be called wholly "right" or wholly "wrong." When confronted with something like the German "Der Preis ist heiss" (The Price is Hot) as a translation of "The Price is Right," we might say "**Yes, but . . .**," and then add doubts about taste or source-text fidelity ("hot" does not mean "right," however loose). Alternatively, we might greet the translation with "**No, but . . .**," followed by expressions of personal appreciation. For Pym (1992b), these judgments are **non-binary, since they involve more than "right" vs. "wrong"** (i.e. more than two terms). This is the general form of problems that concern translation rather than something else (e.g. referents or authoritative terminology). Translation, by its very nature, is indeterminate. As translators proceed, they are confronted by numerous points where their rendition could be one of several possible translations, and the decision to opt for one of the possibilities depends on more than what is in the source (as we said in the introduction, the translator has to theorize when making these decisions).

Imagine that a text being translated comprises a set of points requiring major decisions. Because the text is a text, all those points presumably have something to do with each other. A decision made at one point may have consequences for decisions made at other points. The Czech translation theorist **Jiří Levý** (1967/2000) explained this, using the example of the Brecht play *Der gute Mensch von Sezuan*. The title of the play is sometimes rendered as *The Good Woman of Sezuan*, since the main character is a woman. But the German word *Mensch* can mean "man" or "person," perhaps "guy" (it has a colloquial register), or even "creature" (in the sense of us all being "creatures before God"), and much more. This ambiguity becomes functional in the play, since the main character is a woman who pretends to be a man. According to Levý, the way the translator chooses to render *Mensch* in the title will have repercussions for the way that this and similar terms are rendered throughout the text. **One decision becomes a determinant for others**. The result is that translating is determined not just by the source text, but by the patterns of the translator's own decisions. Levý thus saw translating as being akin to playing a game with finite information (e.g. chess). His aim was to apply **game theory** to the translator's decision-making process.

Indeterminism should probably take us further than Levý's example. Is translating a text really like playing chess? On the chessboard, every move probably does have some consequence for all future moves. In translating, however, no more than a handful of textual items are usually strung together in this way. In the case of Brecht's play, translators into English may not want to choose between a man or a woman in the title (is it really a binary problem?), so they opt for the more neutral *The Good Soul of Sezuan*. More important, if we take Quine's uncertainty seriously, translators will never have anything like complete information about these games. They might be playing the stock market rather than chess. After all, the translator calculates risks and takes chances without really being aware of how the elements will fit together in the mind of the end receiver. Indeterminacy means the translator has no certainty that all possible options have been seen, nor that future decisions will be entirely determined by the previous ones.

Taken in that sense, as an approach to decisions made on the basis of *incomplete* information, game theory might also teach us to live with indeterminacy. That link opens on to the huge field of **risk management**, which has not been fully explored by translation theorists.

6.4.6 Theories of semiosis

What happens if we accept, along with Heidegger and quite a few others, that we do not have access to any intention behind an utterance? Let us say we have the word *gavagai* and we want to know what it means. We are really asking what the word "stands for"; we are treating it as a "sign." However, we can only produce *interpretations* of whatever it stands for, and those interpretations will be further signs, which will then be subject to further interpretations. At no point can we be sure that our intention corresponds to anything that was there before the sign was produced (e.g. the speaker's idea). Our renditions thus constantly move meaning onward, rather than back to anything in the past. This would be despite the backward-looking positions adopted by thinkers like Heidegger. In terms of the nineteenth-century philosopher **Charles Sanders Peirce**, what we are involved in here could be called "**semiosis**":

> By semiosis I mean an action, an influence, which is, or involves, a cooperation of three subjects, such as a sign, its object and its interpretant, this tri-relative influence not being in any way resolvable into pairs.
>
> (Peirce 1931/1958: 5.484)

That sounds abstruse, but the concept could be of importance for translation within **semiotics** (the study of signs) (see Gorlée 1994; Stecconi 2004). If we follow **Umberto Eco**'s reading of this theory (Eco 1977), the "**interpretant**" is a sign that acts as the interpretation of a previous sign. Semiosis is the process by which signs "grow," as Peirce puts it, potentially in an unlimited way. For example, if we look up a word in the dictionary, we will find that the "meaning" is a set of different words. We could then look up the meanings of those words, and so on *ad infinitum*, until the dictionary is exhausted, the language itself would have changed, and we would have to start again.

Eco (1977: 70) describes the interpretant as assuming many different forms, of which "translation into another language" is just one. Other theories, however, have been inclined to see translation as operating in all types of interpretation, as we shall see later (8.2.1 below). The important point here is that the very nature of semiosis makes the processes keep going. That is what translation, in its widest sense, could be doing in the world.

The Russian linguist **Roman Jakobson** was paraphrasing Peirce's concept of semiosis when he wrote that "the meaning of any linguistic sign is its translation into some further, alternative sign" (1959/2004: 139). This effectively reverses most traditional translation problems: rather than represent a previous meaning, translation would be the active *creation* of meaning, and this would hold for all kinds of meanings. Jakobson, rather like Eco, recognizes translation as operating in a very wide sense. He finds translation both within languages and between them, as well as between different kinds of signs (as when a painting represents a poem, or a picture tells us not to walk on the grass).

Theories of semiosis are not always as revolutionary as they might appear. For instance, Jakobson announces a theory of translation in the widest of possible senses (the creation of meaning itself) and then reduces it to just one kind of "**translation proper**," concerning interpretations across languages. We find the same reduction to "translation proper" in Eco (2001), when he opposes translation to the many other kinds of "rewriting." Neither Jakobson nor Eco want to lose the specific sense of translation that remains in touch with fairly traditional concepts. For Jakobson, "equivalence in difference is the cardinal problem of language and the pivotal concern of linguistics" (1959/2004: 139); for Eco, each text has its own "intention," which is what should be translated (cf. Eco 2001). From the very beginning, the idea of semiosis was present within the discourse of those (including Peirce, Jakobson, and Quine) whose prime search was for certainty, for a sure grounding of thought. In this group of theories, the principle of semiosis has tended to be regarded as dissipation rather than liberation. Yet there were other voices prepared to grant semiosis a far more positive press.

6.5 DECONSTRUCTION

Many of the theories dealt with in this chapter could be associated with what is generally called "deconstruction," a set of critical ideas based on the work of the French philosopher **Jacques Derrida** (see Davis 2001). Deconstruction is a highly indeterminist approach that sets out to **undo illusions of stable meaning** of any kind. Whereas other approaches within the uncertainty paradigm have developed from an earnest search for truth, for a moment of full determinacy, deconstruction proposes that the way to live with language is to accept it as not being transparent to the world. Deconstruction thus does not present itself as a theory (since a theory is supposed to have stable concepts and terms). It is instead a practice, an ongoing use of language on language, revealing the gaps and displacements ("differences") by which semiosis keeps going. The uncertainty that was a problem for other approaches here becomes something that has to be accepted as an invitation to discovery and creation.

For example, Derrida (1985) criticizes **Jakobson**'s use of "translation proper" as just one kind of "translation," as if the meaning of the term were stable in one place (what is "proper," usually defined by something like equivalence) and not in another (the rest). The use of terms like "translation proper" is seen as "essentialism," as the false assumption that words have their true meanings (their "essences") somehow embedded in them. We might now say that deconstruction is a critique of all forms of determinism, remembering that Cratylus believed that things could determine their "correct" names. In enacting this critique, deconstruction necessarily sees **translation as a form of transformation** rather than any kind of meaning transfer. Like Heidegger in this regard (and continuing the same philosophical tradition), Derrida seeks out the **"remainder,"** the potential significations that are omitted in the process of translation.

We see this critique at work when the early Derrida (1968) analyzes translations of Plato. Derrida observes that the Greek term **pharmakon** could be rendered in French as either remède (cure) or poison (poison), but not both terms at the same time (an ambiguity perhaps approximated by the American-English term "drugs," which can be good or bad for the body). This is seen as a problem not just for the translations into French, but for the movement from everyday Greek to philosophical Greek.

Derrida often uses translation to investigate the plurality of source texts, here in a sense of revealing their "semantic richness" rather than with reference to our own term "instability." His oft-cited phrase **"plus d'une langue"** expresses this plurality. It could be translated as "more than one language" or as "let us have no more of one language," and both readings are in the source. Note that in doing this, Derrida does not seek to remove the special status of the source text. In a 1999 text we find him asking how it is possible that Shakespeare could make sense – any kind of sense – well beyond its original historical and cultural location. This apparent mode of translatability is called **"iterability,"** attributed not to anything semantic but to the literary institutionalization of certain meaning effects (see Davis 2001: 30–35). The source text may thus be seen not as a set of obligatory orders (as it would in a deterministic world) but as a **phantom**, an image that organizes the range of translational variants without fixing them in a deterministic way. The source returns, like the ghost of King Hamlet, but only as a spirit that can hope to guide without acting directly (Derrida 1993: 42–43). This kind of source–target relationship has been further explored by the American theorist **Douglas Robinson** (2001), who relates it to mystical theories of **"spirit channeling."** Derrida, however, takes care to distinguish his metaphors from any claim to absolute translatability, which would assume the possibility of sameness, and thus essentialism.

Derrida's most perceptive comments on translation are nevertheless more metaphorical, notably in the texts where he investigates entities that are at once present and absent. This is the context in which we find the discussions of ghosts, afterlife, survival ("living-on"), and the apparently permeable border between life and death (this was a long reflection, carried across Derrida 1979, 1982, 1985, 1993, at least). The concept of translation, as a process more than as a product, enters as a model of how a voice can cross a border and continue, transformed. For this, Derrida picks up the notion of **"afterlife"** (Fortleben, "prolonged life") that **Walter Benjamin** (1923/2004: 76) used to describe the way a translation can continue the life of the source text. That was as a suggestive model, among several other models, and it is one to which we will return in our discussion of "cultural translation" (8.2 below).

On the other hand, when Derrida comes to the discussion of actual translations, he is remarkably conservative. In some early texts he **inferiorizes translation** as "a technique in the service of language, a *porte-parole*" (1967: 17–18; cf. 1972: 226). When analyzing the *pharmakon* example he takes delight in challenging the "official translations" and saying how they should be improved (1972: 80). Even when looking at the French translations of Hamlet (1993: 42–47), Derrida is remarkably traditional and prescriptive, finding no translation on the level of the original, and hence preferring the most literal version. For as much as his theorization went one way, his authoritarian stance tended to prevail in contact with actual translations. But not all translation theorists in this paradigm have wanted to see the range of Derrida's actual practice.

The Brazilian theorist **Rosemary Arrojo** has perhaps been the most consistent in her applications of deconstruction to translation theory. We find her enlisting deconstruction (along with concepts from psychoanalysis and postmodernism) not just in her attacks on all assumptions of meaning transfer (Arrojo 1993) but also against many feminist approaches to translation (1994), against ideal symmetrical relations (1997) and generally against all forms of linguistic essentialism (1998). As in Derrida, Arrojo sees deconstruction not as a set theory but as a practice, a way of using language to analyze language, and thus as a way of using language to translate. For example, Arrojo (1992) proposes the Brazilian term **oficina de tradução** to translate the American term *translation workshop* (the practice class where students work together on literary translations, perhaps with a writer or two present). The translation is then shown to come under the category of "right, but. . . ." The Brazilian *oficina* is the standard equivalent of *workshop*, but the word also has the values of "place of work" or "place for the exercise of a profession (*ofício*)." Arrojo (1992: 7–8) says *oficina* can also mean "laboratory," "place for the machinery or instruments of a factory," and "place where cars are repaired" (*workshop*, indeed). If we translate *workshop* as *oficina*, we are thus bringing slightly different meanings, different images, new questions, to the initial concept. Is this a question of adapting to the new target culture? Interestingly enough, the Brazilian poet and theorist Haroldo de Campos (1962/1976) had previously called for a "text laboratory" where linguists and artists would work together on translations. But an *oficina* is not quite the same thing as a *laboratory* (not even in Brazilian Portuguese). As Quine might have predicted, both can mean *workshop*, but they maintain a dynamic difference. Arrojo's translation can thus continue to produce meaning, moving the semiosis on. It uses indeterminacy as a means of production.

The basic lesson of deconstruction might be that **translation always involves transformation**. That would seem a logical consequence of indeterminacy. The task of the deconstructionist would be to make readers aware of this. Arrojo, for example, gives us an extended discussion of *oficina* vs. *workshop*, presenting materials that the reader can then work with, just as Heidegger does with *ratio* vs. *Grund*, or Derrida does with *pharmakon*. Rather than provide ready-made solutions, the deconstructionist would use indeterminism in order to make readers think. We are made to engage in an experience (perhaps as in Augustine), in a dialogue (perhaps as in Locke, although without final consensus), or in a situation where readers themselves have to create their own knowledge (as in constructivism).

That appears to be the way deconstruction operates in the discourse of philosophy or in the teaching situation. What lessons, though, does indeterminism hold for translators, who often cannot dialogue quite so freely?

6.6 SO HOW SHOULD WE TRANSLATE?

The paradigm of uncertainty would presumably be happiest with translations that have long philosophical prefaces or abundant footnotes on philological variants. It should like translations that talk about translating, as philosophers and teachers tend to do. Failing that, we would try to integrate awareness of indeterminacy into what we do in text. Unfortunately, as we have noted, many theories are not particularly helpful in this regard. Model examples do not abound, and there is a reason for this. In the end, from the perspective of indeterminism, **these things are for each individual translator to decide**. After all, if there is no certainty, how can any theory presume to tell us what to do?

Despite this reluctance to prescribe, some theorists have tried to find some practical benefits in heightened awareness of uncertainty. In his survey of hermeneutic theory, **Simon S. C. Chau** (1984: 76–77) claims that translators might be affected in the following ways (here we paraphrase his list):

- They become more **humble**, as they are fully aware of their existential limitation in relation to the translation.
- They become more **honest**, as they admit that neither their reading nor their rendering are canonical.
- They become more **efficient** interpreters, as they realize that apart from employing various scientific means to understand the source, they must "lose themselves" in the communion before any valid interpretation comes about.
- They become more **confident**, as their personal creativity under the given historical conditions of human existence is affirmed – they know that no translator needs to be haunted by the myth of *the* reading and *the* translation.
- They become more **responsible**, as they realize the active creative role of the interpreter in shaping the meaning of a text.

This is an optimistic list: it does not envisage the translator's "confidence" (perhaps Gadamer's "prejudice") becoming excessive and overriding all the rest; it does not worry that "humility" might lead to self-doubt and inactivity. In this, the list is not as subtle as the kinds of virtues we described in **Antoine Berman**, who optimistically proposes that the hermeneutically trained translator will respect the foreign author as an "other," resisting the temptation to domesticate the marks of foreignness (domestication would be unethical "ethnocentric" translation): "The essence of translation is to be an opening, a dialogue, a cross-breeding, a decentering" (Berman 1984/1992: 4). Translation can thus become metaphorical "inn of the distant" (Berman 1999). This in turn differs from the calculated pessimism of **Paul Ricœur**, who talks about translation in terms of a secret "fear" and even "hatred" of the foreigner (2004: 41) and sees the translator as maintaining "distance within proximity" (2004: 52). We note that all these qualities, good or bad, tend to concern the translator's relation with the *source* text or author, far more than they concern forward-looking relations with clients or readers.

Those aspects concern the translator more than the actual process of translating. If we look for proposals about the way we actually translate, we find that the uncertainty paradigm is broadly compatible with a few prominent ideas that come from elsewhere. The basic point here was in fact raised by the French theorist **Georges Mounin** in 1963: translators tend to **"over-translate,"** to explain everything in order to make texts easy for their readers. This would be on the "domestication" side of **Schleiermacher**'s classical dichotomy of translation strategies. Indeterminism sees this as a shortcoming; it tends to favor **"foreignizing"** strategies, the ones that make the reader aware that the text is a translation. The most developed notion of this preference is perhaps **Philip E. Lewis**'s concept of **"abusive fidelity"** (1985/2004), derived from Derrida's work on translation. Lewis values translations that do *not* adopt the norms of the target culture, and which instead try to follow the source text so closely (hence "fidelity") that the result will sound strange to most readers. This, says Lewis, should be done only at points in a text where there are meanings to be explored ("a decisive textual knot," 1985/2004: 263). "Abusive fidelity" could be a valid recommendation for anyone who wants to develop a philosophical reading of a text, or who sets out to produce a series of metatexts on key philosophical terms. But can it seriously be proposed as a translation method? Perhaps not, given its restriction to selected points in great texts (see Davis 2001: 87ff.) and its apparent indifference to the economies of translating. However, the practice of "abusive fidelity" can bring the receiver into a space between two languages; receivers are made aware that there is no meaning transfer as such. The result would ideally be what **Marylin Gaddis Rose** (1997) calls **"stereoscopic reading,"** taking place in an "interliminal space," which remains in need of clear definition.

Beyond these few concepts, most of the modes of translation that oppose "domestication" or "fluency" might claim to raise awareness of indeterminacy, at least as far as the question concerns translations rather than source texts. We mentioned some of these modes in Chapter 2 on equivalence, picking up a line of thinkers that runs from Schleiermacher through to Gutt and Venuti. It would be wrong to place those thinkers entirely within deconstruction, since none of them consistently doubts the translator's capacity to understand the source text. However, the same theorists would certainly want to make the reader work; they do not want translators to provide ready-made solutions, at least not for all translations. In this they meet up with indeterminism in seeking a complex reception experience. In **Schleiermacher** and the German Romantic school we find calls to translate in ways that allow features of the source text (especially in the case of Greek) to influence domestic syntactic patterns, nominally in the aim of developing the German language. **Gutt**, for his part, would oppose moves to translate the Bible as a modernized story (updating things like cultural practices or units of measurement); he would instead have translators provide readers with enough information ("communicative clues") for them to approximate the source location. As for **Venuti**, his call for translations that "resist fluency" privileges the use of non-standard variants in the target language. One of the theoretical bases for this is a deconstructionist critique of linguistics, since Venuti sees mainstream linguists as excluding the parts of language that are unsystematized and thus count as a **"remainder"** (see Venuti 1998, working from Lecercle (1990), although the concept was already in Heidegger and Derrida). This critique unfairly overlooks much of contemporary linguistics (especially the sociolinguistics of variation), but it does help raise awareness of uncertainty.

Uncertainty is something that translators are often conscious of, along with revisers, editors, translation critics, and indeed anyone else who is able to read both source and translation. They may not have a word for it, but they know when it is at work. They constantly find themselves in situations where they have to decide, without certainty, between different interpretations or renditions. Awareness of indeterminism may be considered in some way **internal** to the profession. **External knowledge**, on the other hand, would characterize a reception process in which no doubts are raised about the way the translation represents a source. Seen in these crude binary terms, awareness of indeterminacy would be well served by any mode of translation able to extend internal knowledge as far as possible into the external sphere.

6.7 FREQUENTLY HAD ARGUMENTS

Given the importance of the uncertainty principle in twentieth-century thought, and of deconstruction within literary studies, one should perhaps be surprised at how little debate these theories have sparked within Translation Studies. Part of the explanation for this could be geographical. **Deconstruction** has been particularly important in literary studies in the **United States**, a country where Translation Studies has been very slow to develop. Across the world, university departments of literature or cultural studies have taken their lead from the United States, and have thus paid due attention to that view of indeterminism, and rather less to translation. Parallel to this, the many institutions where translators are trained have tended to take their lead from **Europe and Canada**, where translation is necessary for the workings of societies and indeterminacy is not especially what those societies want to know about. Few translation analysts or translator trainers have read deconstructionist theory, and even fewer have seen value in its complexities. With isolated exceptions, the problematics of uncertainty have mostly been allowed to go their own separate ways. The paradigms pass like ships in the night.

One remarkable exception is the exchange between **Rosemary Arrojo and Andrew Chesterman** in *Target* (Chesterman and Arrojo 2000). Arrojo generally represents deconstruction; Chesterman offers something like philosophically aware descriptive studies. In their joint article, the two agree on a remarkably long list of things that could and should be done in Translation Studies. They show that an academic discipline can allow for exchange between paradigms. At one point, however, Chesterman argues that the relation between a translation and its source cannot be characterized by difference alone, since **meanings have degrees of stability** (and thus there must be degrees of difference and degrees of similarity, as in the "family likeness" metaphor). Arrojo does not accept this: "Meanings are always context-bound," she argues. "Depending on our viewpoint and our circumstances, we may perceive them to be either 'more' or 'less' stable but all of them are always equally dependent on a certain context" (in Chesterman and Arrojo 2000: Ad.10). There is no question of buying into the "more or less." For Arrojo, for consistent deconstruction, to analyze degrees of similarity would mean accepting the ideal of possible sameness ("more or less," with regard to what?), and thus falling into essentialism. At this point, the two paradigms touch but separate.

Beyond that particular exchange, there has long been a hum of behind-the-back comments, mostly against the role of indeterminism, and often without informed knowledge of the positions concerned. We will summarize a few general complaints as follows.

6.7.1 "The theories are not useful to translators"

As we have noted, theories of indeterminacy offer very few guidelines that might be of practical use to translators. They would seem to be **theories for theorists**, or for philosophers, or even for nitpickers. Translators, it is sometimes argued, have no time for such things; they are rarely paid for showing indeterminacy to the world. We might nevertheless concede that indeterminism could be of some practical consequence for the way in which translators are trained. Then again, opposition to commercial criteria might be one of the paradigm's more profound contributions, and the productive use of translation within philosophical discourses is not inconsequential.

6.7.2 "The theorists are not translators and do not care about translation"

This is a rather crude version of the above. Many of the thinkers cited in this chapter are philosophers or literary theorists, more than they are translators. However, when Heidegger traces differences between German, Latin, and Greek, or when Derrida teases out the various gaps found in translations, who is to say they are not using translation as a way of doing philosophy? Who would say they are not translating?

6.7.3 "The theories lead to a lack of rigor"

A fairly common complaint about **deconstruction** is that it leads to situations where "anything goes" (some wonderful examples are given in Eco et al. 1992). Clever critics can locate any meaning in any text whatsoever, proving nothing but their own cleverness. Part of the problem here is that deconstructionist writing is relatively easy to imitate, and pretentious third-raters can display a thousand trivial interpretations, filling their texts with unbearable puns along the way. There is quite a difference, though, between gratuitously playing with texts and the kind of close, careful reading we find in a master like **Derrida**, marked by punctilious attention to detail and careful tracings of myriad transformations. If anything, Derrida's practice errs by an excess of rigor. Nevertheless, like translation itself, deconstruction has practitioners at all levels, and there is no need to discredit the entire paradigm because of the abundance, in some quarters, of facile extensions.

6.7.4 "Indeterminism is of no consequence"

A further debate might surround the **"So what?" response** we have met with respect to Quine. Here the criticism would be that, no matter what games the theorists play, their concerns have no effect on the actual practice of translation. True, indeterminism quite possibly does not interfere with the everyday practice of translation, but it should nevertheless concern any search for certainty, and thus most kinds of theory. When we make selections between various possible translations, we should realize we are mostly dealing with problems that are more complex than "right" versus "wrong."

6.7.5 "These theories are merely oppositional"

This criticism would take some indeterminist theories to task for being too ready to expose the inadequacies of all other theories. As we have indicated, you cannot simply assume all theories of equivalence to be "transmissionist" or "essentialist." You cannot categorize all theories prior to Derrida as somehow "determinist," "prescriptive," or "authoritarian." Indeterminist theories have been around for a long time, and they interact in quite subtle and contradictory ways with the other paradigms available. As we have noted, determinist theories of expression can give indeterminist theories of translation, whereas indeterminist theories of expression (the arbitrariness of the sign) potentially allow translation to be encoding and decoding. In this situation, simple opposition seems extremely reductive.

6.7.6 "Deconstruction prescribes what translations should be"

This is one of the criticisms made by **Raymond Van den Broeck** (1990), who views Derrida (1985) and Lewis (1985/2004) as calling for little more than a particular kind of "deconstructive translation" (1990: 54). Van den Broeck thus sees deconstruction as being opposed to Descriptive Translation Studies. The critique seems very limited, almost to the point of being a misunderstanding, since the uncertainty paradigm obviously does far more than prescribe one ideal way of translating. If "abusive fidelity" is the mode of translating best suited to deconstruction, this does not mean that indeterminism cannot be found in all modes of translating across the board. Cannot a deconstructionist approach, which is basically a way of interpreting texts, be applied to any translation at all?

6.7.7 "These theories do not help us live with uncertainty"

Many of the theories, particularly those associated with deconstruction, are not only bluntly oppositional with respect to other theories but also fail to seek ways in which professional practice effectively works with indeterminism. Here we have listed Augustinian inspiration, Lockean dialogue, constructivism, and game theory as four possible theories in which we find that practice has come to live with indeterminism. Much more could be done in this regard. We could, for example, look closely at the way disciplines like physics and economics deal with uncertainty. What we find, quite quickly, is the development of theories based on probability and risk, concepts that go well beyond the kind of finite game theory used by Levý. Most empirical sciences are living with uncertainty.

None of these arguments seems strong enough to diminish the importance of the indeterminist paradigm. Whatever kind of translation theory we choose to develop, we must learn to live with uncertainty.

Just as it has been attacked, so the indeterminist paradigm has been able to attack rival approaches to translation. Deconstructionists like Rosemary Arrojo (particularly 1998) tend to see all traditional translation theory as being based on equivalence, which they criticize for being essentialist. That critique is easy enough to make, but it could be extended into the other paradigms as well. When *Skopos* theory names its dominant factor as this *Skopos* we have called "purpose," is that not also an essentialism, an assumption of stable meaning? And when Descriptive Translation Studies presumes to be doing science by separating the object of study from the subjectivity of the researcher, is that not similarly an untenable and essentialist divide? Thus extended, the indeterminist paradigm could claim to be the only satisfactory way to come to terms with uncertainty. There would be no way to turn except "to the text itself and hence to a concern with language" (Andrew Benjamin 1989: 86). Translation theory would be content with tracing the displacements and transformations that occur between languages, in the spirit of Cratylus, Heidegger, and Derrida.

Strangely enough, that is not quite the turn that history is taking.

SUMMARY

This chapter started from the simple idea that translators cannot be absolutely certain about the meanings they translate. This is then seen as a problem of determinism, in the sense that the source text does not fully cause (or "determine") the translation. We have identified two kinds of theories that accept this uncertainty. Some theories assume that the (great) source text is full of meaning in a way to which translations will be adequate. Those theories are thus determinist with respect to expression and indeterminist with respect to translation. Other theories, however, assume uncertainty to be a feature of all communication. They are thus indeterminist with respect to both source texts and translations. Seen in this way, uncertainty becomes a problem that the translator has to resolve. We have identified several ways in which translators can at least come to live with uncertainty. You can, for example, trust that religious faith or mystical illumination will guide you; you could enter into extended dialogues in order to reach social consensus about meaning; you can accept that your position influences what you find in a text, so that you spend time analyzing your own motivations; you can see the very act of translation as the way in which meaning is constructed in the social context of the translator; you can see translating as a game in which we make moves and place bets, in a world where we learn to manage uncertainty. Finally, the practice of deconstruction is one further way of dealing with uncertainty, based on translating or analyzing translations so that the points of indeterminacy are revealed rather than hidden.

SOURCES AND FURTHER READING

The Translation Studies Reader (Venuti 2000/2004) includes texts by Benjamin, Jakobson, Berman, Lewis, and Derrida, with Quine and Levý in the first edition only. On the other hand, Munday (2001/2008) has only five pages on Benjamin and Derrida, perhaps because this is not a paradigm that has produced significant research. The best general introduction is Davis (2001). George Steiner's *After Babel* (1975) gives a lot of room to the hermeneutic tradition and Walter Benjamin's position as a past-looking Kabalistic theory. Steiner's general view is ultimately a classical determinist theory of expression underlying an indeterminist view of reception. There are numerous better commentaries on Walter Benjamin's essay "The Task of the Translator," which has been fetishized by English-language literary criticism. Students are advised to tackle Benjamin's text before and after reading the commentaries. Marylin Gaddis Rose's *Translation and Literary Criticism* (1997) includes an application of Benjamin to the teaching of literary translation, displaying keen awareness of the way indeterminism underlies the "stereoscopic" reading of literary texts. Rosemary Arrojo's books in Portuguese (1992, 1993), along with her articles in English, are a constant demonstration of the way deconstruction can reveal contradictions and inconsistencies in other theories of translation. Numerous other authors in the deconstruction camp are more interested in translation as a metaphor able to question stable meaning, making translating itself into deconstructive practice. At that point, those approaches blend into the "cultural translation" paradigm (Chapter 8).

Suggested projects and activities

The activities listed here are designed to make students think beyond the binarisms of right vs. wrong. However, students should also be invited to challenge many of the certitudes upon which other translation paradigms are based.

1   Return to a translation you have done, in prose and preferably not highly technical. Select a source-text sentence and rephrase it, in the source language, in as many different ways as you can. Now look at your previous translation of that sentence. Did your translation follow the form of the sentence you found, or the form of one of the variations you have now produced? If the former, why?

2   Try the same exercise for a line of verse, and again for a sentence from a highly technical text. What is different in each case? Could we say that the language is more determinate (more fixed, or less open to interpretation) in some cases than in others?

3   Working in small groups, students write two sentences, one that they think cannot be misinterpreted (i.e. is relatively determinate) and one that they think needs to be interpreted (i.e. has ambiguities or is otherwise relatively indeterminate). They then have these sentences translated into a foreign language, then back into the source language (by a student who has not seen the original). The operation can be repeated for as many languages as are available, with the starting point always being the last translation into the source language. The groups then see what has happened to their sentences. They can use this information to answer questions such as the following: (a) Did the most indeterminate source undergo the most changes? (b) So does equivalence apply to some texts? (c) Is indeterminacy a feature of all language use?

4   Repeat activity 3 but use the automatic translation programs Babelfish and Google. Translate for the translations and back-translations. What do you find? At what points do human and machine translation reach a level where the successive translations introduce no new modifications? Why?

5   Activities 3 and 4 are versions of a game called "telephone" in the United States. Look up the other names this game is known by around the world. Why should the same game have so many different names? Should some of the names be changed? Are there correct and incorrect names for the game?

6   Is the linguistic sign arbitrary? Consider the names of the heroes and the villains in films or comics. Could the names be changed, or are some sounds well suited to villains, and others appropriate for heroes? Why is "Darth Vader" such a good name for an evil character (see Crystal 2006)? Do these strangely appropriate sounds work the same way in other languages? If not, how should they be translated?

7   Walter Benjamin says that the French and German words for "bread" cannot translate each other, since they evoke different kinds of bread. Is this really true? Find a sizeable literary text online and do a search for the terms for "bread." How often do those terms really refer to a general kind of bread that is found in one culture only? Are those terms really so difficult to translate? Or are there

established equivalents, as one finds in the two occurrences of "bread" in Baudelaire's *Les Fleurs du mal*? What does this tell us about the linguistic or cultural units that translators actually work on?

8   Do a web search for texts presented as translations of Rimbaud's poem "Voyelles" (in 2009 seven could be found here: http://www.brindin.com/pfrimvoy.htm). Can you find any that you would not call translations? At what point does a version cease to be a translation? What does this say about translation as a constant creation of new meanings?

9   For any source text, compare the translations done in class, noting the points where the solutions are all the same and where they are different (cf. Campbell 2001). What is the relation between indeterminacy and the points with many different translations? Are the points "decisive textual knots" (Lewis)? Are they the most difficult translation problems?

10 Act out an encounter where information is exchanged. At a key point, one of the actors has to request information in as many different ways as possible, and the other actor responds accordingly. Can the same request be made in numerous different ways? Or does each different formulation receive a different response? Compare this with the "so what?" argument formulated by Chomsky and Katz.

11 Some theories of languages as world-views say that translation is impossible. But how can anyone know there is a world-view that is not like their own? Use the Internet to find out about the research done by Humboldt, Sapir, and Whorf. In the course of their research, do you think they used translation in order to learn about a language that was not their own?

12 Do a web search for "Margaret Mead" and the word "hoax." With luck you will find a reference to Freeman (1999) and the claim that the American anthropologist was lied to by the young Samoan girls who were her "native informants." Is this case like Quine's *gavagai* example? Was the hoax due to indeterminacy? What does this case say about ethnography as a kind of translation?

13 Consider the following passage from the American philosopher Richard Rorty:

> The thought that a commentator has discovered what a text is really doing–for example, that it is *really* demystifying an ideological construct, or *really* deconstructing the hierarchical oppositions of western metaphysics, rather than merely being capable of being used for these purposes–is, for us pragmatists, just more occultism.
>
> (in Eco et al. 1992: 102–103)

Is this a fair criticism of the way deconstruction has been applied in translation analysis? On the basis of the description in this chapter, would there be any profound differences between "constructivism" and "deconstruction"? Do an Internet search for these terms and try to characterize the different academic fields in which they are used.

14 Rosemary Arrojo refuses to discuss whether meanings are "more or less" stable. Is she right to do so? Here is her argument on this point:

Meanings are always context-bound. Depending on our viewpoint and our circumstances, we may perceive them to be either "more" or "less" stable but all of them are always equally dependent on a certain context. A proper name such as the University of Vic, for example, only makes sense to those who are familiar with the explicit and implicit context to which it belongs and which makes it meaningful. The same certainly applies to notions such as democracy, which may be perceived by some to be less stable. If we ask Fidel Castro, or Augusto Pinochet, for instance, what "democracy" is, their answers will certainly indicate that there is nothing "unstable" about their definitions of the concept, no matter how different they may end up to be. Both Castro and Pinochet will be sure that each of them has the right, true "definition" and that the other one is wrong. The implications of such statements for translation are certainly essential and far-reaching and they may be summarized as follows: no translation will ever be definite or universally acceptable, no translation will ever escape ideology or perspectivism.

(in Chesterman and Arrojo 2000: Ad.10)

How might this position relate to what can be discovered in activities 1, 2, and 3 above? Do you agree with Arrojo?

CHAPTER 7

Localization

This chapter explores localization as a paradigm of translation theory. Although some see localization as an unconstrained form of adaptation, the way it operates in the localization industry usually involves the use of quite extreme constraints, and it is the role of those constraints that we focus on here. This is partly due to the use of new translation technologies, to various types of "internationalization" as generalized one-to-many translation, and to non-linear modes of text production and reception. Here we run through the main concepts of localization theory and a few of the technologies. At the close of the chapter we ask whether translation is part of localization, or vice versa, and what the cultural effects of localization might be. We will generally argue that the basic concepts of localization theory have a great deal to say about the way translation is working in a globalizing world.

7.1 LOCALIZATION AS A PARADIGM

At the beginning of this course we described a strong paradigm based on equivalence. Since it was supposed to be a scientific, objective paradigm, equivalence was seriously challenged by the principle of uncertainty, one of the major intellectual problems of the twentieth century. From that conflict, translation theorists have developed at least three ways of responding. The purpose-based paradigm including *Skopos* theory responded by moving theory closer to practice, reducing equivalence to a special case, and insisting that translators and their clients negotiate in order to decide how to translate. In parallel, Descriptive Translation Studies made equivalence a quality of all translations, no matter how apparently good or bad, and set about describing the many shifts and transformations that translations produce. A third response would then be the indeterminist paradigm itself, particularly deconstruction, which sets about undoing the many illusions of equivalence as a stable semantic relation.

These three responses all deserve to be called paradigms. Each is coherent within itself, and they are different from each other to the extent that people from any one paradigm genuinely have trouble appreciating theories from the others. If that much can be allowed, we must also recognize at least one further paradigm. The ideas and practices increasingly brought together under the label of "localization" do not constitute a translation theory in any strong academic sense; they are perhaps just a set of names-for-things developed within certain sectors of the language industry. On the other hand, those concepts provide a coherent response to the problem of uncertainty. If languages and cultures are so indeterminate that no one can be sure about equivalence, then one solution is to create

The **main points** covered in this chapter are:

- The localization industry responds to the problem of uncertainty by creating artificial languages and cultures.
- Localization is the preparation of a product for a new locale.
- A locale is a set of linguistic, economic, and cultural parameters for the end-use of the product.
- What makes localization a new paradigm is the key role played by *internationalization*, which is the preparation of material so that it can be translated quickly and simultaneously into many different target languages.
- Although new translation technologies are not to be equated with localization, they enhance the role of internationalization.
- One effect of the new technologies is a tendency to *non-linear* modes of text production, use, and translation.
- Localization theory may be seen as a partial return to equivalence in that it uses fixed glossaries and promotes decontextualized translation. The opposition between "standardization" and "diversification" as localization strategies is also reminiscent of the categories of directional equivalence.

stable *artificial* **languages and cultures** in which relative certitude becomes possible. That is a viable solution. But why it should be called "localization" is far from evident.

7.2 WHAT IS LOCALIZATION?

We start with a tale that simplifies history. Back in the 1980s, the American company Microsoft was developing software for the North American market and then translating that software into the main languages of other markets (English to German, English to French, English to Spanish, and so on). That was fine for as long as there were just a few foreign markets. However, as the number of markets grew, the simple **one-language-to-one-language translation** model was seen to be inadequate and expensive. The software required not just replacement of the pieces of language in the menus, dialogue boxes, and Help files visible to the user, but also attention to a long list of apparently minor details like date formats, hotkeys, and punctuation conventions. Some of these apparently minor items would seem to lie on the border of the tasks we would normally expect of a translator. Some do indeed concern translation; others require the technical expertise of a product engineer; and still others require telecommunications technicians, terminologists, marketing experts, and perhaps lawyers. Together, these tasks are ideally carried out by teams, of which translators are a part. The entire process is then called "localization," of which translation is a part.

   "Localization" can involve a wide range of tasks; it usually concerns information technology and marketing, as well as language skills. The **definitions of "localization"** reflect this by talking about **products rather than texts**, and describing the process in terms of the "preparation," "tailoring," or "adaptation" of the product for a new situation. That shift is important. Some even more significant shifts, however, come from the other terms with which "localization" is associated. The first of these is the small word "**locale**," which denotes a set of linguistic

Language and culture tasks in the localization of software

Manuals for the localization of software give lists of problems and tasks such as the following, only some of which clearly concern traditional translation:

- Time conventions: Different cultures have different ways of presenting clocks and calendars (11.04.05 means November 4 2005 in the United States and 11 April 2005 in virtually everywhere else in the English-speaking world; and Chinese English puts the year first).
- Numbers: Different cultures use different punctuation in the presentation of numbers (so the English number 1,200.01 becomes 1.200,01 in Spanish, and even good translators forget this).
- Currencies are different, as are the ways in which they are presented.
- Some scripts move left to write, others move right to left.
- Hotkeys may be reallocated (for example, in English Control+O opens a document, in Spanish it is Control+A (for "abrir"). But then we have to make sure that the command Control+A is not being used for something else. In fact, the complications are so great that the more professional Spanish programs just stay with Control+O.
- Examples and colors need to be adapted to local tastes.
- Products must conform to local legal, fiscal, safety, and environmental requirements.
- Products also have to be adapted to local standards with regard to telecommunications, measurement units, paper sizes, and keyboard layouts.

and cultural parameters defining the context of end-use. It is a nice short term to replace expressions like "target language and/or culture" found in many translation theories. It also implicitly recognizes that translators have rarely worked for entire languages or cultures; our audiences have always been local markets, locales, for which the term was missing.

The important point is that the paradigm of localization involves far more than the mere term "localization."

The key concepts of localization

The basic terms of localization can be defined in several ways. Here we give the definitions proposed by the Localisation Industry Standards Association (LISA):

- **Localization** (L10n) involves taking a product and making it linguistically and culturally appropriate to the target locale (country/region and language) where it will be used and sold (LISA 1998: 3).
- **Internationalization** (i18n) is the process of generalizing a product so that it can handle multiple languages and cultural conventions without the need for redesign. Internationalization takes place at the level of program design and document development (LISA 1998: 3).
- **Globalization** (g11n) addresses the business issues associated with taking a product global. In the globalization of high-tech products this involves integrating localization throughout a company, after proper internationalization and product design, as well as marketing, sales, and support in the world market (LISA 1998: 3). This meaning is more specific than the general process of economic globalization.

Note that the term "localization" is abbreviated as the letter L, then 10 letters, and the letter N. The other terms follow this rule, although the first letter of the abbreviation for "internationalization" is generally written in lower case so as not to confuse it with the numeral 1 and the upper-case L of L10n.

Other terms

- **One-to-many**: This is our term for a translation process that goes from an internationalized version to many target-language versions simultaneously. It is not to be confused with the term "one-to-several" coined by Kade within the equivalence paradigm to describe the way one source-language item can correlate with many target-language items, or vice versa (see 3.2 above).
- **GILT**: Acronym for the Globalization, Internationalization, Localization, and Translation industries. The term tends to be used by those who want to promote the status of translation.
- **Partial localization**: A localization process in which not all of the user-visible language is translated, usually to save costs when working into a small locale.
- **Reverse localization**: A localization process that goes from a minor language into a major language (see Schäler 2006).
- **CAT**: The traditional acronym for Computer-Aided Translation, sometimes used to describe translation-memory and terminology-management suites as "CAT tools." The term is misleading, since almost all translating is done with computers these days, so all processes are "computer-aided" to some extent.

7.3 WHAT IS INTERNATIONALIZATION?

Thus far, there might appear to be nothing new in localization: the term could simply be referring to traditional translation plus a certain amount of "adaptation." That certainly brought nothing new: *Skopos* theory had already seen that many translators carry out numerous tasks beyond the production of translations (hence the concept of "translatorial action"). There are nevertheless several things that are genuinely new in localization theory.

Let us go back to the American software program that has to be localized for a series of European markets (French, Spanish, German, Dutch, and so on). In many instances, those individual localization projects are going to face the same difficulties, in the same places in the programs, even though their solutions will often be different. These particular places are often of the kind we have listed above: date formats, currency references, number presentations, and so on. Those are also the places where the source text (the American software in our example) turns out to be specific to American cultural preferences (for example, in using MONTH, DAY, YEAR as a date format). At those points there is no real need to translate each time from the American version into all the different target versions. That would involve negotiating a huge number of cultural differences and running enormous risks of error. Greater efficiency comes from **taking the American-specific elements *out* of the program** and replacing them with generic elements as far as possible.

What has happened here? In traditional translation, we move from a source text to a target text (Figure 7.1a). In localization, on the other hand, we move from a source to a general intermediary version. The production of that intermediary version is called

Figure 7.1a   A very simple model of traditional translation

"**internationalization**," and the object produced is called the "internationalized" version. This is a bad name, since nations have nothing to do with it (which is why we have the term "locale," after all); it might more correctly be called "interlocalization" (since it works between locales) or even "delocalization" (since it idealistically involves taking out the features specific to the source locale). But we are not here to correct the terminologies of industry. Our general model is shown in Figure 7.1b. That is, internationalization has prepared the product prior to the moment of translation. This makes the actual translation processes easier and faster. Once internationalization has taken place, localization can work directly from the internationalized version, without necessary reference to the source. This brings greater efficiency, with many localizations happening at the same time, producing many different target versions (Figure 7.1c).

Figure 7.1b   A simple model of translation plus internationalization

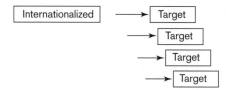

Figure 7.1c   A model of localization

This simultaneous production of target versions has its logic. Economic globalization means that major products (like a new version of Microsoft's operating system) are released at the same time in many locales across the globe, making use of similar marketing formats and publicity campaigns. The age of "**simultaneous shipment**" requires rapid localization, not just of the products but also of the marketing material. It thus tends to work from internationalized versions, without return to any source.

As a general concept, internationalization can take several forms, some of which go beyond what practitioners in the industry might want to recognize as internationalization. At one extreme, it can involve putting **more information and more potential formats** into the product to be localized. The localizer then only needs to consult the glosses or select the appropriate option. Perhaps the most successful model of internationalization of this kind is the development of **character encoding**. Back in the days when software existed in English and little more, the seven-bit ASCII encoding was enough: it allowed for 128 different characters. However, when IBM started to distribute internationally, it found that an eight-bit set was needed to cover all the accents and symbols of Romance languages: this allowed for 256 different characters. Nowadays, with extensive globalization, we have moved to the 32-bit USO or Unicode encoding systems, allowing for over four million characters (for USO) or 65,536 (for Unicode). All characters are now encoded in the more complex way, including those that had simple encoding in the previous systems. The code carrying the information thus expands enormously, but the characters of potentially all locales can thus be represented. This would be the technological logic of internationalization: **expand the source** so that all localization possibilities are allowed for.

At the other extreme, internationalization may make the source language **simpler**, reducing surface-level variation through the use of **controlled language**. When a document has a limited number of syntactic structures and a completely controlled multilingual terminology, as in the case of "Caterpillar English" for heavy machinery, the localization process can happen almost automatically, through the use of machine translation plus reviewing. Later we will return to various modes of internationalization between these two extremes.

Thanks to internationalization, the fundamental message of localization is not just that products need to be adapted to new users in different cultures, as a process that occurs after the product has been developed. The inclusion of internationalization means that those adaptations have to be **thought about from the very beginning**, and planned for at every stage of product development. Translation is usually considered to be something that comes later, after the source text has been produced. Localization, on the other hand, ideally involves a complete rethinking of the way products and texts are produced.

This general restructuring of processes is sometimes called "**globalization**," since it is designed to address a global market. A company might decide to "go global" (cf. Sprung 2000) and thus introduce processes of internationalization and localization. Some care should be taken with this term, however. "Globalization" more generally refers to the development of transnational markets, bringing in a powerful series of economic and financial consequences. Just to confuse the issue, Microsoft tends to use the term "globalization" to refer to what we have called "internationalization," although the marketing jargon takes us through many other words as well. For example, a more recent Microsoft term for an "internationalized" product is "world-ready." Here we will just stay with the few terms so far described: within a company that has been **globalized**, products are **internationalized** so they can then be **localized** quickly and simultaneously, and part of that localization process is **translation**. These four terms can be put together in the abbreviation **GILT** (Globalization, Internationalization, Localization, and Translation), as one sometimes hears in general reference to the "GILT industry."

7.4 IS LOCALIZATION REALLY NEW?

If seen as a process of cultural adaptation, localization probably does not add anything new to existing translation theory. As we have noted, the priorities *Skopos* theory gives to the purpose of a translation can justify a wide range of adaptations. On the other hand, if we see **internationalization** as a key part of localization processes, we do find something new. Is this concept, or anything like it, to be found in any other paradigm of translation theory? One could perhaps argue that the idea of taking out or reducing culture-specific elements may be described by theories of natural equivalence, where a neutral *tertium comparationis* or underlying kernel was once sought as a guarantee that the same thing was being said (see 3.4 above). However, you would have to scour many hundreds of pages to find ideas of working from an intermediary version in a process that is conceptualized from the outset as being **one-to-many**. That, we suggest, is a new element of theory.

This is not to say that one-to-many work cannot be found in the practice of translation. For example, in thirteenth-century Castile a text called the *Escala de Mahoma* was rendered from Arabic into Castilian, and then from Castilian into Latin and French. This means that the Castilian translation could be considered the "internationalized" version. But that is a one-off historical occurrence. More systematically, the use of **relay interpreting** repeats something like the two-step model. In United Nations meetings, for example, speeches in Chinese or Arabic may be rendered into English, and then interpreted into the remaining official languages from that intermediary version. That system, however, does not require any particular changes to the way the texts are produced from the outset, and it need not pay any special attention to cultural adaptation. Something closer to internationalization-plus-localization occurs in **screen translation**. A Hollywood film will usually *not* be translated (for dubbing or subtitling) from the original screen version or from the original script. The translations are increasingly done from a script especially prepared for translators across the globe, which incorporates glosses on culturally specific items, on necessary cross-references within the film text, and indeed any other kind of note that can avoid translation mistakes before they happen. Those prepared scripts might count as internationalized versions.

In similar fashion, many Bible translation projects are carried out nowadays by referring not only to the Hebrew and Greek texts, but to the Paratext software that brings together those texts, other translations into many languages, explanatory glosses, and sophisticated concordancing (basically cross-references to all occurrences of a term in the biblical texts). That might be an instance of internationalization (expanding the source) plus localization. Perhaps more significantly, the actual translations are carried out by teams of native speakers of the many hundreds of minor target languages, with the help of expert "translation consultants" who know the biblical scholarship and who can work with ten or so teams at the same time. The presence and function of the "consultant" might also be seen as a humanized instance of internationalization. That system of Bible translation, however, does not use theoretical concepts like "internationalization" and "localization," and there are clear theological reasons for not accepting that the "source text" has somehow disappeared. Nevertheless, the current practices in this field provide an interesting comparison with software localization.

The models may be taken further still. For instance, consider the way **international news** is put together and translated. An event occurs, producing source reports; those texts are then gathered and put into the format of an international news service like Reuters; those "internationalized" versions are then localized by newspapers, radios, television networks, and websites, some with interlingual translation, others without interlingual translation, all with adaptation. The terminology of localization can describe the overall process. Similarly, **multilingual websites** have to be developed in such a way that the localizations are thought of from the outset, in the initial design and engineering. The localizations then necessarily work from an internationalized version, and the terms of localization are sometimes used to describe what happens.

We thus find a range of translation practices that operate in ways similar to the model of internationalization plus localization. We cannot say that those practices are all new. We can nevertheless argue that the use of localization theory to describe those processes is not only new, but also useful. Once we extend the terms and concepts outward from the software industry, we start to see some general trends in the way economic globalization is affecting translation.

As a rule of thumb, the more global and instantaneous the medium (allowing for simultaneous translation processes), the more we would expect to find practices corresponding to internationalization plus localization. The more traditional, monocultural, and diachronic the medium (sending messages across centuries, for example, as in many literary ideologies), the more we would find traditional binary models, where translation moves from source to target each time. However, even within literary translation, the terms of localization are not completely lost. Popular romance novels, for example, may be produced for different cultures by the one multinational company, with different rules that have to be observed for each locale. The Canadian-based publisher Harlequin, for example, can put out the same novel in some 24 languages and about 100 locales, in each case not just translating but also editing the text to suit local expectations about length, morality, and styles of story-telling (cf. Hemmungs Wirtén (1998), who proposes the term "transediting" for what might also be called localization).

One could still argue that, even within these types of workflows, translation remains translation at each particular step. So perhaps no new theory is needed? Is there really no new paradigm at work here? Yes indeed, translation is probably what it has always been, at some very basic level, but the consequences of localization do not stop at the production of internationalized versions. Technology takes these changes a few steps further.

7.5 THE ROLE OF TECHNOLOGIES

Recent years have seen a tendency to offer courses on "localization" that only teach students how to use a series of tools. The training usually involves translation memories, specific tools for the localization of software or websites, terminology management, and increasingly integrated machine translation, with perhaps a content-management system, globalization management system, or project-management tool as well. Given our definitions above, those tools should not be confused with the nature of localization as a paradigm. The tools are there; they are certainly used in the localization industry; but translation memories and terminology management can be used without any kind of localization going on, and internationalization and localization can be carried out quite independently of the tools. Localization theory is one thing; electronic language-processing tools are something else.

At the same time, careful attention should be given to the way in which these tools are used in localization processes. That is, we have to look at the *intersection* of the tools and the overall work processes. Within that intersection, we find that the tools have several far-reaching consequences. In general, they allow language to be analyzed and processed in a paradigmatic way. That is, they show the alternatives available at particular points in a text. They thus interrupt the syntagmatic or linear dimension of language. That is, they break into the way one sentence flows into another and texts are made into coherent wholes. You might think here of the simplest electronic tools, which are also among the most useful. As we write with word-processing software, a spell-checker automatically compares our words with an electronic dictionary. If we are unsure of the spelling or appropriateness of a word, we can quickly consult a list of suggested spellings or synonyms. The tool thus gives us a vertical list of alternatives, in addition to the horizontal flow of the text. That list is paradigmatic. It interrupts the syntagmatic flow. The technology **imposes the paradigmatic on the syntagmatic**. This may be what all translation technology does.

How does this technology relate to internationalization and localization? To answer this question, we have to consider a few tools in greater detail.

7.5.1 Management systems

Years ago, a team of translators might have been employed to render a whole software program or company website into a particular language. To understand that process, you might consider the user-visible parts of the program or website as a text, and you then assume that translators would render the whole of that text, with each translator more or less aware of the overall product. In short, everyone would be aware of the translation project. Nowadays, software and websites are rarely developed in this way. What we find tends to be a constant flow of **modifications and updates**, as one version gradually evolves into another. Even when we have a new version of the software, or a new format for the website, much of the previous material is reused, usually in slightly modified or updated forms. Just as new translations of the Bible incorporate findings and solutions from previous translations, so new localizations of software and websites make use of the material produced in previous localizations. This means that the translators no longer work on whole texts, not even on whole internationalized versions, but only on the **new additions and modifications**.

The result is a radical change in the way translators are made to think. What they receive is not a text in any sense of a coherent whole. It is more commonly a list of isolated sentences and phrases, or sometimes new paragraphs, one on top of the other, as a set of vertically arranged items. The translator has to render them in accordance with a supplied glossary, which is another paradigmatic document, with items one on top of the other. The work of the translator is thus doubly vertical, paradigmatic, rather than horizontal, syntagmatic, or following the lineal flow of the text.

Where is the technology here? Imagine a company that has countless documents about all its products and operations. The company markets its products in seven different languages, contacting its customers through a multilingual website, user manuals, and publicity material. When an updated version of a product is being prepared, the company is obviously not going to rewrite and translate the entirety of all its previous documents. It somehow has to isolate the additions and modifications, and to coordinate them so that the end output is appropriate to all the media in which it is going to communicate. The real problem is not so much to get the translations done, but to keep track of all the pieces. To do this with any degree of efficiency, the company has its information ("**content**") broken down into units, usually of one or several paragraphs ("**chunks**"), in such a way that these units can be updated individually and combined in new ways to suit new purposes. **Content management systems** allow this process to be controlled with some efficiency in one language; **globalization management systems** allow content to be coordinated in many language versions. A change introduced in an English segment might thus automatically signal that changes are needed in the corresponding segments in other language versions. This is a wonderful vision of an entirely coordinated multilingual information flow.

What the management system prepares for translators are the vertical lists of "translatables," and the vertical list of glossary entries that are to be respected. The translators no longer have access to any global vision of the text or the project. They have no possibility of carrying out the extra-translational tasks envisaged by *Skopos* theory, since they have very few clues about what the communicative purpose is. In effect, all questions of strategic planning have moved to the project manager or perhaps to a marketing expert, while the global project as a set of texts is now held by the technology, in the management system, which offers the possibility of coordinated control.

How does this resemble internationalization? The management systems convert all the company's content into one large multilingual database. Using this database, any new version of a manual or promotional documentation necessarily becomes an internationalized version, ready to have its new and modified elements localized into many target languages. It clearly cannot be seen as a source text in any traditional sense of the term. In fact, since all content is potentially a rewriting of previous content, there are quite possibly no clear sources held within the system. Alternatively, our theories have to revise their definitions of "source."

7.5.2 XML

Another level of the same vision of coordinated control is made possible by XML (eXtensible Markup Language), which is a technical standard used to exchange content. Basically, information is tagged so that it can be retrieved later. The following is an example of a simple XML text:

```
<item>
<title>Pride and Prejudice</title> was written by <author>Jane Austen</author> in
<year>1813</year>.
</item>

<item>
<title>Alice in Wonderland</title> was written by <author>Lewis Carroll</author> in
<year>1866</year>.
</item>
```

By tagging texts in this way, we can later retrieve just the information on authors, for instance, for a textbook on literature. We might also retrieve information on dates, perhaps to create a chronology of publications between 1800 and 1850. XML is thus a way of writing texts so that their elements become available for easy reuse in future texts. This is another case of paradigmatic technology, where text reuse becomes the key.

When management systems and XML are used in localization projects, something quite profound happens to the nature of the texts involved. On many levels, and in many ways, texts are being broken down into fragments that then become available for reuse. New texts are pieced together from those fragments in a way that is no longer linear: the text producer does not start from a beginning, move to a middle, and finish at an end, as Aristotle assumed in his *Poetics*. Texts become **reorganizations of reusable content**. Nor are these texts *used* in a linear way, starting at the beginning and moving toward the end. Think of how you use a software Help file, or an operation manual for an appliance, or a website. The use of these texts (no longer a "reading" of the texts) is mostly non-linear, based on indices, hyperlinks, or a Find function. This is not wholly new in itself. The paradigmatic links are basically like the concordances developed long ago for the study of biblical texts. What seems new is the extent to which this is done.

When texts are regularly *produced* in a non-linear way, and *used* in a non-linear way, it comes as no surprise that they are *translated* in a non-linear way.

When working on modifications to a software program or a website or production documentation, what does the translator receive as the source text? Obviously, only those segments that are either new or require modification, perhaps elements that have been tagged and separated using XML. As we have noted, in such cases the translator has no vision of the overall text. To take a fairly banal example, the translator may have to render the simple English term "Start," which could be a noun or a verb, depending on the co-text (other neighboring words in the text) or context (situation of future use). What happens when the translator can see neither co-text nor context? Do you translate the noun or the verb? This is where the relation between localization and translation becomes problematic. Note, however, that the problem is *not* in the ideological schema of internationalization-plus-localization (ideal internationalization would have the term tagged with a grammatical function). It ensues from the complexity of the work process itself, and from the nature of the technologies able to handle that complexity.

The change is far-reaching: it touches the fundamentals of translation theory. Once upon a time, in the days of comparative linguistics and natural equivalence, translators were seen as working on terms and phrases (see the examples in Vinay and Darbelnet, in 2.3 above). With the development of text linguistics and functionalist approaches, translators were increasingly seen as working on *texts*. With the contribution of the purpose paradigm, where importance is attached to the client's instructions and different communicative aims, the translator was viewed as working on a *project* (text plus instructions, and perhaps plus information on a few cultural and professional contexts). This vision holds true in the field of localization, of course, since the projects have become so complex that they are handled by specialized project managers. From the perspective of the translator, however, the possibilities of that overall vision have largely been lost. In cases where the work involves an ongoing series of updates and modifications, the translator might be engaged in a **long-term localization "program,"** rather like the maintenance programs that we use to have our cars serviced regularly. When that does happen, the ideal is to have the same translators work on the same products or for the same clients on a regular basis, so that they do indeed build up a general vision of where their work is going and what it is supposed to do. When that does not happen, however, translators may simply receive a set of one-off updates, without source context or target purpose, and perhaps without co-text. Their frame of work has moved from text or project right back to where we started: translators work on terms and phrases, as in the good old days of comparative linguistics, or of phrase-level equivalence.

In some respects this means that translators are going "back to basics." The new frame nevertheless requires careful understanding. If we are returning to a kind of equivalence, it would not seem to be the natural and directional equivalence of the earlier paradigms.

7.5.3 Translation memories

Since localization projects are complex, they are frequently allied with technologies that are useful for controlling complexity. Not by chance, the technologies have evolved at the same time as localization practices (commercial translation memories date from the early 1990s). The catch is that the technologies (like the content management systems we considered above) do something quite different from the ideal of cultural adaptation that would seem to be invested in the term "localization." This is one of the major contradictions of the paradigm.

Electronic language technologies are all based on enhanced **memory capacity**, which is why they enable reuse. Language produced in one place and time can be remembered and reproduced in another place and time. Of course, writing has always done this to a degree, and printing even more so. Indeed, systemic language itself is designed for the reuse of structures on all levels (Derrida's *écriture* is prior to the material fact of writing), but the non-linearity has never been to quite the extent that has become commonplace within localization.

Management systems are based on no more than memory, at least in the sense of keeping track of where all the pieces of language are. **Translation-memory tools**, as the name suggests, do much the same thing, but in a way far closer to the process of translation. Translation memories basically store previously translated sentences or phrases ("segments"). This is quite different from machine-translation tools, which are designed to piece together new translations for new texts. Translation memories are less ambitious and currently more useful in the professional environment. As the translator moves through a text, all the segments that have been translated previously can be brought up on to the screen; they do not have to be translated again. The translator effectively only has to translate the new segments. The idea is simple and effective. For text genres that are highly repetitive (and the material of localization projects tends to be), there are real gains in the translator's **productivity**. More significant, though, is the way translation memories tend to impose uniform terminology and phraseology across projects, ensuring that different translators ultimately use the same kind of language. From the client's perspective, and for many of the managers coordinating the work of translation teams, this is one of the major benefits of translation memories: **increased consistency** can be just as important as any gain in productivity.

This means of control is further extended when the translation-memory suites are integrated with **terminology tools**. The translator receives not only the translatables and the translation memory, but also the terminology to be followed when carrying out the translation. Figure 7.2 is a screen-shot of DéjàVu X, where the source-text segments are on the left, the pre-translated segments are brought up in the column in the middle (under "Spanish"), and the suggested translations for near-matches ("fuzzy matches") are at the bottom-right. Remarkably little of the screen is left for the actual work of the translator.

What has changed when translators work this way? The **non-linearity** is clear enough: both source and target texts are broken into segments; the translator need only focus on the segments that are new or have been modified. The **non-visibility** of co-text and context is also fairly evident: the document formatting has been converted into a series of numbered tags, which the translator is not supposed to touch. The degree of control over the translator might also be clear in situations where the translator is instructed to respect the terminology database and all the full-matches, even if those terms and matches appear to have errors in them. But that concerns the way the technology is used, and not necessarily the technology itself.

7.5.4 Technology and the return of equivalence

Here we return to the fundamental question: Are these memory technologies necessarily part of the localization paradigm? As we have said, there seems little justification for any straight correlation. After all, some translators can use Trados or Déjà Vu to translate novels

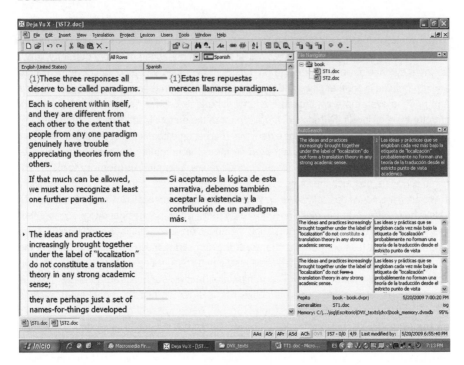

Figure 7.2   The translation-memory suite DéjàVu X

in quite a traditional way. In such cases, the translation-memory tool simply offers a convenient way of having the source and target texts appear on the screen; it also keeps the names of characters and places remarkably consistent. There seems to be no reason, on the level of translation theory, why such uses should be called "localization."

Clearly, we have to ask what specific *uses* localization processes make of technology. The following points may now be made:

■   When translators receive a source text along with translation memories and term databases, the effect on translation is functionally similar to internationalization. That is, the text-reuse technologies are operating as forms of pre-translation: just as Unicode and controlled writing attempt to resolve localization problems before they surface, so translation memories and term bases do translation work before the translator enters the scene. The generality of repetition (text reuse) precludes the specificity of situation (this translator, with this text, for this purpose). In effect, **the technologies are being used for a wider kind of internationalization**, and to that extent have become fundamental to what is new in localization.

■   When translators are simply calling up memories of their own previous translations, they are usually free to *alter* the matches and keep the improved memory as part of their work capital. However, when companies use online translation memories for projects involving teams of translators, those translators have no effective **ownership of the memories** and thus little self-interest in correcting false matches. Indeed, translators are often instructed *not* to alter the full matches, no matter how wrong the matches appear, and the translators are consequently not paid for those matches (although they are paid at varying rates for fuzzy matches). When this happens, the actual work process of the translator is altered substantially: since the previous matches are not looked at, textual linearity all but disappears, and equivalents are cognitively restricted to segment level.

■ Even when translators do have significant interest in improving on full matches (i.e. in creating translation equivalence in a contextual way), the use of the technology is such that they do not always do it. This has been shown in a pilot experiment by Bowker (2005), and has been partly replicated in other experiments. The new cognitive constraints mean that items like numbers and punctuation are **particularly susceptible to non-correction**.

■ Translation decisions within localization projects also involve **conflicts of authority**. Where text reuse technologies present an "authorized" solution (since it comes with the job), the translator is likely to opt for it, even when alternative solutions are readily available or even clearly necessary, if the translator has the time and the disposition to think about it. It may be that translators correct the memories only when they have the self-assuredness of experience in the particular field: perhaps a healthy pay-check, no deadlines, and ideally a strong ethical dedication to quality communication, all of which would seem to be a combination of factors rare within the frame of localization. Note that such corrections, which go from the specific situation to the general database, run counter to the underlying logic of internationalization, which would ideally have all movements flow from the database to the situation.

■ In projects where several translators are involved simultaneously, the reuse technologies result in texts where sentences or segments will be culled from different co-texts and contexts, probably rendered by different translators. Bédard (2000) notes the consequent degradation of text quality resulting in a "**sentence salad**" – the target text will have stylistic features from several different translators and probably many different discursive situations.

■ Because of these problems, localization projects tend to include extensive **product testing** and **document reviewing or revision**, depending on the level of quality required. In this way, the negative effects of the internationalization processes (all pre-translation) are to some extent countered by a series of checking processes (post-translation). Reviewing becomes an extremely important part of the translation process, meriting its own theorization.

If we now ask what kind of **equivalence** is involved in localization, the answer must depend on what particular part of the localization process we are talking about. With respect to internationalization, and indeed from the perspective of the language worker employed as a translator and nothing but a translator, the reigning ideal is undoubtedly equivalence at sentence or phrase level, reinforced by equivalence at product function level (either the user pushes the right button or they don't – and that is often what really counts). However, if we compare this with the theories of the 1960s and 1970s, we find that this "internationalized" equivalence is no longer "natural" (contextualized by the dynamics of social language and culture) or "directional" (with one-off creativity). It has become fundamentally **standardized, artificial**, the creation of a **purely technical language and culture**, in many cases the language of a particular company.

That much may be said of the way technology intersects with localization: we enter an age of artificially produced equivalence. At the same time, however, we have tried not to equate the technology with localization as a paradigm, and there is much more happening in discussions about how projects should be handled. There are typically two alternatives. On the one hand, the multilingual contents may be strongly centralized and reproduced in all target languages, resulting in an extreme **standardization** of localization projects. On the other, contents may be highly adapted to the specific norms and tastes of the target locales, in accordance with a decentralized **diversification** approach to multilingual communication. In terms of the models touched on in this chapter, "standardization" would mean that internationalization plays a key role, whereas "diversification" should give greater scope to localization as adaptation. The underlying choice is also fundamental in the organization of international advertising campaigns, which has its own theorization. What is intriguing here, however, is that the opposition between standardization and diversification recalls the classical oppositions we found in theories of **directional equivalence** ("formal" vs. "dynamic," etc.: see 3.4 above). We thus discover a certain return to the modes of thought used with respect to both natural equivalence (in the consequences of technology) and directional equivalence (in the alternatives facing communication policies).

We hasten to add that localization does include moments (in text composition based on content management and in post-translation editing) in which equivalence is certainly *not* the order of the day. In those moments, **addition and omission are legitimate strategies**, to an extent not envisaged in classical theories of equivalence. Further, cultural adaptation may require degrees of transformation that go well beyond the classical limits of translation but can be justified within the purpose paradigm. Far more can happen within localization than was contemplated by the standard theories of equivalence. The catch, of course, is that the new things, the adapting and the editing, tend not to be done by people employed as translators.

7.6 TRANSLATION WITHIN LOCALIZATION?

We are now in a position to deal with an apparent **contradiction between the discourse and the work processes of localization**. The ideology of localization is based on cultural diversification, yet the principle of text reuse is that language is *not* dependent on specific situations, and thus, in theory, does not have to be adapted. The contradiction is more apparent than real because different things are happening at different levels, or at different stages: text reuse is an affair of technology and internationalization, whereas adaptation is something that tends to be done by policy-makers or marketing experts. For us, the more problematic aspect is where translation fits into those stages.

A localization project may involve numerous tasks, from the moment the material is received through to "post-mortem" discussion with the client. Those are the things that project managers have to consider. Translation is usually presented as just one or two of those steps, so the managers logically conclude that **translation is a small part of localization**. Seen in terms of the lists of tasks, that is entirely correct. Translation has become the replacement of user-visible natural-language strings (i.e. the parts of non-code with which users of the product will have to interact). That is quite probably the least interesting part of localization, both for practitioners and for theorists. Sprung (2000) consistently demonstrates that the real costs (and the real profits) are in tasks that are wider than simple translation: product internationalization, the identification and extraction of translatables, structuring hierarchies

Tasks in the localization of software

The following is a model of the steps taken when localizing software (adapted from Esselink 2000; cf. Pym 2004b: 6):

Analysis of Received Material
Scheduling and Budgeting
Glossary Translation or Terminology Setup
Preparation of Localization Kit (materials for the translators)
Translation of Software
Translation of Help and Documentation
Processing Updates
Testing of Software
Testing of Help and Publishing of Documentation
Product QA and Delivery
Post-mortem with Client.

of target languages in terms of market priorities, organizing complex language-service teams, drawing up schedules, testing localized products, post-editing translations, creating cooperative working relations between specialized service companies, using or developing appropriate software for localization, and working with controlled writing. In short, no matter which model of localization you choose, the replacement of natural-language strings ("translation") is going to look like a minor part. The breakdowns of budgets often rate "translation" at about one-third of the total costs at best, with the remaining two-thirds split between "product re-engineering" and "project management."

This operative reduction of translation lies behind the new sense of "artificial" equivalence. It also effectively separates translation from the wider fields of action sought by the purpose paradigm, even when the fundamental concept of localization would be in agreement with those approaches. Needless to say, it has no place for uncertainty, and little time for descriptions of different kinds of translation practice. The localization frame brings translation right back to square one.

Another question is whether we *should* go along with this reduction. If all translation is a part of localization processes, this does not mean that translation has suddenly stopped happening outside of those processes. Just consider the number of people that translate in speech or writing every day, within bilingual families, multilingual communities, in social services, the courts, business meetings, news services, as well as in literary translation, the larger conferences, and multilingual dreams. Those multiple forms of translation have not suddenly disappeared under the growth of the localization industry. So there is no reason why the whole of translation theory should suddenly accept the frame of localization. In fact, there may be some social nobility in resisting the reduction.

Either we go along with the reduction (accepting that localization is something far wider than translation), or we argue against it (saying that it is all translation after all). We could, for instance, argue that the step-by-step models have always been present in larger translation projects, and they are not the aspect that most distinguishes localization from translation. Gouadec's *Translation as a Profession* (2007) is full of procedural models, and they are not described as "localization." There is no real consensus on this point. In the meantime, there is probably some commercial advantage in talking about "translation and localization," some intellectual legitimacy in studying both terms as aspects of "cross-cultural communication," and a definite need to train translators in the broad range of tasks that make up the localization process. After all, if technical translation is being turned into dehumanized phrase replacement, we should ensure that our translators can reach work that is more rewarding than that, both intellectually and financially, no matter how we choose to name that work.

7.7 FREQUENTLY HAD ARGUMENTS

Although these dilemmas concern nothing less than the fundamental concept of translation, there has been remarkably little debate about localization among translation theorists. This is partly due to the nature of localization discourse, which is the stuff of guru experts, new terms for new trends, hype about technological advances, quick industry surveys, and ideologies straight from globalizing capitalism. The industry experts have no need for careful theoretical concepts, and little time for extensive empirical research within the frame of such concepts.

Perhaps for the same reasons, academics have shown remarkably little inclination to take the localization industry seriously, at least not in any sense that could threaten fundamental beliefs about translation. Rather more has been said about the technologies associated with localization. Researchers generally agree that increased productivity is only part of the logic behind the technology, and that consistency and control are major factors as well. But those findings scarcely reach the heart of localization.

A relatively informal and underinformed milieu thus provides the background for the current arguments.

7.7.1 "Localization is a part of translation"

The localization industry generally sees translation as part of localization; theorists from other paradigms sometimes see the relation the other way around – for them, localization is just a special kind of translation. What is at stake here is the nature and status of translation theory, which is nothing less than the subject of this book. Then again, it could be enough that different speakers explain exactly what they mean when they use the term "translation," as Locke would have us do. We have given a kind of answer on this point above.

7.7.2 "There is nothing new in localization"

This statement is the main weapon used by those who see localization as a part of translation (i.e. standard translation theorists, particularly from *Skopos* theory). We have argued above that the effectively new element in localization is actually internationalization (in its many forms and with its many technologies) and the consequent process of one-to-many translation. Others tend to argue that the various text-reuse technologies are what is really new, and that the technologies are not specific to the localization industry. From the perspective of that argument, the imposition of the paradigmatic on the syntagmatic changes the way translation works across the board, and all paradigms have terms and concepts able to address those changes.

7.7.3 "Localization belittles translators"

This statement brings together various aspects: the restricted sense of translation as segment replacement, the tendency to ensure that (web-based) translation memories cannot be owned by the translators who produce them, the distribution of costs and financial rewards away from translation, and the extreme time constraints typically placed on group translation work. Some within the localization industry claim that these are advantages: translators are now able to focus on what they apparently do well (translation), without having to worry about all the technological aspects of product engineering and formatting, and without having to concern themselves with aspects better handled by marketing and engineering experts. On the other hand, voices within the industry also claim that translators have the intimate cultural knowledge that might ensure the success of products in new markets, and that they should thus be listened to at more than phrase level.

7.7.4 "Localization leads to lower qualities of texts and communication"

There are several points here. Many people within the industry express concerns about the linguistic qualities of translations due to the use of team translating with translation memories. Others are more worried about the accumulation of errors in the translation memories that translators have no motivation to correct. Still others focus on the relative invisibility of graphic text and of the communication situation, assuming that this will lead to decontextualized communication. At present, none of these doubts is based on irrefutable empirical evidence, and all appear to concern the use of translation memories rather than the key concepts of localization itself.

7.7.5 "Standardization reduces cultural diversity"

This criticism is sometimes made of the localization industry in general. We should recognize, however, that standardization more properly belongs to the "internationalization" side of localization, and that considerable cultural adaptation is still conceivable in terms of the localization paradigm. The argument should focus not so much on the communication strategies as on the **range of cultures and languages** that are affected by the localization industry. For the more global products, the lists are impressive (for instance, check the "language and region" settings in Microsoft Office), since an increase in end-use locales correlates with more potential sales. Beyond commercial self-interest, that is not a minor virtue. The **entry of a language into electronic communication**, with standardized scripts and Unicode identity, may well do more to enhance its longevity than will several hundred studies by well-intentioned cultural theorists. The very existence and relative prosperity of the localization industry could thus enhance linguistic and cultural diversity, quite independently of the standardized or diversified communication strategies that are adopted within individual localization projects. At the same time, however, the major act of cultural change is probably the introduction of electronic communication itself, the consequences of which can be far-reaching and are quite possibly common to all cultures that adopt the medium. The tendency toward non-linearity, for example, would seem to be written into the technologies. One might expect it to become a feature of certain genres in all societies that adopt electronic communication.

On most of these issues, the jury is still out.

7.8 THE FUTURE OF LOCALIZATION

A few final words may be appropriate on the importance and possible evolutions of localization theory. To the extent that the term is associated with a major multinational industry, it is not likely to disappear as have many other flavor-of-the-month slogans. Whether or not we like the ideas, the industry will be with us for the long haul. Underlying this is the close relation between localization and **economic globalization**. Elsewhere we have called localization the "showcase communication strategy of multinational capitalism" (Pym 2004a: 47). Why should that be so?

Globalization, we suggest, is the result of technologies that reduce the costs of transport and communication. There is thus increased mobility of capital, merchandize, and labor (although not to equal degrees), and this requires massive crossings of cultural and linguistic boundaries. Those crossings tend to require language learning (when the relation is long term, as in the movement of labor) and translation (when they are short term, as is increasingly the case in the movement of capital and merchandize). The **long-term relations** tend toward the use of lingua francas, especially in the relations of production. Experts from different professions and different primary cultures will come together to work in a multinational space, where they will speak English, or Chinese, or whatever is the dominant language to be learned. Thus far, there is little need for translation, let alone localization.

Short-term relations, however, are better served by translation. No one is going to learn a language just to sell one product over six months, or just to buy a product. The whole commercial logic of translation could be based on the calculation that, in the short term, it is marginally cheaper to use translation than to learn whole languages.

We thus have some languages being learnt as second or third languages over the long term and by people from many different provenances. Those become the languages of globalized production. Then there are other languages that are used in strong and advanced relations of production on the national level, or that form large and/or wealthy locales. Those become languages of both production and consumption: end-users will demand products in their languages. Finally, at the extreme, some languages are virtually only learnt by mother-tongue speakers and the occasional translator. Where they are not associated with enough wealth to form a viable market, those languages may effectively be excluded from consumption. If you speak Ao-Naga and you want to use a computer, you learn enough English or Bangla to do so.

What we have outlined here is the translational logic of what has been called the "**world language system**" (de Swaan 2002). The general picture is of a hierarchy of languages where some are central and used for production, others are semi-central and impose strong constraints on consumption, and still others are virtually excluded from the relations of production, consumption, and translation. In this, we might rediscover some of the dynamics and ideologies of the **medieval hierarchy of languages**. The profound asymmetries are by no means new.

Within this hierarchy, translation tends to move from centralized production to semi-central consumption. This often means going from English to all the major languages of the world. There are some similar movements from other languages, for instance, from Japanese for video games (a larger market than Hollywood films), or from Korean for computers, cars, and ships produced by *chaebol*. English is certainly not the only language of international production, yet the logic of the one-to-many movement remains the same. Economic globalization can thus explain why the one-to-many configuration is so important, and why a key role is played by internationalization as a set of technological processes allowing that pattern. That is why the logic and ideologies of localization are pinned to the development of economic globalization.

Localization is thus marked by a **strong directionality**, moving from the central languages toward the more peripheral languages. So strong is this directionality that movements in the other direction have been called "**reverse localization**" (Schäler 2006). For example, we might find translations *into* English for (1) specialist sectors that require information on other cultures, including feedback on consumption patterns, and (2) easy exchange into third cultures, in a situation where the central language becomes a kind of "**clearing house**" (a Romanian bank will announce investment opportunities in English; French philosophy is sold in English in Eastern Europe; for that matter, Newton wrote in Latin, still the clearing-house language for scientific production in his day). Only the second of these reasons bears relation to localization, where it acts as yet another kind of internationalization. Note, however, that these examples of "reverse localization" do not have the initial one-to-many configuration that we consider so important in the localization paradigm. On the contrary, these examples suggest a preliminary pattern of "many to one" before the stronger sense of localization can begin. As economic globalization increases, we might expect the phenomenon of reverse localization to become more important.

More problematic, however, is what happens at the other end of the scale, with languages that are marginal with respect to both production and consumption. In software localization, for example, the larger locales receive **full localization** (meaning that all user-visible language is translated and items like hotkeys are adapted); secondary locales will have **partial localization** (perhaps the main menus are translated, but not the hotkeys or the Help files), and still smaller locales receive products that are merely "**enabled**" (you can work in the local language with them but the menus and Help files remain untranslated). And then there are the countless languages for which enabling is not yet possible, since the languages do not have standard written forms, or their written forms as yet have no place in our character-encoding systems, or our technologies do not yet work on the basis of voice alone. This rational commercial logic means that the users who most need Help files and pop-up explanations on the menus are precisely the ones who do not have that information in their own language.

In this way, localization configures relations between cultures quite differently depending on which part of the hierarchy you are looking at. Between the central languages, a regime of successful yet artificial equivalence may reign, largely thanks to internationalization. Further down the hierarchy, directionality means that equivalents are imposed through calques or straight loans, as was the case with the downward directionality in the medieval hierarchy of languages. Further down still are decisions to localize or not play a role in the drama of language survival, which is one of the major tragedies of our age.

If localization simply followed economic globalization, all cultures might conceivably be caught up in the maelstrom of product internationalization. At the same time, as we have argued, the localization industry has an active interest in the defense of linguistic and cultural diversity, in the strength of locales, since that is where markets can be expanded. Beyond the commercial logic, many of our government documents and services are now provided online, using communication systems that follow the concepts and the tools of localization projects. **Accessibility** thus becomes an issue of **democracy** and **social ethics**, and a large part of accessibility is the availability of information in one's own language. Whether in the commercial or the governmental sectors, the processes of localization incorporate powerful technologies that can do much to influence the future of diversity. Rather than spread a regime of sameness, the localization paradigm might actively participate in the saving of difference.

No matter what traditional translation theorists think of localization, there are good social and ethical reasons for taking it seriously, and for seeking out the good as well as the bad in the world that it promises.

SUMMARY

This chapter has presented localization as something more than a synonym for "adaptation" or a use of new translation technologies. Instead, localization introduces a new paradigm owing to the key role played by "internationalization" in allowing one-to-many patterns of translation. This key one-to-many processing allows the localization industry to meet the needs of globalizing economic relations, and is thus closely related to the "globalization" described in business models. Further, the one-to-many processing is enhanced by a series of technologies that have far-reaching effects on the way we produce, use, and translate texts, imposing the paradigmatic on the syntagmatic. The actual way translators work is thus altered considerably. The global consequence of localization may be an increasing standardization of cultures. However, the paradigm also allows for considerable cultural adaptation, going well beyond the confines of traditional equivalence-based translation. In most respects, the actual cultural effects of localization remain to be seen.

SOURCES AND FURTHER READING

Localization is dealt with in the second edition of Munday (2001/2008) in a chapter on "new media" (which strangely includes corpus studies). Most of the book-length publications on localization are manuals or otherwise describe professional practice and tools. This includes Esselink's *Practical Guide to Localization* (2000), *Perspectives on Localization* (2006) edited by Keiran J. Dunne, and the volume *Translating into Success* (2000), edited by Robert Sprung. The latter gives numerous case studies of the way in which localization has transformed how companies communicate; it lacks studies of the many mistakes and occasional disasters that can also be associated with localization. The rate of change in the localization industry means that these publications are dating quickly. Insight into recent developments is better sought in the online industry journal *Multilingual*, in the refereed journal *Localisation Focus*, or in industry websites such as LISA, which carries the online magazine *The Globalization Insider*.

Suggested projects and activities

1   Check your software programs for the presence of "locales." How many locales can you find for your language? In Word, check for the available dictionaries and thesauri. In Windows XP and Vista, go to Control Panel/Regional settings and languages. Should we describe these locales as languages or cultures?

2   Offer an explanation for the localization problem in the Catalan dialogue box shown in Figure 7.3 (you do not need to know Catalan to see it!). Would this error occur in a traditional translation process? How could you solve the problem? For how many languages should you solve it? (Note: Microsoft Vista solves the problem by using basic internationalization.)

Figure 7.3   Catalan calendar from Microsoft XP

3   Look at the website of a large international organization or company (especially vendor sites like Ikea.com or organizations like the World Bank). Compare the different localized versions. What parts of the localization could be called translation? What parts go beyond translation? Are there any examples of partial or incomplete localization? Is the general strategy one of standardization or diversification (see 7.5.4 above)? Can you tell which version was the source for others?

4   Once you have completed Task 3, select a *national* company or agency that has a multilingual website (most banks do). It will help if the national company is in the same sector as the multinational one. What are the differences in

communication strategy between the national company and the multinational one? Is there more or less adaptation in the case of reverse localization?

5   Write-down and define the full versions of the following terms: L10n, i18n, g11n, GILT. What might the full version of t9n be? Can it be found with an Internet search engine? If not, why not?

6   Do an Internet search for companies in your country that advertise "localization" services (the local term is probably from English). Do they also offer "translation"? How do they present the relation between "localization" and "translation"? What particular economic sectors do these companies seem to work for?

7   Look at the official website of your local town or city. If it is multilingual, have the different language versions been localized? If it is not multilingual, what languages do you think it should be localized in? Would you translate all the content on the site, or would you select content of interest to non-residents? Would you add new content in some language versions?

8   Should a multilingual website use standardization or diversification as its strategy? What will be the long-term effect on the world's cultures?

9   Check the portals of Google and Yahoo! in as many languages as you can. Do they use standardization or diversification as a general strategy? In what way does Google try to combine the two strategies?

10   Can team translation produce good results? Check to see the way Facebook is translated.

CHAPTER 8

Cultural translation

Localization theory came from industry and has incorporated elements of the equivalence paradigm. At about the same time, a significant number of theories have been heading in precisely the opposite direction. This chapter looks at several approaches that use the word "translation" but do not refer to translations as finite texts. This means that there are no entities that could be related by equivalence. Instead, translation is seen as a general activity of communication between cultural groups. This broad concept of "cultural translation" may thus be used to address problems in postmodern sociology, postcolonialism, migration, cultural hybridity, and much else.

8.1 A NEW PARADIGM FOR THE NEW CENTURY?

A journal called *The New Centennial Review*, founded in 2001, opens its programmatic statement as follows:

> The journal recognizes that the language of the Americas is translation, and that questions of translation, dialogue, and border crossings (linguistic, cultural, national, and the like) are necessary for rethinking the foundations and limits of the Americas.

This use of "translation" is difficult to situate in terms of the paradigms we have looked at so far. How can a whole language be translation? There seems to be no equivalence involved, no goal-oriented communicative activity, no texts or even translators to describe, and nothing definite enough for anyone to be uncertain about it. What is meant, one suspects, is that **colonial and postcolonial processes** displaced and mixed languages, and this displacement and mixing are somehow related to translation. But to call that "translation" sounds willfully metaphorical: it is "as if" every word were the result of a translation, and "as if" all the colonizers and colonized were translators. Either that, or our perplexity marks the passage to a new paradigm.

Numerous examples may be found of "translation" being used in this way. The purpose of this chapter is to survey them and see if they might be parts of a new paradigm. We will start from the basics of postcolonial theory, from a reading of the influential theorist Homi Bhabha. This will map out a sense of "cultural translation." We will then step back and consider previous calls for wider forms of Translation Studies, most of them direct extensions of the paradigms we have seen in this book. Our survey then takes us through uses of the term "translation" in ethnography (where the term "cultural translation" was first used), postmodern

The **main points** covered in this chapter are:

- "Cultural translation" may be understood as a process in which there is no source text and usually no fixed target text. The focus is cultural processes rather than products. The prime cause of cultural translation is the movement of people (subjects) rather than the movement of texts (objects).
- The concepts associated with cultural translation can complement other paradigms by drawing attention to the intermediary position of the translator, the cultural hybridity that can characterize that position, the cross-cultural movements that form the places where translators work, and the problematic nature of the cultural borders crossed by all translations.
- There have been several prior calls for wider forms of Translation Studies, and for close attention to the cultural effects of translation.
- Cultural translation can draw on several wide notions of translation, particularly as developed in (1) social anthropology, where the task of the ethnographer is to describe the foreign culture, (2) actor-network theory ("translation sociology"), where the interactions that form networks are seen as translations, and (3) sociologies that study communication between groups in complex, fragmented societies, particularly those shaped by migration.

The paradigm thus helps us to think about a globalizing world in which it is no longer possible to assume that the "source" and "target" sides are stable and separate.

sociology, and a little psychoanalysis. Can all these things constitute just one paradigm? Should the narrow sense of "translation" be extended in all these directions? The chapter will close with brief consideration of the political questions at stake.

8.2 HOMI BHABHA AND "NON-SUBSTANTIVE" TRANSLATION

The idea of "cultural translation" was most significantly presented by the Indian cultural theorist **Homi Bhabha** in a chapter called "How Newness Enters the World: Postmodern Space, Postcolonial Time and the Trials of Cultural Translation" (Bhabha 1994/2004). The part of the chapter that most concerns us is a discussion of the novel *The Satanic Verses* by the Indian-born British novelist **Salman Rushdie**. Bhabha is concerned with what this kind of mixed discourse, representative of those who have migrated from the Indian subcontinent to "the West," might mean for Western culture. He sets the stage with two possible options, which we might simplify as follows: either the migrant remains the same throughout the process, or they integrate into the new culture. One or the other. That kind of question is strangely reminiscent of some of the major oppositions in translation theory: should the translation keep the form of the source text, or should it function entirely as part of the new cultural setting (cf. the oppositions in 3.4 above)? Or, in another register: Should localization projects seek "diversification" or "standardization" (cf. 7.5.4 above)? Bhabha's use of the term "translation" might be justified owing to those traditional oppositions.

Nonetheless, his basic question more directly concerns fundamental dilemmas faced by migrant families, especially in the second and third generations: for example, which language(s) do we use in the home? Rather than take sides on these questions, Bhabha sets out to see how they are dealt with (or better, performed) in Rushdie's novel. You can imagine Bhabha reading and citing Rushdie, then commenting on other fragments of postcolonial experience, and doing all that with reference to translation, looking for some kind of solution to the basic cultural problems of migration. He does not, however, cite the classical oppositions we have just referred to; he turns only to Walter Benjamin's essay on translation (see 6.3.2 above) and Derrida's commentary on it (with very fleeting reference to de Man). One of the difficulties of reading Bhabha is that he presupposes that everyone has a working knowledge of all these texts, as professors of literature tend to assume. Another difficulty is that he invites us to think that these are the only translation theorists with which he has to engage, as readers of this book can hopefully now not assume.

So what does "**cultural translation**" mean here? By the time Bhabha gets to this chapter of *The Location of Culture* (1994/2004), he has accumulated quite a few uses of the term in a vague metaphorical way. He has talked about "a sense of the new as an insurgent act of cultural translation" (10), "the borderline condition of cultural translation" (11), the "process of cultural translation, showing up the hybridity of any genealogical or systematic filiation" (83), "cultural translation, hybrid sites of meaning" (234), and so on. In this chapter, though, a more serious attempt is made to relate the notion to translation and to translation theory. Bhabha is remarkably uninterested in the translators of *The Satanic Verses*, even though they were the ones who bore the brunt of the *fatwā* or Islamic condemnation of the novel: Hitoshi Igarashi, the Japanese translator, was stabbed to death on July 11, 1991; two other translators of the novel, Ettore Capriolo (into Italian) and Aziz Nesin (into Turkish), survived attempted assassinations in the same years. No matter: Bhabha is more concerned with the novel itself as a kind of translation. What set off the *fatwā*, he claims, is the way the novel implicitly translates the sacred into the profane: the name "Mahomed" becomes "Mahound," and the prostitutes are named after wives of the prophet. Those examples do indeed look like translations; the blasphemy may fairly be described as "a transgressive act of cultural translation"; there is thus some substance to the claim that a certain kind of cross-cultural writing can be translational. Then again, what kind of theorization can allow those few words to become representative of whole genres of discourse?

What Bhabha takes from translation theory is not any great binary opposition (the dilemmas of migration present plenty of those already) but the notion of **untranslatability**, found in Walter Benjamin's passing claim that "translations themselves are untranslatable" (Benjamin 1923/1977: 61; 6.3.2 above). Benjamin actually talks about this untranslatability as being due to the "all too great fleetingness [*Flüchtigkeit*] with which meaning attaches to translations" (1977: 61), and we prefer to see this as a reference to the momentary subjective position of the translator (see our commentary in 6.3.2 above). Bhabha nevertheless wants nothing of this "fleetingness" (and thereby forgoes numerous possible puns on *Flüchtling* as a "displaced person," a "refugee," an "escapee"). For him, that untranslatable quality of translations is instead a point of **resistance**, a negation of complete integration, and a **will to survival** found in the subjectivity of the migrant. As such, it presents a way out of the binary dilemmas. This, we suspect, is the great attraction of translation as a metaphor or way of thinking, here and throughout the whole of Cultural Studies.

To get to the association of resistance with survival, however, Bhabha has to mix this "untranslatability" with the part of Benjamin's essay that talks about translations as extending the life of the original. Benjamin does indeed say that translations give the original an "**afterlife**" (*Fortleben*, "prolonged life"), which, says Benjamin, "could not be called that unless it were not a transformation and a renewal of something living – the original undergoes a change" (Benjamin 1923/2004: 77). But to get from "afterlife" to "survival," you have to have read Derrida's commentary in *The Ear of the Other* (1982/1985: 122–123), where the claim is made that (1) Benjamin uses the terms *Überleben* and *Fortleben* (does Derrida miss *Nachleben*?) interchangeably to mean "living on," and (2) the one French term *survivre* ("survive," but literally "on-live," "to live on") translates both Benjamin's terms (the topic is also developed in Derrida 1979, 1985). Benjamin's "prolonged life" (*Fortleben/Nachleben*) can thus become "survival" (*Überleben, survie*) in the eyes of Bhabha, and both are related to being on, or in, the problematic border between life and death. In this chicane of interlingual interpretations, of course, a few nuances have been shaved off with alarming certitude: what for Benjamin was "fleeting" has become "resistance"; what was a discussion of *texts* in Benjamin and Derrida has become an explanation of *people*; what was an issue of *languages* has become a concern within *just one language* (Bhabha writes as a Professor of English discussing a novel written in English); what was the border between life and death for Derrida has become the cultural borders of migration, and what was generally a theory of translation as linguistic transformation has now become a struggle for new cultural identities. In short, the previous theorization of translation has been invested in one word ("survival") and applied to an entirely new context. Bhabha knits this together as follows:

> If hybridity is heresy, then to blaspheme is to dream. To dream not of the past or present, nor the continuous present; it is not the nostalgic dream of tradition, nor the Utopian dream of modern progress; it is the dream of translation as "survival," as Derrida translates the "time" of Benjamin's concept of the after-life of translation, as *sur-vivre*, the act of living on borderlines. Rushdie translates this into the migrant's dream of survival; an *initiatory* interstices [sic]; an empowering condition of hybridity; an emergence that turns "return" into reinscription or re-description; an iteration that is not belated, but ironic and insurgent.
>
> (Bhabha 1994/2004: 324)

There is no explicit attempt here to relate the notion of survival to anything we might find in the equivalence or purpose paradigms of translation. Perhaps we should not insist too much on Rushdie's use of blasphemous names as actual translations. In Bhabha's reading there is no particular source, no particular target, no well-defined mission to accomplish anything beyond "resistance." All those things (source, target, purpose, life-and-death) surely belong more to the *fatwā* as a flying arrow designed to punish mistranslations. However, if Rushdie's resistance is indeed a kind of translation, it must also recognize the reading embedded in the *fatwā*, even if only to contest it. Indeed, it is only through negation of that reading that the object of cultural translation can properly be described as "**non-substantive translation**," as Bhabha himself is reported as calling it (in Trivedi 2007: 286). What we have, though, looks more like a diffuse kind of longing ("to dream") that comes from **the position of a translator**, situated on or perhaps in the **borders between cultures**, defined by **cultural hybridity**. From that perspective, something of Benjamin's "fleetingness" can then be recuperated on Bhabha's next page, where it is related to the indeterminacy of the hybrid: "The focus is on making the linkages through the unstable elements of literature and life – the dangerous tryst with the 'untranslatable' – rather than arriving at ready-made names" (Bhabha 1994/2004: 325). This is then generalized in the formula: "Translation is the performative nature of cultural communication" (1994/2004: 326), which can perhaps only be understood in terms of Bhabha's closing winks to all kinds of borders between and within cultures, not just those due to migration but also those of all minority cultures: Bhabha mentions feminism, gay and lesbian writings, and something called the "Irish question." Wherever borders are crossed, cultural translation may result.

As a piece of theorizing, Bhabha's text does not choose between the alternatives it presents. Should migrants remain unchanged, or should they integrate? What should be their home language? How should mainstream Western culture react to cultural hybridity? Such questions are not solved; they are dissolved. Bhabha simply points to this space between, elsewhere termed the "third space," where the terms of these questions are enacted. Once you see the workings of that space, the questions no longer need any kind of "yes" or "no" answer.

The sense of "translation" here is far wider than the texts we call translations. This theoretical approach is quite different from the descriptive studies that look at the way translations have been carried out in colonial and postcolonial contexts. We are not talking about a particular set of translations, but of a quite different sense of translation.

We can perhaps now understand why the American journal bravely declared that "the language of the Americas is translation." In fact, such claims may now be rather tame. In a world where major demographic movements have undermined apparently stable categories like "a society," "a language," "a culture," or "a nation," any serious study requires new terms to describe its objects. "Translation" is one of those convenient terms, but so too is "emergence" (things are not simply there; they are emerging and submerging in history), "hybridity" (extending Bhabha, every cultural object is a hybrid), and "minoritization" (which would recuperate the role of all elements excluded by the supposition or imposition of a linguistic or cultural "system"). Translation is thus only one of a number of alternatives, but it has become a popular one. And Bhabha is only one of a number of theorists working in this field, but he is perhaps the most influential.

Now, does this theorizing have anything to offer the other paradigms of translation theory? One may be tempted to dismiss Bhabha's contribution as no more than a set of vague opinions presented in the form of fashionable metaphors. On the other hand, if we do accept this as a paradigm of translation theory, it reveals some aspects that have been ignored or sidelined by the other paradigms:

- This view of translation is from the **perspective of the (figurative) translator**, not the translations. No other paradigm, except perhaps parts of *Skopos* theory, has talked about the position of someone who produces language from the "between space" of languages and cultures (one could also talk about "overlaps").
- The focus on **hybridity** surely has something to say about the general position of translators, who by definition know two languages and probably at least two cultures, and it might say something basic about the effects that translation has on cultures, opening them up to other cultures. Bhabha does not say that translations are hybrid; he merely finds a translatory discourse that enacts hybridity.
- The link with migration highlights the way translation ensues from **material movements**. Bhabha would not want his view of translation to be bound to any materialist determinism. Nonetheless, the framing of translation by the material movement of people seems not to have been the focus of any other paradigm.

■ Bhabha sees that the movements cross the **previously established borders** and thereby question them. No other paradigm has so vigorously raised the problem of the two-side border figured by translations (see 3.5 above), although the uncertainty paradigm certainly questions the way in which borders produce illusory oppositions.

These are all very valid points; they indicate important blind-spots in the other paradigms; they justify calling "cultural translation" a new paradigm. Perhaps more importantly, these points concern quite profound problems ensuing from the increasingly fragmented nature of our societies and the numerous mixes of our cultures, not all of which are due to migration (communication technologies also play a powerful role). Further, these points are raised in a way that seems a little different from what we have called the uncertainty paradigm: whereas Benjamin and Derrida, for example, were ultimately engaged in reading and translating *texts*, attempting to bring out multiple potential meanings, Bhabha makes rather more programmatic statements about the world without much heed for second thoughts (e.g. "Rushdie translates this into the migrant's dream of survival"). Rather than a hermeneutics of texts, "cultural translation" has become a way of talking about the world.

Now for the down-to-earth questions: Do we really have to go through Rushdie, Benjamin, and Derrida to reach the tenets of "cultural translation"? Or have all these things been said before, in different places, from different perspectives? And are they being said in other places as well, as different but similar responses to the underlying phenomenon of globalization?

8.2 TRANSLATION WITHOUT TRANSLATIONS: CALLS FOR A WIDER DISCIPLINE

One of the things that "cultural translation" theory does best is move beyond a focus on translations as (written or spoken) texts. The concern is with general cultural processes rather than with finite linguistic products. This is the sense in which we can talk about "translation without translations." Now, was this wider view of translation invented by Homi Bhabha in 1994? Probably not. Previous paradigms have envisaged projects for the study of translation without translations, albeit without undoing the concept of "a translation" (product) as such. Here we recall just a few of those projects.

8.2.1 Jakobson and semiosis

When discussing the development of hermeneutics within the uncertainty paradigm (6.4.6), we mentioned **Roman Jakobson**'s statement that "the meaning of any linguistic sign is its translation into some further, alternative sign" (1959/2004: 139). This is the key point of a theory of **semiosis**, where **meaning is constantly created by interpretations** and is thus never a fixed thing that could be objectified and transferred. As we noted, rather than represent a previous meaning, translation would be the active *production* of meaning. This was in 1959, from within a kind of linguistics that at that stage wanted to become semiotics, the wider study of all kinds of signs.

Jakobson's 1959 paper attempts to draw out some of the consequences of semiosis. One of those consequences is his list of three kinds of translation, which he claims can be

Separating the terms

After Bhabha, we associate the term "cultural translation" with material movement, the position of the translator, cultural hybridity, and the crossing of borders. Used in this way, the term is not to be confused with several other formulations that sound similar but mean different things. We thus attempt to define the terms as best we can:

- **Cultural translation (Bhabha)**: In the sense of Bhabha (1994/2004), a set of discourses that enact hybridity by crossing cultural borders, revealing the intermediary positions of (figurative) translators. This is the most general sense, and the one in which we are using the term to describe a paradigm.
- **Cultural translation (ethnography)**: In the tradition of British social anthropology, a view of ethnography as the description of a foreign culture. That is, the ethnographer translates the foreign culture into an ethnographic description.
- **Cultural turn**: A term proposed by Snell-Hornby (1990) and legitimated by Lefevere and Bassnett (1990) whereby Translation Studies should focus on the cultural effects of translations. For Snell-Hornby, the "translation unit" (the unit taken for each analysis) should move from the text to the culture. The thrust of this view does not challenge traditional uses of the term "translation" and had long been a part of the intellectual background of the descriptive paradigm. Other versions see the "turn" as the use of cultural variables to explain translations, which has also long been part of the descriptive paradigm.
- **Translation culture** (*Übersetzungskultur*): Term used by the Göttingen group (see Frank 1989) to describe the cultural norms governing translations within a target system, on the model of *Esskultur*, which would describe the way a certain society eats. This concept applies to what a society does with translations and expects of them; it does not challenge traditional definitions of translations and it does not focus on the translator. The concept works clearly within the descriptive paradigm.
- **Translation culture** (*Translationskultur*): Defined by Erich Prunč as a "variable set of norms, conventions and expectations which frame the behavior of all interactants in the field of translation" (Prunč 2000: 59; cf. Pöchhacker (2001), who renders the term as "translation standards"), considered a "historically developed subsystem of a culture" (Prunč 1997: 107). This concept focuses on translators and associated social actors, but strangely does not place them on a border between cultures. Developed with clear sympathies with *Skopos* theory, the concept is basically descriptive.
- **Cultural Studies**: A diffuse set of academic studies that adopt a critical and theorizing approach to cultural phenomena in general, emphasizing heterogeneity, hybridity, and the critique of power. Bhabha's postcolonial use of "cultural translation" fits into this frame. The researcher is generally involved in the object under study (as is the case in Bhabha).
- **Culture research**: The term preferred by Even-Zohar for the study of the way cultures develop, interact, and die. On this view, cultures are seen as systems that need transfer (exchange) for their maintenance of energy and thus survival. The researcher generally adopts an objective stance as far as possible.
- **Professional interculture**: A cultural place where people combine elements of more than one primary culture and do so in order to facilitate or carry out cross-cultural communication. For Pym (2004b), professional intercultures are the places where the borders between primary cultures are defined. They include most of the situations in which translators work. This concept is sociological.

"intralingual" (i.e. any rewording within the one language), "interlingual" (rewording between languages), or "intersemiotic" (interpretation between different sign systems, as when a piece of music interprets a poem). That is, once you decide that translation is a process rather than a product, you can find evidence of that process virtually everywhere. Any use of language (or semiotic system) that rewords or reworks any other piece of language (or semiotic system) may be seen as the result of a translational process. And since languages are based precisely on the repetition of utterances in different situations, producing different but related meanings, just as all texts are made meaningful by intertextuality, **all language use may be seen as translation**. The consequences of this view are perhaps far wider and more revolutionary than what Bhabha has to say. That is why we have positioned Jakobson's insight on the threshold of deconstruction, and why we might also find a foundational place for him in the paradigm of cultural translation.

Perhaps the most eloquent enactment of Jakobson's position is to be found in the French philosopher **Michel Serres**. His volume *La Traduction* (1974), part of a series of books on general communication, considers the ways different sciences translate concepts from each other, then how philosophy is translated from formal langauges, then how painting can translate physics (Turner translates primitive thermodynamics), and how literature translates religion (Faulkner translates the Bible). Serres does not claim to be studying any set of texts called translations; he is more interested in translation as a process of communication between domains otherwise thought to be separate. His practice of "general translation" would become important for French sociology, as we shall see later.

Jakobson, however, did not want to travel too far down that path. His typology retains the notion of "translation proper" for "interlingual translation," and his description of "intersemiotic translation" privileges verbal signs (like those of "translation proper") as the point of departure. In this, he was preceded by the Danish semiotician **Louis Hjelmslev**, whose view of intersemiotic translation was similarly directional:

> In practice, a language is a semiotic into which all other semiotics may be translated – both all other languages and all other conceivable semiotic structures. This translatability rests on the fact that all languages, and they alone, are in a position to form any purport whatsoever.
>
> (Hjelmslev 1943/1963: 109)

As we noted in 5.4.6, the Italian theorist **Umberto Eco** (2001) also classified translatory movements between semiotic systems, at the same time as he privileged the place of "translation proper" as a finite textual product of interlingual movements. Jakobson and Eco could both envisage a wide conceptual space for "translation without translations," yet they did not want to throw away or belittle the translations that profesional translators do.

8.2.2 Even-Zohar's call for transfer theory

Jakobson's 1959 paper is one of the starting points for Itamar Even-Zohar's repeated call to extend translation beyond translations (1981/1990, 1997). Even-Zohar thereby seeks to extend the scope of Translation Studies. Here is a key passage from his 1981 "call for transfer theory":

Types of translation without translations?

Roman Jakobson recognizes three kinds of translation (1959/2004: 139):

1 *Intralingual translation* or rewording is an interpretation of verbal signs by means of other signs of the same language.
2 *Interlingual translation* or translation proper is an interpretation of verbal signs by means of some other language.
3 *Intersemiotic translation* or transmutation is an interpretation of verbal signs by means of signs of nonverbal sign systems.

These categories may be compared with the different forms Umberto Eco describes for the interpretant (1977: 70):

■ An equivalent sign in another semiotic system (a drawing of a dog corresponds to the word *dog*).
■ An index directed to a single object (smoke signifies the existence of a *fire*).
■ A definition in the same system (*salt* signifies *sodium chloride*).
■ An emotive association which acquires the value of an established connotation (*dog* signifies "fidelity").
■ A "translation into another language," or substitution by a synonym.

> As systems are no longer conceived of as homogeneous, static structures, transfer mechanisms, that is, the procedures by which textual models in one system are transferred to another, from canonized to non-canonized literature for example, constitute a major feature of systems.
>
> (Even-Zohar 1981: 2)

The prose is difficult but the idea is simple enough. Since all systems are heterogeneous and dynamic, there are always movements of "textual models" from one to another, and translation is only one type of such movements:

> Some people would take this as a proposal to liquidate translation studies. I think the implication is quite the opposite: through a larger context, it will become even clearer that "translation" is not a marginal procedure of cultural systems. Secondly, the larger context will help us identify the really particular in translation. Thirdly, it will change our conception of the translated text in such a way that we may perhaps be liberated from certain postulated criteria. And fourthly, it may help us isolate what "translational procedures" consist of.
>
> (Even-Zohar 1990a: 74)

The term "transfer" here means that a textual model from one system is not just used in another; it is *integrated* into the relations of the host system and thereby both undergoes and generates change (1997: 374). Thus "transfer . . . is correlated with transformation" (Even-Zohar 1990b: 20). Perhaps more importantly, **transfer is seen as occurring both within and between systems**, since "[i]nter-systemic and intra-systemic transfers will be regarded as homologous" (Even-Zohar 1981/1990: 6). This effectively maps out a kind of study in which there are many movements between systems, only some of those movements can be seen in translations, and the same kinds of movements are crossing borders *within* systems as well.

The scope of the project is thus comparable to what we have seen of Bhabha's "cultural translation," except that:

■   What is transferred here is limited to "textual models" (although Even-Zohar's more recent work refers to "goods," "technologies," and "ideational energy").
■   In these formulations there is no particular focus on the human element, on the position and role of the mediators, and thus no attention to anything like a "third space".
■   As a consequence, the model remains one of systems separated by borders, no matter how many borders (and thus subsystems) there may be within each system.
■   As a further consequence, the human researcher remains clearly external to the systems under investigation, with all the trappings of scientific discourse.

Perhaps because of these choices, Even-Zohar's proposed "transfer theory" has had little effect on the general development of translation theory. Many of those who have opened the paths of "cultural translation" would perhaps be surprised at the extent to which Even-Zohar addressed similar problems years before them. We hasten to add that Even-Zohar's *Ideational Labor and the Production of Social Energy* (2008) does show greater interest in human intermediaries, and generally sees transfer as necessary for cultural survival, not in Bhabha's sense of worrying about who Salman Rushdie really is, but with respect to whole cultures disappearing for want of transfers from other cultures. That is a rather more perturbing sense of survival.

8.2.3 Pym's movements

We have noted that theories of cultural translation can call attention to the material movements at the basis of any translation. This is clear enough in the case of postcolonial approaches, where it is not hard to find claims like Salman Rushdie's: "Having been borne across the world, we are translated men" (1992: 17). Although not mentioned by Bhabha, Rushdie's proposition has been picked up by other theorists (for example, Duarte 2005; Trivedi 2007) and has been related to translation theory.

In what sense **can a person be translated**? The term "translation" here can operate in the sense of the Latin verb *transferre*, to move or carry across, which is indeed where the English term comes from, as indeed does "transfer." The usage nevertheless remains problematic. As the Indian theorist Harish Trivedi notes, Rushdie "neglected to tell us as to whether, before he became a translated man, he was at any stage also an original man" (2007: 283). In terms of most current cultural theory, certainly in the shadow of what we have termed the uncertainty paradigm, there is no original or authentic culture; hybridity would be everywhere, and so too, potentially, would be translation.

The reference to the physical movements of people should nevertheless not be underestimated. Pym (1992a) tried to build a whole view of translations as textual responses to the **movement of objects** across time and space. After all, if nothing moved, there would be no need for translations. At the time, the movements were called "transfers" (Pym (2004a) opts for the less ambiguous term "distribution"), and a distinction was made between **text**

transfers (the movements of goods, including cultural products like translations) and **subject transfers** (the movements of people). Pym (1992a) initially proposed that Translation Studies was focused more on the texts than on the people, which in hindsight was probably his greatest political mistake. Nonetheless, in subsequent work he has produced time-space maps of both kinds of transfer (Pym 1998) and has described the person-to-person networks and negotiations of **professional intercultures**, seen as formations of intermediaries, including translators, that develop in the overlaps of cultures (see Pym 1998). There has thus been a development from the study of translations as texts to research on translators as people, and this has gone hand-in-hand with calls for a "humanization" of Translation Studies. At the same time, Pym has never accepted that all texts are translations or that they all share the general condition of cultural hybridity. In fact, he has argued that **translations tend to be less hybrid than non-translations** (Pym 2001), and that, inasmuch as they allow the functional illusions of equivalence, translations generally support discourses that operate in precisely the opposite way to the ideas of cultural translation (2004b). That is, **translations construct cultural borders**, no matter how many human translators might be operating in the overlaps around those borders. Although not exactly an adept of "cultural translation" theory, Pym has certainly shifted his research questions as the world has changed.

8.3 ETHNOGRAPHY AS TRANSLATION

None of the above approaches uses the term "cultural translation"; all of them can be associated with other paradigms of translation theory; none of them (barring passing winks to Jakobson) are mentioned by the theorists of cultural translation. A more powerful antecedent, however, may be found in the tradition of ethnology or "social anthropology," which is where the term "cultural translation" appears to have been coined. How might this relate to the new paradigm?

The basic idea here is that when ethnologists set out to describe distant cultures (thus technically becoming "ethnographers," writers of descriptions), they are in fact translating the cultures into their own professional language. In some cases the translations are remarkably like the traditional cases dealt with in the equivalence paradigm: they may concern a cultural concept, a place name, or a value-laden phrase. In other cases, however, we are dealing with issues that have more to do with the philosophy and ethics of cross-cultural discourse. In very basic terms, the ethnographer can neither suppose radical cultural difference (in which case no description or understanding would be possible) nor complete sameness (in which case no one would need the description). In between those two poles, the term "translation" could have something to say.

The earlier Western anthropologists were generally unaware of their descriptions being translations, since they tended to assume that their own language was able to describe adequately whatever they found (see Rubel and Rosman 2003). **Talal Asad** (1986) notes that in the British tradition the task of social anthropology has been described as a kind of "translation" since the 1950s. Following the historical survey, Asad goes back to Walter Benjamin (he would probably have been more sure-footed going to Schleiermacher) in order to argue that good translations show the structure and nature of the foreign culture; he thus announces a "call to transform a language in order to translate the coherence of the original" (Asad 1986: 157), especially in situations where there is a pronounced asymmetry in the power relations of the languages involved.

Note that the term "cultural translation" here fundamentally means the **translation of a culture**, and translation theory (not much more than Benjamin) is being used in an argument about how this should be done. This is not quite the same sense as we have found in Bhabha, where "cultural translation" is more closely related to the problematics of hybridity and border-crossing. Asad's argument about a "better" mode of translation certainly pushes "cultural translation" toward a more hybrid kind of space, opening up the more powerful language to those of the less powerful cultures being described. One hesitates, however, to equate Bhabha's usage of "cultural translation" with this simpler and more traditional sense of "describing other cultures."

Some translation theorists have taken due note of the way the term "translation" has been used in ethnography. **Wolf** (1997) allows that this is a kind of translation, but she notes that ethnographers are typically engaged in a two-stage mode of work, first interpreting the spoken discourse of informants, then adapting that interpretation for consumption in the dominant culture. Two-stage work involving oral then written mediation may of course be found in mainstream translation history (the practice was noted in Hispania in the twelfth and thirteenth centuries). The prime difference is that the ethnographer does not usually have a materially fixed text to start from. In this sense, ethnographic translation might yet fit under Bhabha's "non-substantive translation."

Some rather more interesting things have been done either within the ethnographic frame or with reference to it. **James Clifford** (esp. 1997) has elaborated an approach in which **travel** becomes the prime means of contact between cultures, configuring the spaces in which cultural translation is carried out. Within literary hermeneutics, this kind of approach is seen as reducing the asymmetries of intercultural alterity and risking a tendency toward sameness (see, for example, the essays in Budick and Iser (1996), where translation theory returns to various prescriptive stances). Clifford's line of thought nevertheless remains extremely suggestive for future research. The way translations (in the narrow or broad sense) represent cultures through travel and for travelers is a huge area that remains virtually untapped.

A position closer to Bhabha is announced by **Wolfgang Iser**, who sees translation as a key concept not just for "the encounter between cultures" (1994: 5) but also for interactions within cultures. Iser uses the notion of **untranslatability** not as the resistance of the migrant, as it is in Bhabha, but as the use of cultural difference to change the way descriptions are produced. In translation, says Iser, "foreign culture is not simply subsumed under one's own frame of reference; instead, the very frame is subjected to alterations in order to accommodate what does not fit" (1994: 5).

At this level, the references to ethnography as translation enter general debates about how different cultures should interrelate, and any sense of translations as a specific class of texts has virtually been lost. We have reached the space of intellectuals opining in a room, where most feel free to prefer foreignization.

8.4 TRANSLATION SOCIOLOGY

We have mentioned the work of Michel Serres as a mode of "generalized translation." Serres' work influenced a group of French ethnographers of science, notably **Michel Callon** and **Bruno Latour**, who developed what they term a "sociologie de la traduction" (cf. Akrich et al. 2006), also known as "**actor-network theory**." We render this here as "**translation**

sociology" rather than "the sociology of translation" because, for us, the "translation" part refers to the method of analysis rather than to the object under analysis (although the theory would reject this distinction). This is despite the fact that the term "the sociology of translation" has long been used in English by these same sociologists (e.g. in Callon 1986). What should be made very clear here is that members of this group are not at all involved in explaining interlingual translations, and they are not particularly interested in the historical and ethical issues of "cultural translation" as Bhabha would see it. They have instead been using a model of translation to explain the way negotiations proceed and networks are formed between social actors, particularly with respect to power relations involving science. And they have been doing this since at least 1975.

For example, **Michel Callon** (1986), in what is now seen as a seminal paper, studies the way marine biologists sought to stop the decline in the population of scallops by influencing the social groups involved. This involved not just forming networks, but at the same time producing and extending social discourses on the problem. At each stage in the analysis, from the actions of the scallops to those of the fishermen, of the scientists, and indeed of the sociologist, there is a common process by which one actor or group is taken to represent (or speak on behalf of) others. The result is a rather poetic leveling out where the one process ("translation") applies to all, including the scallops. This is a key point, and one that should be of interest to translation theory. Translation, for Callon, is at base the process by which one person or group says things that are taken to be "on behalf of" or to "stand for" another person or group. That might simply be another version of Jakobson's view of linguistic meaning, or of semiosis, except that in this case the representation process is seen as the formation of social power. Here are Callon and Latour on something a little more general than scallops, namely the **social contract** sought by the seventeenth-century English philosopher Thomas Hobbes:

> The social contract is only a particular instance of the more general phenomenon known as translation. By "translation" we mean the set of negotiations, intrigues, acts of persuasion, calculations, acts of violence by which an actor or a force accords or allows itself to be accorded the authority to speak or to act in the name of another actor or force: "your interests are our interests," "do what I want," "you cannot succeed without me." As soon as an actor says "we," he or she translates other actors into a single aspiration [*volonté*] of which she or he becomes the master or spokesperson.
>
> (Callon and Latour 1981/2006: 12–13; our translation)

The word "translation" in this citation has a footnote referring to Serres 1974 and Callon 1975.

Seen in these terms, translation becomes the basic building block of social relations, and thereby of societies, the object of sociology. Thus set up, this sociology is exceptional in that it tries *not* to assume any pre-existing categories of boundaries. It would simply follow the translations, the budding nodes in networks, in order to observe the actual institution of any boundaries. There is thus no need to question what is being translated. Indeed, for Bruno Latour (1984/1988: 167), "[n]othing is, by itself, either knowable or unknowable, sayable or unsayable, near or far. Everything is translated." Similarly, there is no "society or social realm," only translators who generate "traceable associations" (Latour 2005: 108). Translation becomes the process through which we form social relations.

With respect to the theory of translations as texts, and indeed within the paradigm of cultural translation, translation sociology has an appeal on several grounds:

■ The **refusal to recognize pre-established social and cultural boundaries** is essentially what the discourses of cultural translation would be doing when they position themselves in the in-between space of cultures. Translation sociology challenges the borders to manifest themselves, as indeed would the hybrid discourses of cultural translation.

■ The emphasis on **translation as the formation of power relations** clearly also fits in with postcolonial problematics, particularly as far as relations between cultural groups are concerned.

■ If the building block of power relations is the process by which one social actor presumes to or is made to **"speak on behalf of another,"** is this not precisely what all translations are presumed or made to do? This might pose the interesting question of why not all translators accrue the social power gained by those who presume to speak on behalf of science.

■ The **networks** in which translators tend to work are so small, so intercultural, and so marked by cultural hybridity that they are ill-served by the classical sociologies of societies or indeed sociologies of systems (cf. Luhmann) and structurally defined social groups (cf. Bourdieu). Translation sociology would seem well suited to such an object.

■ The recognition that **networks extend to and include the sociologist** (or any other analyst) fits in not only with the general sense of involvement found in the theorists of cultural translation, but also with action research (largely influencing the field of translator education) and indeed psychoanalytical approaches.

This does not mean that translation sociology is automatically a part of the paradigm of cultural translation. There are many other things going on. We could say, however, that the work of Callon and Latour has responded to an increasing fragmentation of social categories, just as theorists like Bhabha have done from other perspectives. Some attempts have been made to apply translation sociology to the networks in which translators operate (e.g. Buzelin 2007), and much more can be done. It would be a sad mistake, however, to think that translation sociology should be applied to professional translators simply because the term "translation" appears in both. That word has very different meanings in the two places.

A more effective connection between translation sociology and cultural translation might be found in a group of Germanic sociologists and translation theorists. For example, in the general line of translation sociology, **Joachim Renn** (2006a, 2006b) argues that our postmodern societies are so culturally fragmented that translation is the best model of the way the different groups can communicate with each other and ensure governance. "Cultural translation" may thus be associated with the way cultural differences are maintained and negotiated within complex societies, as both the institution and resistance to what a more standard systems sociology would call "boundary maintenance" (after Parsons 1951). Since this generally involves the cultural displacements of people rather than any kind of text, it is just a few steps from there to the view of migration itself as a form of translation (see Papastergiadis 2000; Vorderobermeier and Wolf 2008), which ultimately returns us to the postcolonial frame. The work of Germanic scholars, many of them brought together in a 2009 issue of the Routledge journal *Translation Studies*, thus bridges the gaps that initially separated the translation sociology of Callon and Latour from the kind of cultural translation we find in Bhabha.

8.5 SPIVAK AND THE POLITICAL PSYCHOANALYTICS OF TRANSLATION

One final strand should be mentioned here before we move to a general consideration of cultural translation. Quite a few authors have explored the relations between psychoanalysis and translation, although few have done so to make any original contribution to translation theory as such. The general idea is that psychoanalysis concerns the use of language, translation is a use of language, so in translations we can find traces of the unconscious. Other approaches consider the terms Freud used for the workings of the unconscious (Andrew Benjamin 1992), many of which may be seen as modes of translation. This effectively makes translational processes anterior to meaning formation, thus concurring with many of the views held within the uncertainty paradigm. None of this particularly concerns cultural translation of the kind we have been considering in this chapter. An intriguing bridge is built, however, in the way the Indian postcolonial theorist **Gayatri Chakravorty Spivak**, resuming the psychoanalytical approach of Melanie Klein, describes a primal kind of translation:

> The human infant grabs on to some one thing and then things. This grabbing (*begreifen*) of an outside indistinguishable from an inside constitutes an inside, going back and forth and coding everything into a sign-system by the thing(s) grasped. One can call this crude coding a "translation".
>
> (Spivak 2007: 261)

Translation, in this sense, would describe the way the infant enters culture and forms subjectivity; it is spatially a dynamic by which borders are enacted. In Spivak, this sense of translation may be applied to all subsequent entries into all further cultures. Translation is thus also the movement from aboriginal cultures in Australia or Bengal to standard cultures of their regions, or indeed of any of the other cultural movements involved in what we have seen as "cultural translation" (although Spivak does not use the term in the paper we are citing from).

Although Spivak avows openly that this is not the literal sense of the word "translation" – "a term I use not for obscurity, but because I find it indispensable" (2007: 264) – she does stretch it to include her own work as a translator of philosophy (notably Derrida) and literature (most interestingly the Bengali woman writer Mahasweta Devi). This is perhaps the closest we come to a psychoanalytical description of translation from the perspective of a translator:

> When a translator translates from a constituted language, whose system of inscription, and permissible narratives are "her own", this secondary act, translation in the narrow sense, as it were, is also a peculiar act of reparation – towards the language of the inside, a language in which we are "responsible", the guilt of seeing it as one language among many.
>
> (Spivak 2007: 265)

The one primal narrative thus manages to account for the various senses of the word "translation."

Part of the interest of Spivak's view of translation is not just her experience as a translator but her preparedness to experiment with modes of translation that go beyond the reproduction of sentences. Her self-reflexive and informative prefaces and peritextual material (particularly in the translations of Devi) not only make the translator highly visible but inscribe the context of a wider cultural translation. Spivak's is one of the few proposals that might relate the paradigm of cultural translation to the actual practice of translators.

Spivak's message, however, is not univocal. As we have seen (in our comments on Asad, above), the general view derived from the many readings of Walter Benjamin is that translations should manifest cultural differences, rather than standardize national cultures. Such would be the politics of identity as resistance. Spivak takes issue with this (just as elsewhere she reclaimed the right to use essentialism within deconstruction):

> The toughest problem here is translation from idiom to standard, an unfashionable thing among the elite progressives, without which the abstract structures of democracy cannot be comprehended.

> (Spivak 2007: 274)

The democracy of Bengal, we might assume, requires common understanding of shared standard terms. The same might be true of democracies everywhere. This is one of the most important debates with which theories of cultural translation should engage.

8.6 "GENERALIZED TRANSLATION"

Within and beyond the above frames, there is certainly no shortage of metaphorical uses of the word "translation." Language is a translation of thought; writing translates speech; literature translates life; a reading translates a text; all metaphors are also translations (*metapherein* is one of the Greek terms for "translation"), and as the Lauryn Hill song puts it, "everything is everything." Such references have long been present in literary theory and they are increasingly present in cultural theory. Here we just pick at a few threads lest anyone accuse us of not being *au fait*:

■ Translation is the displacement of theory from one topographic location to another (e.g. Miller 1995); it is the figure of intellectual nomadism, moving from discipline to discipline (e.g. Vieira 2000; West 2002), but that was already in Serres.
■ Translation is "a metaphor for understanding how the foreign and the familiar are inter-related in every form of cultural production" (Papastergiadis 2000: 124).
■ Translation is part of all meaning production; there is no non-translation (Sallis 2002), but the proposition was already in Jakobson and Latour.
■ Translation plays a key role in the transmission of values from one generation to the next, and is thus part of all "literary invigoration" (Brodski 2007).
■ Translation is "a means of repositioning the subject in the world and in history; a means of rendering self-knowledge foreign to itself; a way of denaturalizing citizens, taking them out of the comfort zone of national space, daily ritual, and pre-given domestic arrangements" (Apter 2006: 6).
■ And a long etcetera (see further references in Duarte 2005).

This generalization may be liberating and exciting to many; it could seem dissipating and meaningless to others. Let us simply note that many (although not all) of the above references are from the United States or are in tune with the development of Literary Theory and

Comparative Literature in the United States. At the same time, the United States is a country with remarkably few translator-training institutions and thus with relatively little demand for the kind of translation theory developed within the equivalence or *Skopos* paradigms, and scant development of Translation Studies as envisaged in the descriptive paradigm. In terms of academic markets, if nothing else, the United States has provided a situation where what we have called the uncertainty paradigm could flourish into several modes of generalized translation.

Most of the above references do not actually refer to "cultural translation," since that term tended to come later. They have, however, opened up huge conceptual spaces for the paradigm. Once its moorings to equivalence have been severed, "translation" risks becoming a drunken boat.

8.7 FREQUENTLY HAD ARGUMENTS

The positive points of the cultural translation paradigm are roughly those we outlined with reference to Bhabha (in 8.2 above): it introduces a human dimension, seeing translation from the perspective of the (figurative) translator; it concerns translation as a cultural process rather than a textual product; its focus on hybridity undoes many of the binary oppositions marking previous translation theory; it relates translation to the demographical movements that are changing the shape of our cultures; it can generally operate within all the critiques ensuing from the uncertainty paradigm.

Those are not minor virtues. The existence of "cultural translation" as a paradigm is nevertheless illustrated by the many places in which others do not see the point, or do not accept its redefinitions of basic terms. The following arguments are part and parcel of its emergence as a paradigm among paradigms.

8.7.1 "These theories only use translation as a metaphor"

Many of the theorists we have cited here freely recognize that they are using the term "translation" in a metaphorical way. They are drawing ideas from one area of experience (the things translators do) to a number of other areas (the ways cultures interrelate). This can be productive and stimulating for both the fields involved, as we have suggested. On the other hand, the generalized production of metaphors may risk expanding the term "translation" until it becomes meaningless (Duarte 2005), or indeed of losing track of the original referent. Michaela Wolf points out the risk of developing "a sociology of translation without translation" (2007: 27).

It would be dangerous, though, to defend any original or true sense of the word "translation." Is there anything really wrong with the metaphors? Is there anything new in their workings? After all, metaphors always map one area of experience on to another, and when you think about it, the words we use for the activities of translators ("translation," "Übersetzen," etc.) are no less metaphorical, since they propose images of movement across space (more than time) (see D'hulst 1992). Perhaps the problem is that they have become dead metaphors, images that we somehow accept as self-evident truths. The more conscious metaphors of "cultural translation" may thus help us think more critically about all kinds of translation.

8.7.2 "Cultural translation is an excuse for intellectual wandering"

Here we translate **Antoine Berman**'s term "vagabondage conceptuel" (1985: 42–43), which he used as a complaint against the proliferation of metaphors and "generalized translation" he found in George Steiner and Michel Serres (and which has become even more general since then). Berman recognizes that translations will always produce cultural change, and there will thus always be the temptation to associate change with translation. However, he warns against the way this can lead to a view where everything can translate everything else, where there is "universal translatability." To oppose this, indeed to oppose excessive theorizing, he argues for a concept of "restrained translation" that respects the letter of the foreign text (see Godard 2002).

Berman's view nevertheless does not seem to account for the many theorists of cultural translation who emphasize untranslatability, resistance, and maintenance of foreignness in all processes of translation. That is, many would agree with his politics, but not with his strategy. Indeed, many would accept "intellectual wandering" as a compliment.

8.7.3 "Cultural translation is a space for weak interdisciplinarity"

Associated with criticism of "generalized translation" is the suspicion that the scholars dealing with cultural translation do not know anything about interlingual translation, or are not interested in it. From this perspective, the various theorists of culture would be stealing the notion of translation, without due appreciation of any of the other paradigms of translation theory. Wolf (2009: 77–78) retorts:

> [T]he question arises "who is the owner of the translation term?" I argue that banning a metaphorical variant of the translation notion – i.e. what has been called "cultural translation" – from the field of research of Translation Studies would ultimately mean rejecting any sort of interdisciplinary work in this respect.

Can any discipline own a word? Obviously not. Can it attempt to stop others using the word? It is difficult to see how. Yet there is an obvious question here: Why should we work with other theorists simply because they use the same word as us? If we are producing a theory of forks as tools for eating, would we have to work in an interdisciplinary way with experts in "forks in the road" or "tuning forks" or "fork" as a situation in chess? The analogy is perhaps not as far-fetched as it sounds.

One kind of solution here may be found in the difference between a word ("translation") and a term ("translation" plus a set of defining characteristics, such as the ones mentioned in 5.4 above). If a term is defined precisely, as a conceptual tool for working on a particular problem, then perhaps it can indeed be owned by a discipline. Of course, no one can then stop other disciplines using words any way they want.

Wolf's second argument here is that if we do not accept this **interdisciplinarity**, then we must refuse all interdisciplinarity. This is the kind of argument reminiscent of binary political activists: "If you are not with us, you are against us." There seems to be no reason why translation scholars might choose to work with some disciplines (e.g. sociology, psychology, linguistics) and not others (e.g. cultural studies, philosophy, psychoanalysis), so long as the cooperation is suited to the problem being worked on. Alternatively, one could choose not to work with a set of theories because, for example, they are based on no empirical data, display imprecise and contradictory thought, betray a short-term consumption of fashionable concepts, are ploys in search of academic power, and are deployed by fly-by-night intellectuals who will move on to something else next year anyway.

8.7.4 "Cultural translation can be studied entirely in English"

Once the term "translation" loses the interlingual element of its definition, it can be studied without reference to different languages. In fact, everything can be studied within the major languages, often just within English (or French, or German): as we have noted, Homi Bhabha was writing as a Professor of English about a novel in English. The result is a paradoxical eclipse of alterity, as seen by **Harish Trivedi**: "Rather than help us encounter and experience other cultures, translation would have been assimilated in just one monolingual global culture" (2007: 286). This critique fits in with Berman's fear of "global translatability," and indeed with a mode of theorization where the model "postmodern society" somehow fits all societies, and the one kind of "translation correctly understood" (after reading Walter Benjamin in English) accounts for all translation. The theories of cultural translation would thus be sweeping away the very otherness that they generally proclaim to espouse.

To be fair, this risk of reduction is perhaps inherent in all theorizing. A discussion of equivalence can easily move into mathematics or logic, just as debates about purposes seem to become the stuff of philosophy and ethics. Even within the descriptive paradigm, which should perhaps keep us close to texts and languages, the use of "comparable corpora" means that translation can apparently be discerned by looking at English alone. The reduction of alterity is not just a problem of cultural translation.

8.7.5 "Cultural translation is not in touch with the translation profession"

This is part of a general reproach made of translation theory: the people who theorize do not actually know how to translate, so they do not really know about translation. The criticism might be more acute in the case of "cultural translation" since the theorists are talking about much more than translations as texts, and there is the associated argument that they are more interested in their power in the academy than in anything to do with other minority cultures. We have noted that there is very little concern for actual translators (Rushdie's translators took the bullets for him, while Bhabha calmly declares that Rushdie's resistance is "untranslatable"), and we might more generally lament that the dynamics of cultures swamp any focus on specific "translation cultures" or "professional intercultures." In a sense, the paradigm is too powerful to empower translators in any clear way.

On the other hand, some of the theorists are indeed translators, and very innovative ones at that (Spivak, certainly, and Venuti), and most of the others live and work across multiple cultures. They are not unaware of the kinds of situations in which translators work. More promisingly, the connection with migration helps us consider the many new translation situations, with a focus on "social needs" rather than market demands. There is no theoretical reason why the paradigm of cultural translation should exclude a closer focus on translators.

The above are real arguments, of significance for the future of translation theory. Some of them are profound enough to threaten any attempt to see cultural translation as a coherent paradigm; others are debates that ensure the dynamism and contemporary relevance of the paradigm. You might run through them and keep a scorecard of good and bad points. On balance, for us, the virtues of cultural translation are significant enough to have been included in this book.

SUMMARY

This chapter started from a reading of the way Homi Bhabha uses the term "cultural translation" in his chapter "How newness enters the world." We have then questioned how new the concept really is. We have reviewed earlier views of processes wider than text-based translation, particularly in Jakobson, Even-Zohar, and Pym, and we have seen how the term "cultural translation" developed from social anthropology. The wider view can also draw on actor-network theory (translation sociology) and German work on communication between different cultural groups in complex societies, particularly in contexts involving immigration. If something new has entered the world of translation, it is probably from the migrations and changes in communication patterns, to the extent that we can no longer assume separate languages and cultures. The basic spaces that once set up equivalence theory are no longer there. Cultural translation might thus offer ways of thinking about the many situations in which translation now operates in the world.

SOURCES AND FURTHER READING

The Translation Studies Reader (Venuti 2000/2004) includes texts by Berman, Spivak, Appiah, and Derrida (although the latter is not highly representative of Derrida's uses of translation). Munday (2001/2008) touches on this paradigm in three separate chapters, courageously attempting to distinguish between culture, ideology, sociology, and philosophy. Homi Bhabha should be basic reading for anyone interested in cultural translation. Where you go from there depends very much on what questions are of interest. The volume *Nation, Language, and the Ethics of Translation*, edited by Bermann and Wood (2005), gives samples of the work being done in the United States. Many of the more international strands are being brought together in the Routledge journal *Translation Studies*, which plays an active role in the formation of the paradigm.

Suggested projects and activities

1   Do a web search for the term "cultural translation." How many different meanings can you find? Would they all fit into the one paradigm?
2   If a novel by Salman Rushdie can be considered an act of cultural translation because of its active use of hybridity, could the same be said of all novels? Are there any non-translational uses of language?

3 Consider the statement that "the language of the Americas is translation." Could the same be true of all languages? (Is there any language that has not been displaced?) How many different natural languages are spoken in the Americas? What could be the ideological effect of saying that they are all really the one language?

4 Even-Zohar wants "transfer studies" to look at the movements from culture to culture of basic technologies like the horse or the alphabet. Should such things be considered by translation theory?

5 Locate one of Spivak's translations of Mahasweta Devi (or any literary translation that has a substantial preface by the translator). How does the translator describe the source languages for the translation processes? How many source languages are there in the content of the text (i.e. what languages are the ideas coming from)? Are the sources assumed to be more authentic than the translations? Can the sources be seen as translations?

6 Callon and Latour see translation as an act where someone speaks on behalf of someone else, making themselves indispensable and thus accruing power. Is this the case for all translations? Could it be the case for the relation between Bhabha and Rushdie, or Spivak and Devi?

7 Emily Apter is an American Professor of Comparative Literature and French who associates translation theory with a "new Comparative Literature" (2006). In doing so, she acknowledges the following "pioneers in the field of translation studies": "George Steiner, André Lefevere, Antoine Berman, Gregory Rabassa, Lawrence Venuti, Jill Levine, Michel Heim, Henri Meschonnic, Susan Sontag, Richard Howell, and Richard Sieburth" (2006: 6). Who are all these people? What do they have in common? Why have so few of them been mentioned in this book?

8 Go to the website of the European Institute for Progressive Cultural Policies (eipcp) and look up its various activities involving "cultural translation." What kind of translation has produced this superb multilingual website? What is the relation between what the authors say about translation and the way they use translations? What language does the siglum "eipcp" make sense in? Why are there so few references to the "pioneers" mentioned by Apter?

9 Can translation be studied by looking at one language only? Should it be studied by people who know only one language?

10 In 1928, in full Surrealist swing, the Brazilian poet Oswald de Andrade proclaimed his *Manifesto antropófago* for Brazilian culture. Here is a taste:

Only Cannibalism unites us. Socially. Economically. Philosophically.
The only law of the world. Masked expression of all individualisms, of all collectivisms. Of all religions. Of all peace treaties.
Tupi, or not tupi that is the question.
Against all catechisms. And against the mother of the Gracchus brothers.
I am only interested in that which is not mine. Law of the human. Law of the cannibal.

(Andrade 1928/1980: 81; our translation)

In 1978 the Brazilian poet Augusto de Campos applied this to translation, listing his favorite foreign poets and declaring, "[m]y way of loving them is to translate them. Or to swallow them down, in accordance with Oswald de Andrade's Cannibal Law: I am only interested in that which is not mine" (1978: 7; our translation).

Compare these statements with the inner/outer dynamic described by Spivak. Are they talking about the same kind of translation? Now compare it with the guilt described by Spivak, or with the power of "speaking on behalf of" mentioned by Callon and Latour. Do the degrees of guilt or power depend on the directionality of the translation? Could they have anything to do with your own experience when translating?

11 Compare the statements by Andrade and de Campos with the accounts of postcolonial cannibalism theory in Vieira (1999), Munday (2001: 136–137, now web-based extra material for the 2008 edition), or Gentzler (2008). Do the above statements actually present a theory of translation, or a clear translation theory? Do the commentaries by Vieira, Munday, or Gentzler present much more evidence than the above? Have the commentaries somehow constructed a whole school of thought ("the strong Brazilian translation-studies community," says Munday 2001: 136) without reference to actual translation practices in Brazil (cf. Milton and Bandia 2008: 12)?

12 Look for information on the translation services (not) provided for immigrants in your country. Are immigrants obliged to become translators themselves? What role do children play? What is the position of women with respect to the various languages? Are these problems and forms of translation addressed by any other paradigm of translation theory?

Postscript
Write your own theory

This is where I move to the first person, to address you, the person who is going to do something with translation theory. I will try to position myself with respect to the various paradigms (since there can be no neutral description), then I will suggest how you might go about positioning yourself.

What do I think of these paradigms? Equivalence, for me, is a social illusion but a necessary one. People believe in it just as they believe in the value of the money they carry in their pockets; we believe in these things even when we know there is no linguistic certainty behind equivalence and not enough gold to back up our money. We thus have to try to understand the way *equivalence beliefs* work. From that point, I can accept all the other paradigms as having valid things to say. *Skopos* theory, for me, is a collection of quite evident things, unfortunately unable to solve ethical problems involving competing purposes. The descriptive paradigm stands at the center of translation research and cannot be ignored, but it must be made to reflect critically on the role of the describer. The uncertainty paradigm has good and bad in it – I accept the lessons of deconstruction and I am looking for ways to live with them, but I do not go along with theories that assume supremacy of the source text, and I have trouble with the hermeneutic tradition which stares in that direction (and which includes part of Walter Benjamin). I am more interested in the aspects of the uncertainty paradigm that can help create a future. As for localization, I am fascinated by the effects of technology which is offering us a better future, just as I am appalled by the naïve way in which equivalence has returned in that paradigm in all its deceptive simplicity. Cultural translation then opens up new avenues for the understanding of translation in social contexts. For me, however, the paradigm ceases to function as translation theory when it can no longer offer a critique of equivalence. Worse, the perspective of "generalized translation" forgoes the valuable contact with translation and interpreting as professions, and I feel that much of the work done on cultural translation would be better branded as "intercultural studies."

If I can take all those positions, I clearly do not belong to just one paradigm. I do not think anyone has to be situated in one place or another. We should feel free to move between the paradigms, selecting the ideas that can help us solve problems. That is the way I think translation theories should develop.

For example, I am currently working on translation processes as risk management. This means that instead of saying that different translation solutions are "right" or wrong," or are instances of one kind of equivalence or another, I try to assess how much risk they involve. The work of the translator becomes an exercise in risk management. On that basis I can set about reinterpreting all previous theories. The various modes of equivalence are different ways of reducing or transferring risk; the risk is measured in relation to the *Skopos* of the task, which at its most general ethical level is to offer mutual benefits to all participants (a theory I cannot go into here); translation norms also become ways of reducing risk; the proposed universals of translation are similarly all risk-reduction measures; risk analysis enables us to live with uncertainty by assuming it and calculating it; localization technologies tend to fail whenever there is no way of distinguishing between high-risk and low-risk text; and the study of cultural translation has a lot to say about the kinds of values and benefits that are at stake in a globalizing world. I have no need to stop reading any of the paradigms. Some parts of previous theories are more useful than others, and some significant gaps appear. For instance, very little theoretical work has been done on the psychology of translation processes, or rather, most of that work is on conference interpreting and concerns the paradigms of cognitive science. It has not really connected with translation theory (and has thus not found a place in this book). Or again, all the proposed laws and universals suggest that translators are risk-averse. Is that necessarily so? Do translators sometimes take risks? No one has really asked. Some of the most stimulating ideas concerning this problem actually come from the paradigm of cultural translation, which offers a wider view of cross-cultural communication. Of course, when I theorize these problems I am also drawing on concepts from outside of translation theory, as many others have done. I try to think about the fundamental ethics of communication, then about what might be specific to cross-cultural communication, and then about translation as a particular kind of cross-cultural communication. Others might want to go the other way, from translation to all communication, and that can be equally as valid.

Here, then, is my one piece of advice. When theorizing translation, when developing your own translation theory, first identify a problem – a situation of doubt requiring action, or a question in need of an answer. Then go in search of ideas that can help you work on that problem. There is no need to start in any one paradigm, and certainly no need to belong to one.

References

Akrich, M., M. Callon, and B. Latour (2006) *Sociologie de la traduction. Textes fondateurs*, Paris: Presses de l'École des Mines.

Ammann, M. (1994) "Von Schleiermacher bis Sartre. Translatologische Interpretationen," in M. Snell-Hornby and K. Kaidl (eds) *Translation Studies. An Interdiscipline*, Amsterdam and Philadelphia: Benjamins, pp. 37–44.

Andrade O. de (1928/1980) "Manifesto antropófago," in J. Schwartz (ed.) *Literatura comentada*, São Paulo: Abril, pp. 81–83.

Appiah, K. A. (2000) "Thick Translation," in L. Venuti (ed.) *The Translation Studies Reader*, London and New York: Routledge, pp. 417–429.

Apter, E. (2006) *The Translation Zone. A New Comparative Literature*, Princeton and Oxford: Princeton University Press.

Arrojo, R. (1992) *Oficina de tradução. A teoria na prática*, second edition, São Paulo: Ática.

Arrojo, R. (1993) *Tradução, Deconstrução e Psicanálise*, Rio de Janeiro: Imago.

Arrojo, R. (1994) "Fidelity and the Gendered Translation," *TTR* 7: 147–163.

Arrojo, R. (1997) "Asymmetrical Relations of Power and the Ethics of Translation," *TEXTconTEXT* 11: 5–25.

Arrojo, R. (1998) "The Revision of the Traditional Gap between Theory and Practice and the Empowerment of Translation in Postmodern Times," *The Translator* 4: 25–48.

Asad, T. (1986) "The Concept of Cultural Translation in British Anthropology," in J. Clifford and G.E. Marcus (eds) *Writing Culture. The Poetics and Politics of Ethnography*, Berkeley, Los Angeles, London: University of California Press, pp. 141–164.

Augustine of Hippo (Aurelius Augustinus) (*c*. 400/1969) "De catechizandis rudibus," *Aurelii Augustini Opera*, vol. 13.2, Turnout: Brepols.

Bascom, B. (2007) "Mental Maps and the Cultural Understanding of Scripture," Unpublished paper presented to the conference *Translation, Identity, and Language Heterogeneity*, San Marcos University, Lima, December 7–9.

Baumgarten, S. (2001) "Uncovering Ideology in Translation: An Analysis of English Translations of Hitler's *Mein Kampf*," *CTIS Occasional Papers* 1: 21–54.

Bédard, C. (2000) "Translation Memory Seeks Sentence-oriented Translator . . .," *Traduire* 186.

Benjamin, A. (1989) *Translation and the Nature of Philosophy. A New Theory of Words*, London and New York: Routledge.

Benjamin, A. (1992) "Translating Origins: Psychoanalysis and Philosophy," in L. Venuti (ed.) *Rethinking Translation: Discourse, Subjectivity, Ideology*, London: Routledge, pp. 18–41.

Benjamin, W. (1923/1977) "Die Aufgabe des Übersetzers," in *Illuminationen: Ausgewählte Schriften*, Frankfurt am Main: Suhrkamp, pp. 50–62.

Benjamin, W. (1923/2004) "The Task of the Translator," trans. H. Zohn, in L. Venuti (ed.) *The Translation Studies Reader*, second edition, London and New York: Routledge, pp. 75–85.

Berger, K., and C. Nord (trans.) (1999) *Das Neue Testament und frühchristliche Schriften*, Frankfurt: Insel.

Berman, A. (1984/1992) *The Experience of the Foreign. Culture and Translation in Romantic Germany*, trans. S. Heyvaert, Albany: State University of New York Press.

Berman, A. (1985) "La traduction et la lettre, ou l'auberge du lointain," in *Les Tours de Babel: Essais sur la traduction*, Mauvezin: Trans-Europ-Repress, pp. 35–150.

Berman, A. (1995) *Pour une critique des traductions: John Donne*, Paris: Gallimard.

Berman, A. (1999) *La traduction et la lettre ou l'Auberge du lointain*, Paris: Seuil.

Bermann, S., and M. Wood (eds) (2005) *Nation, Language, and the Ethics of Translation*, Princeton: Princeton University Press.

Bhabha, H. (1994/2004) *The Location of Culture*, Routledge Classics Edition, London and New York: Routledge.

Bigelow, J. (1978) "Semantics of Thinking, Speaking and Translation," in F. Guenthner and M. Guenthner-Reutter (eds) *Meaning and Translation. Philosophical and Linguistic Approaches*, London: Duckworth, pp. 109–135.

Blum-Kulka, S. (1986/2004) "Shifts of Cohesion and Coherence in Translation," in L. Venuti (ed.) *The Translation Studies Reader*, London and New York: Routledge, pp. 290–305.

Blum-Kulka, S., and E. A. Levenston (1983) "Universals of Lexical Simplification," in C. Faerch and G. Casper (eds) *Strategies in Inter-language Communication*, London and New York: Longman, pp. 119–139.

Bowker, L. (2005) "Productivity vs. Quality? A Pilot Study on the Impact of Translation Memory Systems," *Localisation Focus* 4: 13–20.

Brislin, R. W. (1981) *Cross-cultural Encounters. Face-to-face Interaction*, New York: Pergamon.

Brodski, B. (2007) *Can These Bones Live? Translation, Survival, and Cultural Memory*, Stanford: Stanford University Press.

Budick, S., and W. Iser (eds) (1996) *The Translatability of Cultures: Figurations of the Space Between*, Stanford: Stanford University Press.

Bühler, K. (1934/1982) *Sprachtheorie. Die Darstellungsfunktion der Sprache*, Stuttgart and New York: Gustav Fischer.

Burge, T. (1978) "Self-reference and Translation," in F. Guenther and M. Guenther-Reutter (eds) *Meaning and Translation. Philosophical and Linguistic Approaches*, London: Duckworth, pp. 137–153.

Buzelin, H. (2007) "Translations 'In the Making'," in M. Wolf and A. Fukari (eds) *Constructing a Sociology of Translation*, Amsterdam and Philadelphia: John Benjamins, pp. 135–160.

Callon, M. (1975) "L'opération de traduction," in Pierre Roquepio (ed.) *Incidence des rapports sociaux sur le développement des sciences et des techniques*, Paris: Cordes, pp. 105–141.

Callon, M. (1986) "Some Elements for a Sociology of Translation: Domestication of the Scallops and the Fishermen of St-Brieuc Bay," in J. Law (ed.) *Power, Action and Belief: A New Sociology of Knowledge?*, London: Routledge, pp. 196–223.

Callon, M., and B. Latour (1981/2006) "Unscrewing the Big Leviathan; Or How Actors Macrostructure Reality, and How Sociologists Help Them to Do So," in K. D. Knorr and A. Cicourel (eds) *Advances in Social Theory and Methodology. Toward an Integration of Micro and Macro Sociologies*, London: Routledge & Kegan Paul, pp. 277–303.

Caminade, M., and A. Pym (1995) *Les formations en traduction et interprétation. Essai de recensement mondial*, Paris: Société Française des Traducteurs.

Campbell, S. (2001) "Choice Network Analysis in Translation Research," in M. Olohan, (ed.) *Intercultural Faultlines. Research Models in Translation Studies I: Textual and Cognitive Aspects*, Manchester: St. Jerome, pp. 29–42.

Campos, A. de (1978) "Verso, reverso, controverso," in *Verso, reverso e controverso*, São Paulo: Perspectiva, pp. 7–8.

Campos, H. de (1962/1976) "Da tradução como criação e como crítica," reprinted in *Metalinguagem*, São Paulo: Cultrix, pp. 35–36.

Catford, J. C. (1965) *A Linguistic Theory of Translation: An Essay in Applied Linguistics*, London: Oxford University Press.

Chau, Simon S. C. (Chau Suicheong) (1984) "Hermeneutics and the Translator: The Ontological Dimension of Translating," *Multilingua* 3(2): 71–77.

Chesterman, A. (1996) "On Similarity," *Target* 8(1): 159–163.

Chesterman, A. (1997) *Memes of Translation. The Spread of Ideas in Translation Theory*, Amsterdam and Philadelphia: Benjamins.

Chesterman, A. (1999) "The Empirical Status of Prescriptivism," *Folia Translatologica* 6: 9–19.

Chesterman, A. (2005) "Where is Similarity?," in S. Arduini and R. Hodgson (eds) *Similarity and Difference in Translation*, Rimini: Guaraldi, pp. 63–75.

Chesterman, A. (2006) "Interpreting the Meaning of Translation," in M. Suominen et al. (eds) *A Man of Measure. Festschrift in Honour of Fred Karlsson on his 60th Birthday*, Turku: Linguistic Association of Finland, pp. 3–11.

Chesterman, A., and R. Arrojo (2000) "Forum: Shared Ground in Translation Studies," *Target* 12(1): 151–160

Chomsky, N. (1980) *Rules and Representations*, New York: Columbia University Press.

Cicero, M. T. (46CE/1996) "De optimo genere oratorum," in F. Lafarga (ed.) *El discurso sobre la traducción en la historia*, bilingual edition, Barcelona: EUB, pp. 32–44.

Clifford, J. (1997) *Routes: Travel and Translation in the Late Twentieth Century*. Cambridge, MA: Harvard University Press.

Coseriu, E. (1978) "Falsche und richtige Fragenstellungen in der Übersetzungstheorie," in L. Grähs, G. Korlén, and B. Malmberg (eds) *Theory and Practice of Translation*, Bern, Frankfurt am Main, Las Vegas: Peter Lang, pp. 17–32.

Croce, B. (1902/1922) *Aesthetic as a Science of Expression and General Linguistic*, London: Noonday.

Crystal, D. (2006) *Words, Words, Words*, Oxford: Oxford University Press.

Davis, K. (2001) *Deconstruction and Translation*, Manchester and Northhampton, MA: St. Jerome.

Delabastita, D. (2008) "Status, Origin, Features: Translation and Beyond," in A. Pym, M. Shlesinger, and D. Simeoni (eds) *Beyond Descriptive Translation Studies*, Amsterdam, Philadelphia: Benjamins, pp. 233–246.

Delabastita, D., L. D'hulst, and R. Meylaerts (2006) *Functional Approaches to Culture and Translation. Selected Papers by José Lambert*, Amsterdam and Philadelphia: Benjamins.

Delisle, J. (1988) *Translation: An Interpretive Approach*, trans. P. Logan and M. Creery, Ottawa: University Press.

Delisle, J., and J. Woodsworth (eds) (1995) *Translators through History*, Amsterdam, Philadelphia: Benjamins.

de Man, P. (1986) *The Resistance to Theory*, Minneapolis: University of Minnesota Press.

Derrida, J. (1967) *De la grammatologie*, Paris: Minuit.

Derrida, J. (1968) "La pharmacie de Platon," *Tel Quel* 32: 3–48; 33: 18–59.

Derrida, J. (1972) *Marges de la philosophie*, Paris: Minuit.

Derrida, J. (1979) "Living On: Border Lines," in H. Bloom (ed.) *Deconstruction and Criticism*, New York: Seabury, pp. 75–176.

Derrida, J. (1982/1985) *The Ear of the Other: Otobiography, Transference, Translation: Texts and Discussions with Jacques Derrida*, trans. P. Kamuf, New York: Schocken Books.

Derrida, J. (1985) "Des Tours de Babel" (French and English versions), in J. F. Graham (ed.) *Difference in Translation*, Ithaca, NY: Cornell University Press, pp. 165–207, 209–248.

Derrida, J. (1993) *Spectres de Marx: l'état de la dette, le travail du deuil et la nouvelle Internationale*, Paris: Galilée.

Derrida, J. (1999) "Qu'est-ce qu'une traduction 'relevante'?," in *Quinzièmes Assises de la Traduction Littéraire*, Arles: Actes Sud, pp. 21–48.

D'hulst, L. (1992) "Sur le rôle des métaphores en traductologie contemporaine," *Target* 4(1): 33–51.

Duarte, J. F. (2005) "Para uma crítica de retórica da tradução em Homi Bhabha," in A. G. Macedo, and M. E. Keating (eds) *Colóquio de Outono. Estudos de tradução – Estudos pós-coloniais*, Braga: Universidade do Minho, pp. 89–100.

Dunne, K. J. (ed.) (2006) *Perspectives on Localization*, Amsterdam, Philadelphia: Benjamins.

Eco, U. (1977) *A Theory of Semiotics*, London, Basingstoke: Macmillan.

Eco, U. (2001) *Experiences in Translation*, trans. A. McEwan, Toronto, Buffalo, London: University of Toronto Press.

Eco, U., et al. (1992) *Interpretation and Overinterpretation*, Cambridge: Cambridge University Press.

Eliot, T. S. (1933/1975) "The Use of Poetry and the Use of Criticism," in F. Kermode (ed.) *Selected Prose of T. S. Eliot*, Orlando: Harcourt, pp. 79–06.

Esselink, B. (2000) *A Practical Guide to Localization*, Amsterdam and Philadelphia: Benjamins.

Even-Zohar, I. (1978a) "The Position of Translated Literature Within the Literary Polysystem," in J. S Holmes et al. (eds) *Literature and Translation*, Leuven: Acco, pp. 117–127.

Even-Zohar, I. (1978b) *Papers in Historical Poetics*, Tel Aviv: Porter Institute. Available at http://www.tau.ac.il/~itamarez/, visited November 2008.

Even-Zohar, I. (1981/1990) "Translation Theory Today: A Call for Transfer Theory," *Poetics Today* 2(4): 1–7; revised as "Translation and Transfer," *Poetics Today* 11(1): 73–78.

Even-Zohar, I. (1986) "The Quest for Laws and its Implications for the Future of the Science of Literature," in G. M. Vajda and J. Riesz (eds) *The Future of Literary Scholarship*, Frankfurt am Main: Peter Lang, pp. 75–79.

Even-Zohar, I. (1990a) "Translation and Transfer," *Poetics Today* 11(1) [Special Issue on Polysystem Studies]: 73–78.

Even-Zohar, I. (1990b) "Polysystem Theory," *Poetics Today* 11(1): 9–26.

Even-Zohar, I. (1997) "The Making of Culture Repertoire and the Role of Transfer," *Target* 9(2): 355–363.

Even-Zohar, I. (2008) *Ideational Labor and the Production of Social Energy: Intellectuals, Idea Makers and Culture Entrepreneurs*, Tel Aviv: Porter Chair of Semiotics. Available at http://www.tau.ac.il/~itamarez/, visited March 2009.

Fawcett, P. (1997) *Translation and Language. Linguistic Theories Explained*, Manchester: St. Jerome.

Fedorov, A. V. (1953) *Vvedenie b teoriu perevoda*, Moscow: Literaturi na inostrannix iazikax.

Folkart, B. (1991) *Le Conflit des énonciations. Traduction et discours rapporté*, Montreal: Balzac.

Frank, A. P. (1989) "Translation as System and Übersetzungskultur, On Histories and Systems in the Study of Literary Translation," *New Comparison* 8: 85–98.

Freeman, D. (1999) *The Fateful Hoaxing of Margaret Mead: A Historical Analysis of her Samoan Research*, Boulder: Westview Press.

Gadamer, H. G. (1960/1972) *Wahrheit und Methode: Grundzüge einer philosophischen Hermeneutik*, Tübingen: Mohr.

Genette, G. (1976) *Mimologiques. Voyage en Cratylie*, Paris: Seuil.

Gentzler, E. (1993/2001) *Contemporary Translation Theories*, revised version, Clevedon: Multilingual Matters.

Gentzler, E. (2008) *Translation and Identity in the Americas*, London and New York: Routledge.

Godard, B. (2002) "L'Éthique du traduire: Antoine Berman et le 'virage éthique' en traduction," *Meta* 14(2): 49–82.

Gorlée, D. L. (1994) *Semiotics and the Problem of Translation, with Special Reference to the Semiotics of Charles S. Peirce*, Amsterdam, Atlanta, GA: Rodopi.

Gouadec, D. (2007) *Translation as a Profession*, Amsterdam, Philadelphia: Benjamins.

Grice, H. P. (1975) "Logic and Conversation," in P. Cole and J. L. Morgan (eds) *Syntax and Semantics*, vol. 3, New York: Academic Press, pp. 41–58.

Gutt, E-A. (1991/2000) *Translation and Relevance. Cognition and Context*, second edition, Manchester: St. Jerome.

Halverson, S. (1998) "Translation Studies and Representative Corpora: Establishing Links between Translation Corpora, Theoretical/Descriptive Categories and a Conception of the Object of Study," *Meta* 43(4): 459–514.

Halverson, S. (2007) "Translations as Institutional Facts: An Ontology for 'Assumed Translation'," in A. Pym, M. Shlesinger, and D. Simeoni (eds) *Beyond Descriptive Translation Studies*, Amsterdam, Philadelphia: Benjamins, pp. 343–362.

Hatim, B., and I. Mason (1990) *Discourse and the Translator*, London: Longman.

Hatim, B., and I. Mason (1997). *The Translator as Communicator*, London, New York: Routledge.

Heidegger, M. (1927/1953) *Being and Time*, trans. J. Stambaugh, Albany: State University of New York Press.

Heidegger, M. (1957) *Der Satz vom Grund*, Pfullingen: Neske.

Heisenberg, W. (1927) "Über den anschaulichen Inhalt der quantentheoretischen Kinematik und Mechanik," *Zeitschrift für Physik* 43: 172–198.

Hemmungs Wirtén, E. (1998) *Global Infatuation. Explorations in Transnational Publishing and Texts*, Uppsala: Uppsala University.

Hermans, T. (ed.) (1985) *The Manipulation of Literature: Studies in Literary Translation*, London, Sydney: Croom Helm.

Hermans, T. (1997) "Translation as Institution," in M. Snell-Hornby, Z. Jettmarová, and K. Kindl (eds) *Translation as Intercultural Communication*, Amsterdam, Philadelphia: Benjamins, pp. 3–20.

Hermans, T. (1999) *Translation in Systems. Descriptive and Systemic Approaches Explained*, Manchester: St. Jerome.

Hjelmslev, L. (1943/1963) *Prolegomena to a Theory of Language*, trans. F. J. Whitfield, Madison: University of Wisconsin.

Hoffman, E. (1989) *Lost in Translation. Life in a New Language*, New York: Penguin.

Holmes, J. S. (1970) "Forms of Verse Translation and the Translation of Verse Form," in J. S Holmes, F. de Haan, and A. Popovič (eds) *The Nature of Translation. Essays in the Theory and Practice of Literary Translation*, The Hague, Paris: Mouton de Gruyter, pp. 91–105.

Holmes, J. S., F. de Haan, and A. Popovič (eds) (1970) *The Nature of Translation. Essays in the Theory and Practice of Literary Translation*, The Hague, Paris: Mouton de Gruyter.

Holmes, J. S., J. Lambert, and R. van den Broeck (eds) (1978) *Literature and Translation: New Perspectives in Literary Studies with a Basic Bibliography of Books on Translation Studies*, Louvain: Acco.

Holz-Mänttäri, J. (1984) *Translatorisches Handeln. Theorie und Methode*, Helsinki: Academia Scientiarum Fennica.

Hönig, H. G. (1997) "Positions, Power and Practice: Functionalist Approaches and Translation Quality Assessment," *Current Issues in Language and Society* 4(1): 6–34.

Hönig, H. G., and P. Kussmaul (1982/1996) *Strategie der Übersetzung. Ein Lehr- und Arbeitsbuch*, Tübingen: Narr.

House, J. (1997) *Translation Quality Assessment. A Model Revisited*, Tübingen: Narr.

Iser, W. (1994) "On Translatability," *Surfaces* 4: 5–13.

Jakobs, C. (1975) "The Monstrosity of Translation," *Modern Language Notes* 90: 755–766.

Jakobson, R. (1959/2004) "On Linguistic Aspects of Translation," in L. Venuti (ed.) *The Translation Studies Reader*, second edition, London, New York: Routledge, pp. 138–143.

Jakobson, R. (1960) "Closing Statement: Linguistics and Poetics," in T. A. Sebeok (ed.) *Style in Language*, Cambridge, MA, New York, London: MIT Press, John Wiley & Sons, pp. 350–377.

Kade, O. (1968) *Zufall und Gesetzmässigkeit in der Übersetzung*, Leipzig: VEB Verlag Enzyklopädie.

Kamenická, R. (2007) "Explicitation Profile and Translator Style," in A. Pym and A. Perekrestenko (eds) *Translation Research Projects 1*, Tarragona: Intercultural Studies Group, pp. 117–130.

Katz, J. (1978) "Effability and Translation," in F. Guenthner and M. Guenthner-Reutter (eds) *Meaning and Translation. Philosophical and Linguistic Approaches*, London: Duckworth, pp. 191–234.

Kiraly, D. C. (2000) *A Social Constructivist Approach to Translator Education. Empowerment from Theory to Practice*, Manchester: St. Jerome.

Klaudy, K. (2001) "The Asymmetry Hypothesis. Testing the Asymmetric Relationship between Explicitations and Implicitations," paper presented to the *Third International Congress of the European Society for Translation Studies*, Copenhagen.

Koller, W. (1979/1992) *Einführung in die Übersetzungswissenschaft*, Heidelberg and Wiesbaden: Quelle & Meyer.

Kuhn, T. (1962) *The Structure of Scientific Revolutions*, Chicago: University of Chicago Press.

Latour, B. (1984/1988) *The Pasteurization of France*, Cambridge, MA, London: Harvard University Press.

Latour, B. (2005) *Reassembling the Social: An Introduction to Actor-network Theory*, Oxford: Oxford University Press.

Laygues, A. (2006) "Pour une réaffirmation de l' 'être-ensemble' par la traduction," *Meta* 51: 838–847.

Lecercle, J. J. (1990) *The Violence of Language*, London, New York: Routledge.

Lefevere, A. (1992) *Translation, Rewriting, and the Manipulation of Literary Fame*, London, New York: Routledge.

Lefevere, A., and S. Bassnett (1990) "Introduction: Proust's Grandmother and the Thousand and One Nights: The 'Cultural Turn' in Translation Studies," in S. Bassnett and A. Lefevere (eds) *Translation, History and Culture*, London, New York: Pinter, pp. 1–13.

Leuven-Zwart, K. van (1989) "Translation and Original: Similarities and Dissimilarities, I," *Target* 1(2): 151–182.

Leuven-Zwart, K. van (1990) "Translation and Original: Similarities and Dissimilarities, II," *Target* 2(1): 69–96.

Levý, J. (1967/2000) "Translation as a Decision Process," in L. Venuti (ed.) *The Translation Studies Reader*, London, New York: Routledge, pp. 148–159.

Levý, J. (1969) *Die literarische Übersetzung: Theorie einer Kunstgattung*, Frankfurt am Main: Athenäum.

Lewis, P. E. (1985/2004) "The Measure of Translation Effects," in L. Venuti (ed.) *The Translation Studies Reader*, second edition, London and New York: Routledge, pp. 256–275.

LISA (1998) Report of the Education Initiative Taskforce of the Localisation Industries Standards Association. Available http://leit.lisa.org/pubs/public.pdf, visited March 2009.

Locke, J. (1690/1841) *An Essay Concerning Human Understanding*, London: Tegg.

Lotman, Y., and B. Uspenski (1971/1979) "Sobre el mecanismo semiótico de la cultura," trans. N. Méndez, *Semiótica de la cultura*, Madrid: Cátedra, pp. 67–91.

Luhmann, N. (1985) *A Sociological Theory of Law*, trans. E. King and M. Albrow, London: Routledge & Kegan Paul.

Malblanc, A. (1944/1963) *Stylistique comparée du français et de l'allemand: Essai de représentation linguistique comparée et étude de traduction*, Paris: Didier.

Malmkjær, K. (1997) "Linguistics in Functionland and through the Front Door. A Response to Hans G. Hönig," *Current Issues in Language and Society* 4(1): 70–74.

Malone, J. L. (1988) *The Science of Linguistics in the Art of Translation: Some Tools from Linguistics for the Analysis and Practice of Translation*, Albany: State University of New York Press.

Mayoral, R. (2003) *Translating Official Documents*, Manchester: St. Jerome.

Meschonnic, H. (1973) "Propositions pour une poétique de la traduction," in *Pour la poétique II*, Paris: Gallimard, pp. 305–316.

Meschonnic, H. (1999) *Poétique du traduire*, Lagrasse: Verdier.

Meschonnic, H. (2003) "Texts on Translation," trans. A. Pym, *Target* 15(2): 337–353.

Miko, F. (1970) "La théorie de l'expression et la traduction," in J. S. Holmes, F. de Haan, and A. Popovič (eds) *The Nature of Translation. Essays in the Theory and Practice of Literary Translation*, The Hague, Paris: Mouton de Gruyter, pp. 61–77.

Miller, J. H. (1995) *Topographies*, Stanford: Stanford University Press.

Milton, J., and P. Bandia (2008) "Introduction. Agents of Translation and Translation Studies," in J. Milton and P. Bandia (eds) *Agents of Translation*, Amsterdam, Philadelphia: Benjamins, pp. 1–18.

Mounin, G. (1963) *Les Problèmes théoriques de la traduction*, Paris: Gallimard.

Munday, J. (1998) "A Computer-assisted Approach to the Analysis of Translation Shifts," *Meta* 43(4): 542–556.

Munday, J. (2001/2008) *Introducing Translation Studies. Theories and Applications*, London, New York: Routledge.

Muñoz Martín, R. (1998) "Translation Strategies: Somewhere Over the Rainbow," paper presented to the *Fourth International Congress on Translation*, Universitat Autònoma de Barcelona.

Newmark, P. (1988) *A Textbook of Translation*, New York: Prentice Hall.

Newmark, P. (1997) "The Customer as King," *Current Issues in Language and Society* 4(1): 75–77.

Nida, E. (1964) *Toward a Science of Translating with Special Reference to Principles and Procedures involved in Bible Translating*, Leiden: E. J. Brill.

Nida, E., and C. Taber (1969) *The Theory and Practice of Translation*, Leiden: Brill.

Nord, C. (1988/1991) *Text Analysis in Translation. Theory, Method, and Didactic Application of a Model for Translation-Oriented Text Analysis*, Amsterdam, Atlanta, GA: Rodopi.

Nord, C. (1997) *Translating as a Purposeful Activity. Functionalist Approaches Explained*, Manchester: St. Jerome.

Nord, C. (2001) "Loyalty Revisited. Bible Translation as a Case in Point," in A. Pym (ed.) *The Return to Ethics*, Special Issue of *The Translator* 7(2): 185–202.

Nord, C. (2002/2003) "Übersetzen als zielgerichtete Handlung," Interaktiv. Newsletter der German Language Division der American Translators Association 6–12: 5–10.

Oettinger, A. G. (1960) *Automatic Language Translation: Lexical and Technical Aspects, With Particular Reference to Russian*, Cambridge, MA: Harvard University Press.

Olohan, M., and M. Baker (2000) "Reporting *That* in Translated English: Evidence for Subconscious Processes of Explicitation?," *Across Languages and Cultures* 1(2): 141–158.

Papastergiadis, N. (2000) *The Turbulence of Migration: Globalization, Deterritorialization and Hybridity*, Cambridge: Polity Press.

Parsons, T. (1951) *The Social System*, London: Routledge & Kegan Paul.

Peirce, C. S. (1931/1958) *Collected Papers*, Cambridge, MA: Harvard University Press.

Plato (*c.* 400BCE/1977) *Cratylus*, in *Plato in Twelve Volumes*, trans. H. N. Fowler, Loeb Classical Library, London: Heinemann, vol. 4, pp. 6–191.

Pöchhacker, F. (2001) "Translationskultur im Krankenhaus," in G. Hebenstreit (ed.) *In Grenzen erfahren – sichtbar machen – überschreiten*, Frankfurt: Peter Lang, pp. 339–354.

Pöchhacker, F. (2004) *Introducing Interpreting Studies*, London, New York: Routledge.

Pöchhacker, F., and M. Shlesinger (eds) (2001) *The Interpreting Studies Reader*, London, New York: Routledge.

Popovič, A. (1968/1970) "The Concept 'Shift of Expression' in Translation Analysis," in J. S. Holmes, F. de Haan, and A. Popovič (eds) *The Nature of Translation. Essays in the Theory and Practice of Literary Translation*, The Hague, Paris: Mouton de Gruyter, pp. 78–87.

Prunč, E. (1997) "Translationskultur (Versuch einer konstruktiven Kritik des translatorischen Handelns)," *TEXTconTEXT* 11: 99–127.

Prunč, E. (2000) "Vom Translationsbiedermeier zur Cyber-translation," *TEXTconTEXT* 14: 3–74.

Pym, A. (1992a) *Translation and Text Transfer. An Essay on the Principles of Intercultural Communication*, Frankfurt am Main, Berlin, Bern, New York, Paris, Vienna: Peter Lang.

Pym, A. (1992b) "Translation Error Analysis and the Interface with Language Teaching," in C. Dollerup and A. Loddegaard (eds) *The Teaching of Translation*, Amsterdam: Benjamins, pp. 279–288.

Pym, A. (1998) *Method in Translation History*, Manchester: St. Jerome.

Pym, A. (2001) "Against Praise of Hybridity," *Across Languages and Cultures* 2(2): 195–206.

Pym, A. (2004a) *The Moving Text. Translation, Localization, and Distribution*, Amsterdam, Philadelphia: Benjamins.

Pym, A. (2004b) "Propositions on Cross-cultural Communication and Translation," *Target* 16(1): 1–28.

Pym, A. (2007a) "On History in Formal Conceptualizations of Translation," *Across Languages and Cultures* 8(2): 153–166.

Pym, A. (2007b) "On Shlesinger's Proposed Equalizing Universal for Interpreting," in F. Pöchhacker, A. L. Jakobsen, and I. M. Mees (eds) *Interpreting Studies and Beyond: A Tribute to Miriam Shlesinger*, Copenhagen: Samfundslitteratur Press, pp. 175–190.

Pym, A., M. Shlesinger, and Z. Jettmarová (eds) (2006) *Sociocultural Aspects of Translating and Interpreting*, Amsterdam, Philadelphia: Benjamins.

Pym, A., M. Shlesinger and D. Simeoni (eds) (2008) *Beyond Descriptive Translation Studies. Investigations in Homage to Gideon Toury*, Amsterdam and Philadelphia: Benjamins.

Quine, W. V. O. (1960) *Word and Object*, Cambridge, MA: MIT Press.

Quine, W. V. O. (1969) "Linguistics and Philosophy," in S. Hook (ed.) *Language and Philosophy. A Symposium*, New York: New York University Press, pp. 95–98.

Reiss, K. (1971/2000) *Translation Criticism: Potential and Limitations. Categories and Criteria for Translation Quality Assessment*, trans. E. F. Rhodes, Manchester: St. Jerome.

Reiss, K. (1976) "Texttypen, Übersetzungstypen und die Beurteilung von Übersetzungen," *Lebende Sprachen* 22(3): 97–100.

Reiss, K., and H. J. Vermeer (1984) *Grundlegung einer allgemeinen Translationstheorie*, Tübingen: Niemeyer.

Remesal, A. de (1966) *Historia general de las Indias occidentales y particular de la gobernación de Chiapa y Guatemala*, ed. C. Saenz de Santa María, Madrid: Atlas.

Rendall, S. (1997) "Notes on Zohn's Translation of Benjamin's 'Die Aufgabe des Übersetzers'," *TTR : traduction, terminologie, rédaction* 10(2): 191–206.

Renn, J. (2006a) *Übersetzungsverhältnisse. Perspektiven einer pragmatistischen Gesellschaftstheorie*, Weilerswist: Velbrück.

Renn, J. (2006b) "Indirect Access. Complex Settings of Communication and the Translation of Governance," in A. Parada and O. Díaz Fouces (eds) *Sociology of Translation*, Vigo: Universidade de Vigo, pp. 193–210.

Retsker, Y. I. (1974) *Teoria perevoda i perevodcheskaia praktika*, Moscow: Mezhdunarodnii otnoshenia.

Ricœur, P. (2004) *Sur la traduction*, Paris: Bayard.

Robinson, D. (2001) *Who Translates? Translator Subjectivities beyond Reason*, Albany: State University of New York Press.

Rose, M. G. (1997) *Translation and Literary Criticism. Translation as Analysis*, Manchester: St. Jerome.

Rubel, P. G., and A. Rosman (2003) "Introduction. Translation and Anthropology," in P. G. Rubel and A. Rosman (eds) *Translating Cultures. Perspectives on Translation and Anthropology*, Oxford, New York: Berg, pp. 1–22.

Rushdie, S. (1992) *Imaginary Homelands. Essays and Criticism 1981–1991*, London: Granta Books.

Sallis, J. (2002) *On Translation*, Bloomington: Indiana University Press.

Saussure, F. de (1916/1974) *Course in General Linguistics*, trans. W. Baskin, Glasgow: Fontana Collins.

Schäler, R. (2006) "Reverse Localization," *Multilingual* 17(3): 82.

Schleiermacher, F. (1813/1963) "Ueber die verschiedenen Methoden des Uebersezens," in H. J. Störig (ed.) *Das Problem des Übersetzens*, Darmstadt: Wissenschaftliche Buchgesellschaft, pp. 38–70.

Seleskovich, D., and M. Lederer (1984) *Interpréter pour traduire*, Paris: Didier.

Serres, M. (1974) *Hermès III. La Traduction*, Paris: Minuit.

Shlesinger, M. (1989) Simultaneous Interpretation as a Factor in Effecting Shifts in the Position of Texts on the Oral-Literate Continuum, MA thesis, Tel Aviv University.

Shveitser, A. D. (1973/1987) *Übersetzung und Linguistik*, Berlin: Akademie.

Simeoni, D. (1998) "The Pivotal Status of the Translator's Habitus," *Target* 10(1): 1–39.

Snell-Hornby, M. (1988) *Translation Studies. An Integrated Approach*, Amsterdam, Philadelphia: Benjamins.

Snell-Hornby, M. (1990) "Linguistic Transcoding or Cultural Transfer? A Critique of Translation Theory in Germany," in S. Bassnett and A. Lefevere (eds) *Translation, History and Culture*, London, New York: Pinter, pp. 79–86.

Snell-Hornby, M. (1994) Contribution to D. Motas et al., "New Translation Departments – Challenges of the Future," in M. Snell-Hornby, F. Pöchhacker, and K. Kaindl (eds) *Translation Studies, An Interdiscipline*, Amsterdam, Philadelphia: Benjamins, pp. 431–434.

Sperber, D., and D. Wilson (1988) *Relevance. Communication and Cognition*, Cambridge, MA: Harvard University Press.

Spivak, G. C. (2007) "Translation as Culture," in P. St-Pierre and P. C. Kar (eds) *In Translation – Reflections, Refractions, Transformations*, Amsterdam, Philadelphia: Benjamins, pp. 263–276.

Sprung, R. C. (ed.) (2000) *Translating into Success. Cutting-edge Strategies for Going Multilingual in a Global Age*, Amsterdam, Philadelphia: Benjamins.

Stecconi, U. (2004) "Interpretive Semiotics and Translation Theory: The Semiotic Conditions to Translation," *Semiotica* 150: 471–489.

Steiner, G. (1975) *After Babel: Aspects of Language and Translation*, London, Oxford, New York: Oxford University Press.

Swaan, A. de (2002) *Words of the World: The Global Language System*, Cambridge: Polity Press.

Tirkkonen-Condit, S. (2004) "Unique Items – Over- or Under-represented in Translated Language?," in A. Mauranen and P. Kujamäki (eds) *Translation Universals. Do they Exist?*, Amsterdam, Philadelphia: Benjamins, pp. 177–186.

Toury, G. (1980) *In Search of a Theory of Translation*, Tel Aviv: Porter Institute for Poetics and Semiotics.

Toury, G. (1985) "A Rationale for Descriptive Translation Studies," in T. Hermans (ed.) *The Manipulation of Literature: Studies in Literary Translation*, London, Sydney: Croom Helm, pp. 16–41.

Toury, G. (1991) "What are Descriptive Studies into Translation Likely to Yield apart from Isolated Descriptions?," in K. M. van Leuven-Zwart and T. Naaijkens (eds) *Translation Studies: The State of the Art*, Amsterdam, Atlanta, GA: Rodopi, pp. 179–192.

Toury, G. (1992) " 'Everything Has its Price': An Alternative to Normative Conditioning in Translator Training," *Interface* 6(2): 60–72.

Toury, G. (1995a) *Descriptive Translation Studies and Beyond*, Amsterdam, Philadelphia: Benjamins.

Toury, G. (1995b) " 'The Notion of 'Assumed Translation' – An Invitation to a New Discussion," in H. Bloemen, E. Hertog, and W. Segers (eds) *Letterlijkheid, Woordelijheid / Literality, Verbality*, Antwerp and Harmelen: Fantom, pp. 135–147.

Toury, G. (2004) "Probabilistic Explanations in Translation Studies. Welcome As They Are, Would They Count As Universals?," in A. Mauranen and P. Kujamäki (eds) *Translation Universals. Do they Exist?*, Amsterdam, Philadelphia: Benjamins, pp. 15–32.

Trivedi, H. (2007) "Translating Culture vs. Cultural Translation," in P. St-Pierre and P. C. Kar (eds) *In Translation – Reflections, Refractions, Transformations*, Amsterdam, Philadelphia: Benjamins, pp. 277–287.

Van den Broeck, R. (1990) "Translation Theory After Deconstruction," in P. N. Chaffey et al. (eds) *Translation Theory in Scandinavia*, Oslo: University of Oslo, pp. 24–57.

Vázquez-Ayora, G. (1977) *Introducción a la traductologia*, Washington, DC: Georgetown University Press.

Venuti, L. (1995) *The Translator's Invisibility. A History of Translation*, London, New York: Routledge.

Venuti, L. (1998) *The Scandals of Translation. Towards an Ethics of Difference*, London, New York: Routledge.

Venuti, L. (ed.) (2000/2004) *The Translation Studies Reader*, second edition, London, New York: Routledge.

Vermeer, H. J. (1989a) *Skopos und Translationsauftrag*, Heidelberg: Institut für Übersetzen und Dolmetschen.

Vermeer, H. J. (1989b/2004) "Skopos and Commission in Translational Action," in L. Venuti (ed.) *The Translation Studies Reader*, second edition, London, New York: Routledge, pp. 227–238.

Vermeer, H. J. (1996) *Übersetzen als Utopie: Die Übersetzungstheorie des Walter Bendix Schoenflies Benjamin*, Heidelberg: TEXTconTEXT.

Vermeer, H. L. (1998) "Didactics of Translation," in M. Baker (ed.) *Routledge Encyclopedia of Translation Studies*, London, New York: Routledge, pp. 60–63.

Vieira, E. (1999) "Liberating Calibans: Readings of Antropofagia and Haroldo de Campos' Poetics of Transcreation," in S. Bassnett and H. Trivedi (eds) *Post-colonial Translation: Theory and Practice*, London, New York: Routledge, pp. 95–113.

Vieira, E. (2000) "Cultural Contacts and Literary Translation," in O. Classe (ed.) *Encyclopedia of Literary Translation into English*, vol. 1, London, Chicago: Fitzroy Dearborn, pp. 319–321.

Vinay, J-P., and J. Darbelnet (1958/1972) *Stylistique comparée du français et de l'anglais: méthode de traduction*, Paris: Didier.

Vorderobermeier, G., and M. Wolf (eds) (2008) *"Meine Sprache grenzt mich ab ..." Transkulturalität und kulturelle Übersetzung im Kontext von Migration*, Münster: LIT.

West, R. (2002) "Teaching Nomadism: Inter/Cultural Studies in the Context of Translation Studies," in S. Herbrechter (ed.) *Cultural Studies, Interdisciplinarity and Translation*, Amsterdam, New York: Rodopi, pp. 161–176.

Wilss, W. (1982) *The Science of Translation: Problems and Methods*, Tübingen: Gunter Narr.

Wittgenstein, L. (1958) *Philosophical Investigations*, Oxford: Blackwell.

Wolf, M. (1997) "Translation as a Process of Power: Aspects of Cultural Anthropology in Translation," in M. Snell-Hornby, Z. Jettmarová, and K. Kaindl (eds) *Translation as Intercultural Communication*, Amsterdam, Philadelphia: Benjamins, pp. 123–133.

Wolf, M. (2007) "Introduction: The emergence of a sociology of translation," in M. Wolf and A. Fukari (eds) *Constructing a Sociology of Translation*, Amsterdam and Philadelphia: Benjamins, pp. 1–36.

Wolf, M. (2009) "The implications of a Sociological Turn – Methodological and Disciplinary Questions," in A. Pym and A. Perekrestenko (eds) *Translation Research Projects 2*, Tarragona: Intercultural Studies Group, pp. 73–79.

Zellermayer, M. (1987) "On Comments Made by Shifts in Translation," *Indian Journal of Applied Linguistics* 13 (2): 75–90.

Index

References to main mentions are in bold. References to "projects and activities" are in parentheses, so "42(7)" refers to task 7 on page 42.